Struggle and Hope

GENERATIONS

A History of Canada's Peoples

Struggle and Hope:
The Hungarian-Canadian Experience

N.F. Dreisziger

with

M.L. Kovacs

Paul Bődy

and

Bennett Kovrig

Published by McClelland and Stewart Ltd. in association
with the Multiculturalism Directorate,
Department of the Secretary of State
and the Canadian Government Publishing Centre,
Supply and Services Canada.

Catalogue No. Ci44-8-1982E

McClelland and Stewart Limited
The Canadian Publishers
25 Hollinger Road
Toronto, Ontario
M4B 3G2

CANADIAN CATALOGUING IN PUBLICATION DATA
    Dreisziger, Nandor A.F., 1940-
      Struggle and Hope

(Generations, a history of Canada's peoples)
Includes index.
Bibliography: p.
ISBN 0-7710-2895-4 (pbk.)

1. Hungarian Canadians – History.   I. Canada. Multiculturalism Directorate.   II. Title.   III. Series.

FC106.H95D73   971'.00494511   C82-094303-7
F1035.H8D73

Printed and bound in Canada

Contents

Editors' Introduction/*vi*

Introduction/*1*

ONE: The Magyars and their Homeland *Bennett Kovrig/4*

TWO: Emigration from Hungary, 1880-1956 *Paul Böatty/27*

THREE: The Saskatchewan Era, 1885-1914 *M.L. Kovacs/61*

FOUR: Years of Growth and Change, 1918-1929 *N.F. Dreisziger/94*

FIVE: A Decade of Setbacks: The 1930's *N.F.D./139*

SIX: The End of an Era: The 1940's *N.F.D./169*

SEVEN: Toward a Golden Age: The 1950's *N.F.D./195*

EIGHT: A Century of Evolution *N.F.D./220*

Appendix: A Note on Sources/*232*

Bibliography/*236*

Index/*240*

Contributors/*247*

Editors' Introduction

Canadians, like many other people, have recently been changing their attitude towards the ethnic dimension in society. Instead of thinking of the many distinctive heritages and identities to be found among them as constituting a problem, though one that time would solve, they have begun to recognize the ethnic diversity of their country as a rich resource. They have begun to take pride in the fact that people have come and are coming here from all parts of the world, bringing with them varied outlooks, knowledge, skills and traditions, to the great benefit of all.

It is for this reason that Book IV of the *Report of the Royal Commission on Bilingualism and Biculturalism* dealt with the cultural contributions of the ethnic groups other than the British, the French and the Native Peoples to Canada, and that the federal government in its response to Book IV announced that the Citizenship Branch of the Department of the Secretary of State would commission "histories specifically directed to the background, contributions and problems of various cultural groups in Canada." This series presents the histories that have resulted from that mandate. Although commissioned by the Government, they are not intended as definitive or official, but rather as the efforts of scholars to bring together much of what is known about the ethnic groups studied, to indicate what remains to be learned, and thus to stimulate further research concerning the ethnic dimension in Canadian society. The histories are to be objective, analytical, and readable, and directed towards the general reading public, as well as students at the senior high school and the college and university levels, and teachers in the elementary schools.

Most Canadians belong to an ethnic group, since to do so is simply to have "a sense of identity rooted in a common origin . . . whether this common origin is real or imaginary."[1] The Native Peoples, the British and French (referred to as charter groups because they were the first Europeans to take possession of the land), the groups such as the Germans and Dutch who have been established in Canada for over a hundred years and those who began to arrive only yesterday all have traditions and

vi

values that they cherish and that now are part of the cultural riches that Canadians share. The groups vary widely in numbers, geographical location and distribution and degree of social and economic power. The stories of their struggles, failures and triumphs will be told in this series.

As the Royal Commission on Bilingualism and Biculturalism pointed out, this sense of ethnic origin or identity "is much keener in certain individuals than in others."[2] In contemporary Canadian society, with the increasing number of intermarriages across ethnic lines, and hence the growing diversity of peoples ancestors, many are coming to identify themselves as simple Canadian, without reference to their ancestral origins. In focusing on the ethnic dimension of Canadian society, past and present, the series does not assume that everyone should be categorized into one particular group, or that ethnicity is always the most important dimension of people's lives. It is, however, one dimension that needs examination if we are to understand fully the contours and nature of Canadian society and identity.

Professional Canadian historians have in the past emphasized political and economic history, and since the country's economic and political institutions have been controlled largely by people of British and French origin, the role of those of other origins in the development of Canada has been neglected. Also, Canadian historians in the past have been almost exclusively of British and French origin, and have lacked the interest and the linguistic skills necessary to explore the history of other ethnic groups. Indeed, there has rarely ever been an examination of the part played by specifically British – or, better, specifically English, Irish, Scottish and Welsh – traditions and values in Canadian development, because of the lack of recognition of pluralism in the society. The part played by French traditions and values, and particular varieties of French traditions and values, has for a number of reasons been more carefully scrutinized.

This series is an indication of growing interest in Canadian social history, which includes immigration and ethnic history. This may particularly be a reflection of an increasing number of scholars whose origins and ethnic identities are other than British or French. Because such trends are recent, many of the authors of the histories in this series have not had a large body of published writing to work from. It is true that some histories have already been written of particular groups other than the British and French; but these have often been characterized by filio pietism, a narrow perspective and a dearth of scholarly analysis.

Despite the scarcity of secondary sources, the authors have been asked to be as comprehensive as possible, and to give balanced coverage to a number of themes: historical background, settlement patterns, ethnic identity and assimilation, ethnic associations, population trends, religion, values, occupations and social class, the family, the ethnic press, language patterns, political behaviour, education, inter-ethnic relations, the arts and recreation. They have also been asked to give a sense of the way the group differs in various parts of the country. Finally, they have been asked to give, as much as possible, an insider's view of what the immigrant and ethnic experiences were like at different periods of time, but yet at the same time to be as objective as possible, and not simply to present the group as it sees itself, or as it would like to be seen.

The authors have thus been faced with a herculean task. To the extent that they have succeeded, they provide us with new glimpses into many aspects of Canadian society of the past and the present. To the extent that they have fallen short of their goal, they challenge other historians, sociologists and social anthropologists to continue the work begun here.

Jean Burnet
Howard Palmer

---

[1]   *Report of the Royal Commission on Bilingualism and Biculturalism.*
[2]   Ibid. Paragraph 8.

Introduction

In a few years Hungarian Canadians will celebrate the centenary of their beginnings in Canada. Since the arrival of the first Hungarian settlers in the Canadian West in 1885, the group has undergone great changes. It has evolved from small, rural communities of peasant immigrants into a highly urbanized, socially and culturally diverse ethnic group with members scattered over most of Canada. In terms of numbers, Canadians of Hungarian origin have increased from a few thousand, at the turn of the century, to over one hundred and thirty thousand by the time of the 1971 census.

The history of Hungarians in Canada can be divided into three eras according to the times of arrival of the major waves of Hungarian immigrants in this country. The first period, lasting from 1885 to the First World War, might best be called the "Saskatchewan era." It was characterized above all by the establishment of Hungarian colonies on the Prairies by peasant settlers, many of whom came to Canada via the United States. The second major era of Hungarian-Canadian history is the interwar period. It was dominated by a socially more mixed group of newcomers who were largely responsible for the start of new Hungarian communities in the cities of western and, especially, central Canada. Finally, there is the post-1950 era, which has seen the arrival of two more waves of Hungarian newcomers as well as the emergence of a diverse and vigorous Hungarian-Canadian community whose achievements are still very much in evidence. Within these major eras, shorter time spans, such as the Depression years, the World War II period and so on, can be readily identified.

The primary aim of this book is to outline these successive phases of Hungarian-Canadian development. We hope that our survey will serve as a convenient point of departure for researchers, that it will foster a heightened awareness of a rich and varied past in Hungarian Canadians, and that it will result in a better understanding by everyone of the historical and cultural background of Canadians of Hungarian origin.

1

The amount of detail offered in this book decreases as the story approaches the present. This was done deliberately, as we deemed it appropriate to emphasize those periods of Hungarian-Canadian history which have faded from public memory and which can be better placed into proper historical perspective. We have tried also to avoid making value judgements on individual Hungarian Canadians, especially in the case of the living. Since this is a general historical survey and not a specialized monograph, we have taken some liberties with regard to terminology. In most places, we have used the words "Hungarian" and "Magyar" as synonyms. When distinction was required between the two, it was made evident through the context. Our use of the term "the Hungarian community" of this or that town or city is a device of literary convenience and not a reference to a spatially integrated or ethnoculturally homogeneous group of persons. Similarly, the expression "Hungarian Canadians" has been applied throughout, despite the tendency in Hungarian to use the term "Canadian Hungarians" [kanadai magyarok]. In the spelling of Hungarian names the usual diacritical marks have been provided, the exceptions being Anglicized proper names commonly used in Canada, such as Bekevar and Esterhazy. Finally, we have usually dispensed with the citing of the names of organizations and institutions in Hungarian and instead have used their closest or most convenient English equivalents. Those interested in the Hungarian versions should consult our sources.

The researching and publication of this book would have been impossible without the help of public agencies. Our special thanks must go to the Department of the Secretary of State for sponsoring this project and for covering a portion of our research expenses,* to our respective institutions for the use of their facilities for research and administration, and to libraries and archives, as well as other establishments, for permitting access to their holdings.

A great number of individuals have also helped in the completion of this project. A few must be mentioned by name because of their special contributions. Mrs. Kathy Norman, Dr. Zoltán Máté, and Mr. Peter Duschinsky have acted as temporary and part-time research assistants to the principal author. Professor S.B. Vardy of Duquesne University made valuable comments on the book's introductory chapter. Professors Jean Burnet and Howard Palmer have given advice and encouragement beyond the call of duty as the general editors of the series. Mr. Myron Momryk, Mrs. Roberta Russell, and Ms. Yok Leng Chang of the Multiculturalism Directorate have looked after some administrative aspects of our project for many years. Mrs. Karen Brown and Miss Ann LaBrash

* M.L. Kovacs gratefully acknowledges indebtedness to the Canada Council and the Canadian Centre for Folk Culture Studies, National Museum of Man, National Museums of Canada, for the collection under their aegis of research material, which made possible part of his contribution to this study. Paul Bódy is thankful for an IREX Fellowship which enabled him to pursue research in Hungary.

have patiently typed various drafts of our manuscript. Much of our information and documentary and pictorial material derives also from helpful individuals. To all of them we extend our sincere thanks.

The production of a collaborative scholarly work often presents more than the usual number of difficulties. Our book is no exception. One member of our original team of six authors, Professor John Kosa of Harvard University, died before he could begin sociological fieldwork for a chapter on contemporary Hungarian-Canadian society. A further contribution, originally planned by Dr. Ivan Halasz de Beky of the University of Toronto's John Robarts Research Library, had to be dropped when it became evident that an extensive bibliography of Hungarians in Canada could not be included in a modest-sized volume such as this one.** Our book also required extensive editing. To reduce overlap and to achieve reasonable uniformity in style and detail of coverage, some parts of the study had to be considerably revised or abridged. In the case of Chapter Three, for example, the footnotes alone were reduced by about two-thirds, obscuring somewhat the extent of research that had gone into this portion of the volume. The editing, rewriting, and checking of draft manuscripts by authors and editors scattered across half a continent caused many delays. As a result, more than the usual time elapsed between the completion of some chapters and the book's final appearance in print.

In his work on this project, the undersigned has received advice, help, encouragement, and patient understanding from his fellow-authors. For this he is thankful. He would also like to extend special thanks to Professor Kovacs for his numerous and valuable comments on Chapters Four and Seven and the introduction and conclusion.

N.F. Dreisziger
Kingston, Ontario, 1981

** A short list of major works in English was eventually added. As Dr. de Beky was on a European sabbatical at the time, it was prepared by the principal author.

3

ONE

The Magyars and their Homeland

Bennett Kovrig

The Land

At its greatest historical extent, Hungary occupied the entire Middle Danube (or Carpathian) basin. The natural boundaries of this geographic unit were formed by the 1500 km long Carpathian Mountain range, sweeping northeast from the Danube at Pozsony (now Bratislava), a few miles below Vienna, then south and west to encompass the mountainous region of Transylvania. The foothills of the Dinaric and Alpine ranges delineated Hungary's boundaries in the southwest and west. Rich in mineral resources, these mountainous regions formed an economic balance with the fertile agricultural lowlands that they encompassed.

The Danube River, running west to east and then north to south, bisects the bowl enclosed by the mountain ranges, and it forms the nucleus of the drainage basin before it leaves the central lowlands. East of the Danube lie the Great Plains (Alföld), a flat and featureless steppe broken only by the Tisza River, a tributary of the Danube. To the west of the Danube lies the region known as Transdanubia, with a varied topography that includes Lake Balaton, covering 600 sq km, as well as lesser mountain ranges, the Bakony and Vértes to the north and the Mecsek to the south. The northwest Little Plain and the northern middle mountain ranges of the Börzsöny, Cserhát, Mátra (with the highest peak at 1015 m), Bükk, and Zemplén are other distinctive topographic features of the basin. For a time, Hungary had access to the Adriatic Sea through the Dalmatian coastal cities, and more recently through the port of Fiume (now Rijeka).

The present boundaries of Hungary were determined by the Treaty of Trianon of 1920. It reduced the country's territory by 71.4 per cent, to the core of the Middle Danube basin. That core is rich in agricultural land but bears only modest mineral resources in the low mountainous districts. Europe's second most important bauxite deposits are found in the Bakony and Vértes mountains in Transdanubia. There are also some

4

manganese deposits in the Bakony. Black coal and uranium are mined in the Mecsek Mountains, while lignite and brown coal deposits occur in the northern mountain ranges. Other domestic energy sources are a few oil fields, principally in southern Transdanubia, and recently discovered natural gas fields on the Great Plains. Finally, Hungary is singularly well-endowed with mineral and medicinal waters; in the Budapest area alone there are 123 sources of thermal waters.

Historically, Hungary functioned as Central Europe's breadbasket, and at the turn of the nineteenth century close to 90 per cent of the population owed its living to agriculture. That proportion declined steadily as a consequence of industrialization and the mechanization of farming, but agriculture remains an important sector for both domestic consumption and the export trade. Of the total area of 93,030 sq km, 57 per cent is ploughland. Maize and wheat are the most important crops, and most other cereals are grown in quantity, as are vegetables, sugar beets, and tobacco. The climatic conditions also favour fruit-farming and vine-growing, the latter producing such famous wines as the Tokay. Livestock breeding is another major activity important for the export trade.

The Hungarian plain, astride the main waterway linking Western Europe with the Balkans, served as a commercial route as early as Roman times. Hungary's subsequent dependence on Austria influenced the western orientation of the principal road and rail routes. The transportation and communications network fans out from the commercial and industrial centre and capital city, Budapest. Passenger and freight transport is effected by rail and road, internal air service having been recently abandoned as uneconomical. Hungary has 1424 km of navigable rivers, used by both domestic and international traffic.

Hungary's position at the centre of the continent and midway between the Equator and the North Pole predetermines her climate and vegetation. The relatively moderate distance from the Atlantic Ocean and the Adriatic and Mediterranean Seas produces a tempered continental climate marked by cold, dry winters and hot, dry summers, and by irregular precipitation. All four seasons are well-defined, although the changes are less pronounced in Transdanubia than on the Great Plains. The annual average precipitation ranges by region from under 500 mm to over 800 mm; there are from fifteen to thirty snowy days, but the snow cover is generally short-lived. The annual mean temperature varies by region from 8 to 11 degrees C., with the coldest month, January, having an average mean temperature of just under freezing point and the warmest, July, a mean of between 18 and 23 degrees C.

The population, which stood at 10,600,000 in 1978, is divided approximately equally between cities and towns on the one hand and villages and other rural settlements on the other. Budapest, the capital, has over two million inhabitants. Other major cities are the industrial centre of Miskolc, situated in the northeast and counting 200,000 inhabitants; Debrecen (180,000) and Szeged (140,000) in the Great Plains; Pécs

(160,000) in southern Transdanubia; and Győr (120,000) in northern Transdanubia. The overall density of the population is 114 per square kilometre.

The People and Their Language

The ethnic origins of the Magyar people and the roots of their language are difficult to ascertain. The migration of the Magyar ancestors prior to their entry into the Carpathian basin can be traced only approximately, but they were evidently the amalgamation over time of several races and languages. The orthodox classification of the Magyars is in the Ural-Altaic group, but their racial composition encompassed Nordic, Ugrian elements from the Ural region, Turkic elements from Central Asia, and Caucasian as well as Iranian-Mesopotamian elements. Their composite language, with Finno-Ugrian at its core, was logically structured and agglutinative. Distantly related to Finnish and Estonian, modern Hungarian survives as a distinct linguistic entity amidst the surrounding Germanic, Slavic, and Romance languages. There has been much mutual linguistic enrichment; the English word "coach," for instance, is derived from the Hungarian "Kócs," the name of the town where this vehicle was first built. The term "Magyar" is a composite Ugrian-Turkic word meaning "men." The equivalent Western name "Hungarian" stems from the Magyars' link with the Turkic-Onogur-Hun peoples.*

While the Hungarian language remained as the vehicle for a distinctive culture in the Magyars' new homeland in the Carpathian basin, their already complex racial composition became further mixed in the course of European history. The retention of national identity despite recurring threats of annihilation or submersion testified to an amazing resilience, but there are few if any characteristics that can be conclusively ascribed to a Magyar "race." Mesomorphic in physical build, the early Magyars were reputed to be warlike and aggressive nomads; they nevertheless readily adapted to a settled, pastoral, and agricultural existence. National pride, individualism, a highly developed sense of honour, hospitality, even a certain guilelessness have all been cited as characteristic of Hungarians. A brief survey of their history may suggest the enduring as well as acquired values and features of this small nation in the heart of Europe.

Historical Highlights

Around the beginning of Christian times, and after centuries of slow southward migration from what is now the Volga-Kama region of northern Russia, the Ugrian Magyars gradually moved southwest to the Don region, north of the Caucasian Mountains. In the process they came into

---

* Current ethnogenic speculation concerns a hypothetical connection with the ancient Sumerians of Mesopotamia and rests partly on apparent similarities between the Hungarian runic and the Sumerian cuneiform script, and partly on the agglutinative structure of both languages.

contact with and were joined by the Turkic elements noted above. In their new home they preserved a semi-nomadic existence, living in autonomous tribes that became allied with the Khazar Empire. The tribes traded with nearby cultures, were influenced by the Persians and other Islamic peoples, and acquired some familiarity with agriculture. They were renowned for their talents as warriors. Superb horsemen and archers, the Magyars had the peculiar skill of shooting arrows in any direction while at full gallop. They possessed a basically undifferentiated social structure founded on the clan and were familiar with a rudimentary runic script.

The subsequent westward migration of the Hungarians occurred in several phases. One group of Ugrians and Avars reached the Carpathian basin in the seventh century. The others, more of Turkic character, remained behind until the beginnings of the disintegration of the Khazar Empire in the early ninth century compelled them to resume a nomadic existence and to fight their way west in quest of pastureland and security. They came to rest momentarily in a region between the Dnieper and Dniester Rivers (known in Hungarian as the Etelköz) and regrouped for their final westward thrust. According to tradition, the seven tribes, which had been joined in their migration by the Khabars from the Khazar Empire, elected the chief of the strongest Magyar tribe, Álmos, as the ruling prince of their federation. The tribal chiefs allegedly entered into a "Blood Oath" creating a hereditary princeship and undertaking that conquered land would be shared by all, in contrast to the feudal model then prevailing in Europe.

Harassed by the neighbouring Pechenegs, the Hungarians decided to migrate en masse behind the protective line of the Carpathians, a region they had already explored in the various military forays conducted in alliance with the Byzantine and German Empires. Prior to the Hungarians' entry, the Carpathian basin had been occupied by a variety of semi-independent tribes of various origins. The Romans for a time administered the provinces of Pannonia (modern Transdanubia) and Dacia (encompassing modern Transylvania). Attila's Huns incorporated the area into their empire for a brief period in the fifth century. In the sixth century Avar settlers from the East arrived, as did Slavonic immigrants in the north. Finally, as noted earlier, in the seventh century the first wave of proto-Hungarians – the so-called "Late Avars" or "Avar-Magyars" – reached the Carpathian basin. Tradition has it that the major migration was effected under the leadership of Álmos' son, Árpád, in 895-896, when in a two-pronged movement the seven tribes entered Transdanubia and Transylvania. More recent historical research, however, identifies him as only the second-in-command ("Gyula") under the leadership (perhaps only nominal) of Prince Kurszán, who was allegedly the sacred supreme ruler ("Kende") of the Magyars. The Hungarian conquest of the late ninth century was more a settlement than an invasion, for there was no central state or ruler at the time in the Car-

7

pathian basin. Most of the earlier settlers offered no resistance, or indeed welcomed their relations. The northern Slavs, disorganized after the collapse of Svatopluk's Great ("Old") Moravia, fell under Hungarian rule.

The Hungarians established themselves in their new home by distributing land among the members of the seven tribes and creating a state under the loose authority of Árpád and his descendants. Some of the tribal chiefs enjoyed wide autonomy, notably in Transylvania. The pagan Hungarians alternatively served as mercenaries in the wars among the Western states and waged battles against the hostile German and Byzantine Empires. Their raids ranged as far afield as western France and Constantinople. After the German Emperor Otto the Great inflicted a major defeat on the Hungarians in 955, Hungarian raids toward the West ceased. Some years later (973) Prince Géza established a friendly relationship with Emperor Otto, and then Hungary became affiliated with Western Christianity.

The consolidation of a Christian Hungary was accomplished by Géza's son István, or Stephen (later canonized as St. Stephen). In the year 1000 Pope Sylvester II recognized him as an independent Christian king and sent a crown and an apostolic cross as symbols of his temporal and religious authority. To build an efficient kingdom, Stephen brought in foreign advisers, missionaries, and artisans, established a church hierarchy, and gradually replaced the tribal system with a centralized structure based on counties.

The Árpád dynasty ruled over a sovereign and ultimately Christian Hungary for four hundred years. Western influences were promoted by a succession of kings whose dominion encompassed the entire Carpathian basin and, with the subjection of Croatia, reached as far south as the Adriatic. In 1222 the landowning lesser nobility compelled King Endre II to grant a charter, the Golden Bull, that guaranteed their rights against the monarch and his barons. This charter, much as the Magna Carta of 1215, served as the foundation of constitutional law. At the time of the Golden Bull, Hungary had a population of about two million.

The first in a series of devastating blows on the Hungarian nation came with the Mongol invasion of 1241. In their westward drive the Mongols first annihilated those Magyars who had remained behind in the Volga-Kama region (and with whom King Béla IV had just re-established contact through an emissary, Brother Julian); they then laid waste the kingdom of Hungary itself. The Mongols withdrew shortly after their triumph, and Béla returned to rebuild his country, partly by repopulating it with foreigners.

Following the death in 1301 of the last of the Árpád line of kings, Endre III, the Neapolitan house of Anjou acceded to the throne. Previously a feudal relationship had existed principally between noblemen and peasants, but the Anjous curbed the autonomy of the barons and instituted a fully centralized state. The distinction between nobles and peasants was confirmed, the former enjoying inalienable possession of their land regardless of whether they had acquired it as a consequence of the original settlement or by subsequent royal grants. Under the Anjous, Hungary prospered thanks to her mineral resources (notably gold) and location at the trading crossroads of Europe, and the country emerged as a major European power. The second Anjou king, Louis the Great, came to the throne in 1342. Noted for his patronage of scholarship and the arts, he founded at Pécs in 1367 the first Hungarian university. For a time he was also king of Poland, and at the Pope's behest he waged war against the Serbs.

The Anjous' successful rule was followed first by that of the German Sigismund (1387-1437), an absentee monarch who became Holy Roman Emperor and King of Bohemia, then by that of the Polish Prince Wladislas (1440-1444). In the concurrent defensive wars against Turkish expansion a Transylvanian nobleman, János Hunyadi, emerged as a brilliant military leader. Inspired by his Christian faith, he expended his talents and wealth to rally resistance to the Moslem Turks. At the head of an army of ordinary Hungarians galvanized with the help of the Italian Franciscan friar John Capistrano, Hunyadi inflicted defeat on the Turks at the famous battle of Nándorfehérvár (then a Hungarian outpost, now Belgrade) in 1456. Thanks to the Hungarians, Christian Europe had gained a respite.

The plague felled Hunyadi on the morrow of his triumph, and the nation elected as king his son Mátyás, or Matthias Corvinus (1458-1490). The latter's reign was the most brilliant in Hungarian history. A man of learning, Mátyás brought the Renaissance to Hungary, and his court at Buda became a centre of humanistic culture that drew artists and scholars from across Europe. His "Corvina" library was one of the richest collections of illuminated codexes of the time, and in 1473 the printing of books began in Buda. Mátyás' fiscal policies led to a more equitable, general taxation, expanded trade, and improved conditions for the peasantry. Feudalism made way for a more modern social structure in which the clergy and nobility were joined by a third estate, representatives of the emerging urban middle class. The lower classes meanwhile benefited from greater legal protection of their rights. Mátyás used his mercenary "Black Army" to win the Bohemian crown and to acquire Austria, and he conducted minor campaigns against the Turks, but his ultimate goal, the crown of the Holy Roman Empire, eluded him.

When Mátyás died in 1490, the ambitious magnates (the great landowning nobles) chose a weak monarch, Wladislaw Jagiello (also King of Bohemia), who allowed them to undo many of his enlightened predecessor's reforms. In 1514, at the Pope's request, a crusader army was raised from among the peasantry. The magnates ordered its disbandment to retrieve their manpower, whereupon the army rebelled under the command of a Transylvanian nobleman, György Dózsa. The civil war ended in bloody repression, and the ensuing punitive confirmation of serfdom was codified by the jurist István Werbőczi in a long-lived constitutional compendium known as the *Tripartitum*. This divided the Hungarian nation into two unequal parts, the "Natio Hungarica" or nobility, including rich aristocrats as well as poor noblemen, who enjoyed freedom from taxation and military service in offensive wars, and who could elect kings and participate in legislation; and the voiceless "plebs," the masses who were excluded from the ranks of the "Natio" and who were to bear the burden of taxation and be tied to their menial tasks.

The magnates thus weakened Hungary at a time when Turkish pressure was mounting. The rest of Europe was even more reluctant to contribute to the defence of Christianity, and in 1526 an outnumbered Hungarian army led by the young King Louis II was annihilated by the Turks at Mohács in southern Hungary. The King died while fleeing. After the Turks ransacked Buda and withdrew, an ambitious nobleman, János Zápolya, had himself elected king. The Austrian archduke Ferdinand of Habsburg followed suit and had himself elected by a smaller group from the Hungarian nobility, basing his claim largely on his dynastic relationship to the deceased King Louis. The two rivals struggled for supremacy but ultimately it was the Turks who prevailed by incorporating central Hungary into their empire and making – at least for a while – both kings of Hungary their vassals.

For the next century and a half Hungary was divided into three parts. The central, Turkish area was gradually bled of wealth and population; millions of Hungarians perished or were taken away as slaves. The northern and western fringes of the country, known as "Royal" Hungary, remained under Habsburg rule and became a battlefield for the struggle between the Turks and the Habsburgs. In mountainous Transylvania, a succession of Hungarian princes resorted to compromise and diplomacy to preserve a precarious semi-independence until the Turks finally occupied the region in 1660.

This division of Hungary also had a religious dimension. The Turks were largely indifferent to the religion of their infidel subjects, but the Catholic Habsburgs promoted a Counter Reformation in their domain, driving many formerly Catholic Hungarian noblemen to espouse Protestantism in protest. Nevertheless, an enlightened and patriotic prelate, Cardinal Péter Pázmány, did have some success in Royal Hungary with his peaceful though forceful advocacy of Catholicism. In Transylvania, religious tolerance (which encompassed the locally founded Unitarian faith) prevailed under the rule of Protestant princes. Indeed, Transylvania became at this time the bastion of Hungarian culture and the centre of much of Magyar national consciousness. It possessed a constitution that granted equal rights to the "three nations": the Hungarians, the Székelys, who were indigenous Magyars proud of their separate identity, and the German Saxons. Although their peasant-shepherd status prevented them from being accepted as one of the "nations" of Transylvania, the Vlachs (later renamed Romanians) who had settled in Transylvania from the twelfth century onward also benefited from the liberal ethos. Moreover, by being ennobled they could join the ranks of one of the privileged "nations."

The era of Ottoman rule was marked by sporadic battles between the Turks and the Habsburgs. Because this protracted struggle took place largely on Magyar-inhabited territory, they were the ones who suffered the greatest losses. One of the most illustrious leaders of the Royal Hungarians was Count Miklós Zrinyi. They were opposed by those of eastern Hungary (including Transylvania and the Partium) who distrusted the Habsburgs and sought to restore their unified nationhood with the help of the Turks. Calling themselves "Kuruc" (a word derived from the crucifix and first adopted by Dózsa's crusaders) and led by Imre Thököly, they launched attacks on Emperor Leopold's forces in northern and western Hungary. Finally, in 1683 an international army repelled a Turkish attack on Vienna and proceeded to push the Turks out of Hungary. Three years later Buda was recaptured, and by 1697 the Turks had been expelled from the whole country.

The Turks left behind a country depopulated and economically shattered, and the liberating armies had only contributed to the devastation. Turkish rule was replaced by that of the Habsburgs, which turned out to be very severe. Compliant Hungarian magnates were rewarded with estates, but for the rest of the nation, noblemen and serfs, the Habsburgs' absolutist administration brought repression, and for the serfs and burghers heavy taxation as well. In 1703 Kuruc insurgents won the support of Ferenc Rákóczi, a descendant of Transylvanian princes. Educated at the Habsburg court, Rákóczi was nevertheless appalled at his nation's misery, and he assumed the leadership of the fight for independence. Catholics and Protestants, rich and poor, Magyars and other oppressed nationalities were all galvanized together by the slogan "Cum Deo – Pro Patria et Libertate" (With God – For Country and Freedom). With the opportunistic and short-lived encouragement of France's King Louis XIV, Rákóczi's men liberated much of Hungary, but they lacked the resources and organization to pursue their course to victory. Although they won some of their objectives, Rákóczi and his followers, like many earlier and later Hungarian patriots, were driven into exile, and most of them died in Turkey.

The compromise peace treaty of Szatmár (1711) promised amnesty, constitutional rule, and religious freedom. In another compromise twelve years later the Hungarian Diet (parliament) agreed to a "Pragmatic Sanction" assuring the eventual succession of Maria Theresa in exchange for Hungary's legal independence, in fact for a modest degree of domestic autonomy. Transylvania was kept by the Habsburgs under separate administration. Vienna's rule had another far-reaching consequence for Hungary – the settlement of Germans, Slavs, and Vlachs on the depopulated territories, with the result that no more than half of the population was Magyar by origin. Maria Theresa began her reign in 1740 surrounded by enemies, but she succeeded in winning the support of

11

Hungarian noblemen, who in the Diet pledged "vitam et sanguinem" (life and blood) in defence of her imperilled dominions. The grateful queen reciprocated by confirming the nobility's privileges, including their freedom from taxation. However, this also impelled the Habsburgs to put up a tariff barrier between Hungary and Austria, and Vienna's regional development policies conspired with the agrarian conservatism of the Hungarian magnates to confirm Hungary's agricultural character at a time when the Industrial Revolution was unfolding in Austria and Bohemia. The inclination of Maria Theresa and her successor, Joseph II, to effect reforms was met by the self-serving resistance of the Hungarian nobility, and as a result Hungary's social and economic structure was preserved at the price of inequality and stagnation.

At the beginning of the nineteenth century Hungary was by Western European standards a backward country, underdeveloped, in many respects feudal, and with a national culture submerged by the use of German as well as the traditional Latin in administration and education. Its social structure consisted of the entrenched nobility, magnates as well as the poorer gentry, the largely rural masses, and a small and heavily Germanic urban middle class. A conspiracy in the 1790's aiming at national liberation and social reform had been mercilessly crushed, but the Hungarian language nevertheless gradually re-emerged as the vehicle for literary and national self-expression. As a consequence of the nobility's quest for greater political autonomy, the Diet was convoked in Pozsony in 1825 after a lapse of thirteen years. The Austrian chancellor, Metternich, rejected their demands for reform, but the pressure for change mounted.

The most prominent voice of reform was that of a cosmopolitan aristocrat, Count István Széchenyi. He criticized the reactionary conservatism of his fellow magnates and of the Viennese court and promoted a multitude of practical reforms. Széchenyi founded and endowed the National Academy of Sciences, designed to encourage the use of the language in culture and scholarship. He fostered Danubian navigation and had the first bridge built linking Buda, the royal city, with the burgeoning commercial and industrial centre of Pest; the nominal toll levied at the Széchenyi chain bridge (designed by the Scotsman Adam Clark) was the first tax applied to all social strata. Széchenyi was a pragmatist who felt that social and economic reform had to precede any challenge to administration by Austria. The reverse priority was propounded by a group of more radical reformers led by Lajos Kossuth, a Protestant nobleman and lawyer. A brilliant orator, Kossuth denounced feudalism and its aristocratic defenders and agitated for self-rule and parliamentary democracy, for the abolition of the constitutional distinction between noblemen and plebeians, and for economic modernization.

The council of the weak Emperor-King Ferdinand (his title reflected the fact that a Habsburg was both Emperor of Austria and King of Hungary) allowed the 1842 Diet to designate Magyar as the country's official language. The popular revolts that erupted in Paris, and then in Vienna in March, 1848, spurred Kossuth to press the demands of the nationalist reformers, and the Imperial Council consented to the formation of a responsible Hungarian government headed by Count Lajos Batthyány and including Kossuth and Széchenyi. In another concession, Transylvania was to be reunited with Hungary. Concurrently, and unaware of these developments, the youth of Hungary issued its own challenge. On March 15, 1848, galvanized by the radical poet Sándor Petőfi, the so-called "March youth" proceeded to bypass the censors in publishing their demands for independence and democratic rights. A new constitution received royal assent in April. Through the efforts of these various groups Hungary thus became momentarily a self-governing country, though nominally still with a Habsburg king. The nobility more or less willingly renounced its old privileges, the remnants of serfdom were abolished, the power of the guilds was curtailed, and a variety of freedoms were proclaimed.

The implementation of these reforms had hardly begun when the Viennese court, having overcome its panic, resorted to the old "divide and rule" tactic. The national minorities were encouraged to challenge Hungarian predominance, and the Serbs and Romanians mounted sporadic assaults on the Hungarian population. As tempers flared, an irate crowd in Budapest murdered the Austrian military commander. In September, 1848, an Austro-Croatian offensive led by the governor of Croatia, Count Jellašič, was repulsed. Thereupon the Austrians attacked in force and occupied Pest and Buda in early December. Kossuth, at the head of a National Defence Committee in the provincial city of Debrecen, hurriedly assembled an army, and the peaceful revolution turned into a bitter war for independence. The Hungarian national army, led by such outstanding generals as Arthur Görgey and the Pole József Bem, scored early successes in the north and in Transylvania. When in the spring of 1849 the new emperor, Franz Josef, formally revoked Hungary's right to self-government, a Diet convened in Debrecen and proclaimed Hungary's full independence from the Habsburgs. Kossuth was named governor, and for a time the Hungarians seemed to have the upper hand. The tide turned when Russian forces dispatched by Tsar Nicholas I reinforced the Austrians, and in August, 1849, the Hungarians capitulated. There ensued a period of harsh military administration by Austria. Prime Minister Batthyány and thirteen generals, as well as other less prominent patriots, were executed; thousands were imprisoned. Kossuth fled into exile and travelled the world preaching the cause of liberty on behalf of his compatriots and other oppressed peoples.

Over time, as the Empire suffered reverses in Italy and in the Austro-Prussian War, Vienna's direct rule became attenuated. While some leading Hungarians remained true to Kossuth's goal of full independence, others, exemplified by the veteran politician Ferenc Deák (who became known as the "Sage of the Nation"), explored the possibilities of accommodation. The resulting Compromise of 1867 restored the April, 1848, constitution, granting Hungary self-government under a Habsburg king and with joint administration of foreign affairs, defence, and finance.

Hungary was still not fully independent, nor even Austria's equal in the dual monarchy. The ruling Liberal Party, unlike the opposition Independence Party, accommodated itself to this status. In other respects, such as social and economic policy, these two principal groups were almost equally conservative. As in much of the rest of Europe, the franchise was reserved for men of property, a small proportion of the adult population. The legacies of Turkish devastation and Habsburg neglect also remained in evidence. Hungary was the breadbasket of the Empire, industrially underdeveloped compared to Austria and Bohemia. The politically preponderant landed aristocracy was largely satisfied with this state of affairs. The impoverished country gentry gravitated to the state administration. In rural areas, a growing and prosperous freeholder peasant class coexisted with immense estates and over four million landless peasants. The urban middle class, commercial and professional, consisted mainly of Germans and Jews. The industrial working class, whose numbers reached a modest 700,000 by the end of the century, suffered from the relative inefficiency of industry and from the government's hostility to trade unionism and to the infant Social Democratic Party. These social and economic stresses became more acute toward the end of the nineteenth century, leading to the emigration of over two million Hungarian citizens, including nearly one million Magyars in the decades before World War I.

Notwithstanding the shortcomings of the Compromise and the conservatism of their rulers, Hungarians took pride in their national revival, and in 1896 they celebrated with great pomp the millennium of their ancestors' arrival in the Carpathian basin. Patriotic euphoria was in tune with the upsurge of nationalism in nineteenth-century Europe, but in the case of Hungary it confronted the fact that scarcely half the population was ethnically Magyar. Many Hungarian patriots, including Kossuth himself, were of mixed ethnic descent, testifying to the strength of the national culture, but the national awakening of the non-Magyars could not be ignored. The nationalities law of 1868 was a notably liberal charter granting equal rights to the Slovak, southern Slav, Romanian, German, and other minorities. As formulated by Eötvös and Deák, it served the minorities' cultural interests; nor were they subject to economic discrimination. However, the successors of Eötvös and Deák were less conciliatory and, under the impact of modern nationalism, they made attempts at assimilating the other ethnic groups. Meanwhile, some of the minorities were incited by their co-nationals outside of Hungary to join in the fight for self-determination. Kossuth, in exile, propagated the idea of a Danubian federation to accommodate the multinational character of the region, but his sensible proposal was out of tune with the mood of the times.

At the turn of the century the pace of modernization picked up in Hungary. Budapest had already acquired the continent's first subway line, and technological and industrial development proceeded apace. There was also intellectual ferment, exemplified by an emerging "Second Reform Generation" (to distinguish it from the period of Széchenyi and Kossuth). Innovation in the pure and social sciences and in literature, theatre, and journalism went hand in hand with a liberalism that looked to the West for lessons applicable to Hungary. These innovators included such luminaries as the poet Endre Ady, the politician Count Gyula Andrássy, Jr., and the radical sociologist Oszkár Jászi. With varying emphases, they confronted the political aspects of the agrarian problem, the minorities, and educational and cultural conservatism. Their immediate political impact was negligible, for the ruling elite's traditionalism and orthodoxy continued to prevail, although between 1905 and 1910 a National Coalition government of former opposition parties toyed with various reforms, including extension of the franchise.

After the assassination of Archduke Franz Ferdinand at Sarajevo in June, 1914, Count István Tisza, once again prime minister with the Liberal Party back in power, cautioned the Crown Council against war, but to no avail. Fighting on the eastern and southern fronts, the Hungarian armies suffered heavy casualties over the four-year span of World War I, with 660,000 dead and 750,000 wounded out of a population of some twenty million. As the futility of the war became apparent the new emperor, Karl, sought a compromise, but the Entente powers had become committed to the self-determination of the Czech, Slovak, Romanian, and southern Slav minorities, in other words the dismemberment of Austria-Hungary. War weariness, the pacifism and liberalism inherent in President Wilson's Fourteen Points, and the scent of social revolution emanating from Russia all contributed to a malaise in the disintegrating Empire. With military defeat imminent, the leader of the opposition in Budapest, Count Mihály Károlyi, formed a self-styled National Council. On October 31, 1918, a bloodless revolution propelled Károlyi to power, and the King gave his assent to the new regime.

A liberal pacifist, Károlyi had much of the returning army demobilized, then a republic proclaimed. He also promised general elections on a broad suffrage and land reform. His government of liberals and social democrats was confronted not only by domestic chaos, which was fed by masses of refugees and former soldiers and food and fuel shortages, but also by the advancing armies of the Entente's minor allies, the Romanians, Czechs, and Serbs. After the November, 1918, armistice Károlyi tried to negotiate a tolerable settlement but won no sympathy from the French, who were in command of the southern Entente forces. Influenced by the advocates of Czechoslovak independence and of

15

Romania's claim to Transylvania, the victorious powers saw no need to accommodate Hungarian interests and were suspicious of the Károlyi regime's tolerance of domestic radicalism.

Indeed, in November, 1918, a small band of Communists led by Béla Kun had arrived in Hungary. Most of them were former left-wing socialists who as prisoners of war had rallied to Lenin's Bolsheviks. They founded a Hungarian Communist Party and proceeded to exploit the chaos reigning in Budapest by seeking the support of a variety of disaffected elements and of the more radical social democrats. The government took some half-hearted measures to contain their agitation, then resigned in March, 1919, when confronted with an Entente ultimatum to evacuate further Hungarian territories.

The resulting power vacuum was filled by an impromptu coalition of Communists and left-wing social democrats, which on March 21 proclaimed a "Republic of Councils." This government, which received little active support even from the trade unions, was dominated by Kun and his handful of Communists. They set about to replicate the Bolshevik model with soldiers' and other revolutionary councils. Opponents were terrorized by the new political police and by a band of Communist thugs known as the "Lenin boys." The peasantry, unrepresented in the government, was told that land reform would take the form of collectivization and not redistribution. Industry and commerce were precipitously socialized. As a result, the production of the war-torn economy declined further and inflation grew. The regime's radical measures proved generally unpopular and alienated early supporters drawn by the promise of reform. Kun won a modicum of support only when his Red Army, led by former career officers, registered some successes against the Czechs. But he, like Károlyi, failed to extract concessions from Clemenceau and the other Western leaders at the Paris peace conference. An offensive by the Romanians precipitated the collapse of the regime on July 31, 1919.

While the Romanians occupied and sacked Budapest, transitional regimes tried to remedy the excesses of Kun's reign. In the countryside the "red terror" made way for a "white terror" aimed at the Communists and their sympathizers. Finally, a national army led by Admiral Miklós Horthy restored a semblance of order and replaced the Romanians in Budapest. Horthy, a dignified and honourable figure, was ultimately elected Regent, and despite two attempts in 1921 by Emperor Karl to regain the Hungarian throne, Hungary remained a kingdom without a king.

Under Horthy a succession of essentially conservative governments guided Hungary's fortunes until German occupation in 1944. The first task was to conclude peace, and this was codified in the Treaty of Trianon of June, 1920. It was by any standard a harshly punitive dictate. Hungary was reduced to less than a third of her former size; her population was cut by 63.5 per cent. The principles of ethnic homogeneity and national self-determination were applied by the peacemakers to the exclusive benefit of the successor states. As a result, 1,704,851 persons of Magyar mother tongue found themselves in Romania, 1,063,020 in Czechoslovakia, 547,735 in Yugoslavia, and 26,183 in Austria. What remained of Hungary, with a population of eight million, had the smallest ethnic minorities in the region. The country also lost most of her mineral resources, and historic commercial links were severed.

Not surprisingly, the values that came to prevail in interwar Hungary were irredentist nationalism and counter-revolutionary conservatism. The Kun episode had discredited not only Communism but also its unwitting progenitor, liberal democracy, in the eyes of many Hungarians. Károlyi remained in exile, a bitter critic of the new regime. Count István Bethlen, who served as prime minister from 1921 to 1931, was a capable administrator. He pragmatically toned down Hungarian irredentism in order to secure a League of Nations loan and stabilize the country's finances. Industry revived, and the regime made peace with the Social Democratic Party and the trade unions on condition that they abjure the radicalism that had characterized the Republic of Councils. The franchise was extended to some two-thirds of the adult population. A limited land reform effected in 1920-21 raised the proportion of freeholding peasants to 61 per cent. There remained numerous huge estates as well as masses of landless labourers and dwarf holdings, leading to emigration and resettlement in industry. Agriculture still employed half of the adult population. Bethlen's administration enacted a wide range of social measures covering pensions, social insurance, and working conditions. Under the able guidance of Count Kuno Klebelsberg, educational facilities were vastly expanded. The impartial rule of law generally prevailed, although Communist agitation was proscribed. After the disastrous social and economic impact of war, revolution, and truncation, the restoration of stability was a remarkable achievement.

With the onset of the Great Depression Bethlen resigned, and economic distress brought new social tensions and radical proposals. General Gyula Gömbös, who became prime minister in 1932, was sympathetic to fascism, but his corporatist schemes were not well-received by either the conservative elite or the population at large. Tentative alignment with Italy and Germany was inspired by Hungary's political isolation in the Danubian basin, where her latent revisionism was countered by the French-supported Little Entente of Czechoslovakia, Romania, and Yugoslavia. Apart from the heterodox governing party, whose policies reflected the inclinations of succeeding prime ministers, the political spectrum encompassed the Social Democrats and Liberals, who enjoyed some urban support, the Smallholders, who represented mainly the peasant freeholder class, and, ultimately, the far-right Arrow Cross Party.

Intellectual dissent in the 1930's came from an urban-oriented group of progressive writers and from what became known as the populist movement. The populists were primarily concerned with the social and

17

economic distress of the peasantry (particularly the three-million-strong landless agrarian proletariat) in a system controlled by large estates. Most of them reflected the nationalism of the age and venerated the peasantry as the truest embodiment of the virtues of the Magyar race. Populist writers such as Imre Kovács and Géza Féja produced socio-graphic studies of the peasants' plight, and in March, 1937, they issued a proclamation calling for social and economic reform. Official harassment and internal divisions left the populist movement politically impotent, although in 1939 some of its members formed the Peasant Party. A more immediate destabilizing threat was the violent nationalism, racism, and social radicalism of the Arrow Cross, which won substantial support at the 1939 elections. The government, meanwhile, remained almost equally hostile to left and right radicalism.

The changing balance of power in Europe worked momentarily to Hungary's benefit. Economic recovery and industrialization were aided by the expansionist economic and trade policies of Hitler's Germany. Then at Munich in 1938 Britain and France acceded to German demands backed by German power but dismissed Hungary's request that the ethnically Magyar areas of Slovakia be ceded back. This impasse proved to be of capital importance, for it strengthened the hand of those who had preached all along that Hungary's fortunes lay with the Axis powers. Germany and Italy agreed to arbitrate the dispute, and by the Vienna Award of November, 1938 (acknowledged by Britain and France), a predominantly Magyar-inhabited strip was returned to Hungary. The country thereby fell deeper into the embrace of the Axis. In 1939 Hungary signed the Anti-Comintern Pact, left the League of Nations, and reannexed Ruthenia, the easternmost tip of dismembered Czechoslovakia. The government also yielded to right-wing pressures in limiting the proportion of Jews in the free professions; Hungary nevertheless remained a haven for Jews until German occupation in 1944.

Hungary avoided involvement in Hitler's Polish campaign, but in August, 1940, she regained a part of Transylvania through the second Vienna Award. Later that year a pact of friendship was signed with Yugoslavia. However, in April, 1941, Germany demanded Hungary's participation in the anti-Yugoslav campaign and sent its troops across Hungary. Unable to withstand German pressure, and finding no other way out, Prime Minister Pál Teleki committed suicide in protest. His act, observed Churchill, absolved his name before history, but it could not extricate his country from its fateful alliance. In June, following a mysterious aerial bombardment of the city of Kassa, Hungary became an active belligerent against the Soviet Union.

For much of the remainder of World War II Hungary pursued a policy of limited military involvement on the Russian front while preserving her national sovereignty. The promoters of this policy, including the Regent, Miklós Horthy, and Prime Minister Miklós Kállay, were determinedly anti-Soviet, but they also wanted to ward off Nazi rule. The people in

Hungary benefited for a time from this perilous balancing act, but the ill-equipped army suffered heavy losses, notably in the disastrous defeat at Voronezh in January, 1943. An informal "Independence Front" of opposition politicians and other notables pressed the government to seek a separate peace, and Kállay did make secret overtures to the Western allies. These attempts were doomed to failure, however, for the Great Powers had assigned Hungary to the Soviet sphere of military operations and influence.

In March, 1944, the impatient Germans occupied Hungary and forced the appointment of a more compliant prime minister. There followed massive arrests and the deportation of anti-Nazis and Jews. Finally, in desperation Horthy named a more loyal premier and opened negotiations with the Russians. On October 15 he informed his nation of these steps, whereupon the Germans seized him and installed as their puppet the Arrow Cross leader Ferenc Szálasi. By then the Red Army had penetrated well into Hungary, and it completed the country's occupation on April 4, 1945.

Once again the Hungarians found themselves on the defeated side, and the costs were incalculable. The seven-week-long siege of Budapest left the once glittering capital in ruins. The retreating Germans stripped their shrinking territory of equipment and supplies; the advancing Russians looted and raped indiscriminately. Some 200,000 Hungarian servicemen were killed or unaccounted for. Civilian losses and the number of Jews murdered in Nazi concentration camps were greater still. Allied promises of self-determination, made in the Atlantic Charter and the Yalta Declaration on Liberated Europe, seemed illusory in face of the reality of Soviet occupation.

In December, 1944, while battle still raged around Budapest, a provisional government was set up in Debrecen under Soviet auspices. Headed by General Béla Miklós, who had crossed lines following Horthy's armistice proclamation, the government included members of the armistice delegation as well as representatives of such former opposition parties as the Smallholders and the Social Democrats. The Soviet presence ensured that a disproportionate influence would be exercised by repatriated Communists. In the interwar period a few Communists had pursued illegal activities in Hungary. Those who lived in exile, in Moscow and elsewhere, plotted and served the Comintern on assignments such as the Spanish Civil War. Béla Kun and many of his comrades perished in Stalin's great purges. At war's end the party, led by a former commissar in the 1919 revolution, Mátyás Rákosi, developed a strategy for the gradual acquisition of power.

The provisional government concluded an armistice that committed Hungary to declare war on Hitler and pay huge reparations. At home it faced the formidable task of reconstruction. Rákosi seized the initiative in creating a Communist secret police and imposing Communist predominance over the traditionally social democratic trade unions. The government meanwhile hurriedly effected a land reform that redistributed the larger farms and estates. The Communists promoted this measure but soon discovered to their chagrin that the peasantry remained impervious to their ideology. The results of the relatively free general elections held in November, 1945, disappointed the Communists. They received less than 17 per cent of the vote, while the Smallholder Party, which had become the rallying point of most anti-Communists, achieved a clear majority. At the insistence of the Soviet commander, Marshal Voroshilov, a coalition government was maintained. Shortly thereafter, Hungary became a republic.

The Smallholder prime minister, Ferenc Nagy, hoped that a semblance of democracy could be preserved until the peace treaty and the end of occupation, but the race was an uneven one. The Paris Peace Treaty of 1946 dashed Hungarian hopes that the Trianon dictate would be revised on grounds of ethnic self-determination. The Soviet Union opposed all Hungarian claims, and indeed a further territorial fragment was awarded to Czechoslovakia, where the Hungarian minority was already suffering from harsh discrimination. The Communists meanwhile exploited Soviet support to persecute their opponents and to begin the socialization of the economy. In early 1947 they seized upon an alleged conspiracy to decimate the Smallholders, forcing Nagy into exile. Many other democratic politicians and ordinary anti-Communist Hungarians fled the country.

During the general elections in August, 1947, the Communists resorted to fraud but still managed to gain only a reported 22 per cent of the votes. Shortly thereafter, the establishment of the Cominform signalled to the East European Communists Stalin's determination to impose uniform Red rule over his sphere of influence. Rákosi promptly abandoned all pretence at parliamentary government. He nationalized all industrial, commercial, and financial institutions and harassed the divided Social Democrats until in June, 1948, they were absorbed into the Hungarian Workers' (Communist) Party.

As the "Iron Curtain" descended to seal off Stalin's satellites from the West, Rákosi imposed an iron rule and proceeded to replicate the Soviet model in Hungary. A vicious collectivization campaign, an economically irrational concentration on the development of heavy industry, cultural russification, and police persecution characterized the new order. The last surviving institutional bulwark against Communism, the churches, was brought to heel through such measures as the infamous show trial in 1949 of Cardinal Mindszenty. Rákosi emulated Stalin in exercising a pitiless autocracy. He purged his party of most of its indigenous veterans and Social Democratic adherents. His tyranny brought terror, moral degradation, Soviet exploitation, and economic mismanagement to Hungary.

After Stalin's death in March, 1953, Rákosi was compelled by his new Soviet masters to share his power with a more moderate Communist, Imre Nagy. The latter launched a "New Course" that alleviated the former's economic and other excesses. By 1955 Rákosi had regained the upper hand, but the image of an infallible and monolithic party had been shattered. Dissent was spurred on by Khrushchev's anti-Stalin speech in early 1956, and although the Russians finally replaced Rákosi with the scarcely less dogmatic Ernő Gerő, the spirit of opposition spread. Intellectuals and students, including supporters of the disgraced Imre Nagy, began to question openly the party's supremacy and to demand sweeping reforms that ultimately encompassed the withdrawal of Soviet troops. Encouraged by the relatively peaceful revolution under way in Poland, they mounted demonstrations that on October 23, 1956, brought about the first armed clash. Within hours the nation rose to defy its oppressors. Most of the membership deserted the party, and with only the secret police left to defend Communist rule, Gerő called for Soviet assistance. The first battles in the streets of Budapest were inconclusive, but for a time the revolutionaries seemed to have the upper hand. Imre Nagy was appointed prime minister and János Kádár, a home Communist and former victim of Rákosi's purges, head of the renamed Hungarian Socialist Workers' Party. Responding to overwhelming popular pressure, Nagy restored a multi-party government and, as Russian reinforcements crossed Hungary's borders, asked for United Nations recognition of his country's neutrality on November 1. More non-Communists were brought into the government, and the Hungarian people could briefly rejoice in once again being their own masters. They looked forward to the end of Soviet domination and exploitation, to genuine democratic government, to the restoration of human rights, and to some rational form of mixed economy. The Western powers, among which the United States had verbally advocated the liberation of Eastern Europe, were coincidentally embroiled in the Suez crisis, and they offered the Hungarians sympathy but no assistance. The Soviet Union unleashed its forces at dawn on November 4 to crush the revolution, and some 200,000 Hungarians fled the reimposition of Communist rule.

Contemporary Hungary

The new Communist regime was headed by Kádár, who had been persuaded by the Russians to abandon the revolution prior to its final repression. At the start, the loyal rump of the party relied entirely on Soviet support in trying to overcome popular defiance. Workers' councils, the intellectuals, indeed the nation as a whole had to be intimidated by massive arrests, executions, and deportations. The first few years of Kádár's rule were characterized by general repression and economic and cultural stagnation. Between 1959 and 1961 most of the peasantry were driven into collective farms. Imre Nagy and his associates had been kidnapped by the Russians from the Yugoslav embassy, where they had sought refuge after the defeat of the revolution, and Nagy was executed in 1958.

Although the restoration of Soviet hegemony and Communist rule was a painful process, Kádár persistently professed his determination to hew a middle line between the oppressive dogmatism of his Stalinist predecessors and the nationalism and liberalism associated with Imre Nagy. By 1962, with collectivization completed, Kádár felt confident enough to proclaim that the domestic class struggle had come to an end and to invite all Hungarians to join in their country's modernization. "Those who are not against us are with us" – the converse of Rákosi's axiom – became the slogan of the regime's so-called alliance policy. Class discrimination in education was eased, and non-party members were allowed to fill administrative and managerial positions. Most political prisoners were amnestied, internment and internal exile were abolished, the jamming of Western broadcasts was phased out, and the secret police adopted a lower profile.

The key reform within the alliance policy was the New Economic Mechanism (NEM), introduced in 1968. In contrast to the old command model, the NEM provided for a relative decentralization of economic management and for greater flexibility in pricing and investments. The reform did lead to improvement in national income, productivity, and private consumption. The modernization of agriculture was pursued concurrently with some success on the state and collective farms, although the remaining private farms together with the household plots still produced half of the horticultural and livestock output.

Foreign trade is of critical importance to Hungary's economic well-being, for it accounts for 40 per cent of the national income. The socialist common market, Comecon, takes up around 70 per cent of trade, and the Soviet Union alone accounts for 36 per cent. Hungary relies on the Soviet Union for 90 per cent of her oil requirements as well as for a high proportion of other raw materials. Her exports to that country include bauxite and uranium. In the industrial sector the more important products are pharmaceuticals, electrical and communications equipment, and commercial vehicles. The principal components of the expanding trade with Western countries are the export of foodstuffs and the import of technology. To encourage tourism, an important source of hard currency, the government has devoted substantial resources to the renovation of historical landmarks such as the royal palace at Buda. In the mid-1970's the Soviet Union began to raise its Comecon price for oil and raw materials toward world market levels, a step that worked to Hungary's economic disadvantage. Still, the NEM has fostered a degree of affluence and consumer choice that is uncommon in Eastern Europe. Many problems remain, such as a perennial urban housing shortage and a level of industrial productivity well below that found in Western industrial countries. In 1976 Hungary had a GNP per capita of $2,140, which ranked it thirty-sixth in the world.

Hungary's government remains firmly in the hands of the Hungarian Socialist Workers' Party, which is described in the 1972 constitution as the "leading force in society." Marxism-Leninism is the official and exclusive ideology, and the party's monopoly and loyalty to the Soviet Union are unchallengeable. The party's current membership stands at around 770,000, and while the majority of members have joined for reasons other than ideological conviction, Kádár himself has won notable popularity for his skilful pursuit of domestic modernization and tolerance while retaining the trust of the Soviet leadership.

Parliamentary government is more form than substance. Multiple candidacies in general elections are technically permissible, but the party and its mass mobilizing organization, the Patriotic People's Front, will not allow overt political opposition. The National Assembly meets only for some ten days each year and remains a largely symbolic source of legislative authority. The party controls appointments to all important administrative posts. Official promotion of "socialist democracy" has, however, led to a refreshing stress on professional expertise in recruitment to the party leadership and government. Recognized interest groups are no longer simple agents of party propaganda but may represent sectoral interests; this modest degree of pluralism is constrained, of course, by the fact that the socialist system cannot be put in question. The labour code makes no provision for strikes, and the party has tried to channel worker dissatisfaction (and improve productivity) by experimenting with what it calls enterprise democracy.

Cultural life gradually revived after the rigid orthodoxy of the post-revolution period, and it is remarkably rich in all spheres of creativity. Tolerance has its limits, however, particularly in the social sciences, where some intellectuals had to be punished for deviant interpretations of Marxism-Leninism. As a result, most authors and other creative people have learned to practice self-censorship. The regime has also reached a compromise with the churches. Cardinal Mindszenty remained in the haven of the United States embassy until 1971, when the Vatican persuaded him to go into exile; he died in 1975. Faced with the persistence of religious faith, the regime remains doctrinally opposed to religion but tolerates a modest level of church activity while severely constraining the educational role of the churches.

Kádár has balanced his liberalization at home with a consistent, low-keyed support for the Soviet Union's foreign policies. He attempted to mediate in the dispute over the reform movement in Czechoslovakia in the spring of 1968; however, as a dutiful member of the Warsaw Pact, Hungary had to participate in the eventual invasion. Relations with the neighbouring socialist countries are generally cordial at the official level, with the notable exception of Romania, where the over two-million-strong Hungarian minority is subjected to forcible attempts at assimilation by the intensely nationalistic Ceausescu regime; indeed, the fate of the Magyars of Transylvania is a matter of passionate concern to Hungarians at home and abroad. The regime has also pursued the normalization of relations and the expansion of trade with the West and the Third World. Recognizing the merits of Kádár's domestic liberalism in the context of the Helsinki agreement, the United States in 1978 returned to Hungary the ancient crown of St. Stephen, which had been in American safekeeping since the end of World War II.

Considering the circumstances of its imposition in 1956, the Kádár regime has been remarkably successful in creating domestic stability and progress and is the object of envy for other East Europeans. Acknowledging the inevitability of Communist rule as long as their country remains in the Soviet sphere of dominance, most Hungarians have learned to live with Kádár's brand of "proletarian dictatorship." By all evidence, given a free choice they would not opt for a Communist government with its pervasive propaganda, cultural constraints, virtual prohibition of private enterprise, and subordination to the Soviet Union. Patriotism and a certain materialism rather than Marxism-Leninism are the prevalent popular values, and thirty years of Communist rule have exacted a terrible human and material cost. Notwithstanding a pragmatic accommodation to present political realities, national independence and full democratic rights remain the remote but fervent hope of the people of Hungary.

Hungarian Culture and the World

Uniqueness of language and a national pride accentuated by their vulnerability in the heart of Europe have conditioned the cultural evolution of the Hungarians as much as their political history and the cross-currents of major European cultural traditions. Early Hungarian literature consisted mostly of chronicles in Latin. A sixteenth-century nobleman, Bálint Balassa, was the first to write poetry in Hungarian. Some of his works, as well as more modern Hungarian poetry, have been ably translated by the Canadian scholar, Watson Kirkconnell. The wars against the Turks inspired Count Miklós Zrinyi to powerful poetry as well as great military deeds.

The national revival at the turn of the nineteenth-century unleashed a flood of literary creation. A blend of romantic and classical influences suffused, for instance, the epic and lyric poetry of Mihály Vörösmarty. The eloquent patriotism of Sándor Petőfi helped to spark the 1848 revolution, but he also excelled in narrative and love poems. János Arany's realistic folktales in verse and his ballads, as well as the immensely popular novels of Mór Jókai and Kálmán Mikszáth (both widely translated), were among the outstanding literary creations of the late nineteenth century.

The innovative writers and critics identified with the review Nyugat (West) at the turn of the twentieth century included the world-famous poet, Endre Ady. The naturalism of novelist Zsigmond Móricz, the European upper-middle-class perspective of Sándor Márai, the impressionistic stories of Gyula Krúdy, the humanism of priest-poet László Mécs, and the lively novels and plays of Ferenc Molnár represent only a few facets of the vigorous literary life of the interwar period. A critical social outlook characterized the writings of proletarian poet Attila József and the novels of the populist László Németh. Populism and a profound concern for national survival distinguish the work of Hungary's greatest living writer, Gyula Illyés.

Conventional wisdom has it that the Hungarians are an uncommonly musical people. Hungarian folk music has ancient roots and such distinctive features as the pentatonic scale. It differs in its pure form from modern variations, played by gypsy orchestras, which have become somewhat misleadingly identified in the West as Hungarian "gypsy" music. The modern composers Zoltán Kodály and Béla Bartók did extensive research on Hungarian folk melodies and incorporated them in some of their works.

Apart from the folk tradition, classical composers of note range from the sixteenth-century Transylvanian, Bálint Bakfark, to Ferenc Erkel, the nineteenth-century father of Hungarian opera, and world-famous pianist and composer Ferenc Liszt, as well as Bartók and Kodály, the latter being renowned also for his method of musical education for children. Ferenc Lehár and Imre Kálmán composed immensely popular operettas in the Viennese tradition, and Miklós Rózsa, film scores. Hungarian excellence in performance is exemplified by famous conductors such as Eugene Ormandy, Sir George Solti, and George Széll, pianists like Géza Anda and György Cziffra, and violinists of the stature of Joseph Szigeti and Ede Zathureczky.

In the realm of art, each day brings new archeological discoveries testifying to the skills of the Hungarians' Magyar and Avar ancestors. The peasantry subsequently developed a rich and variegated folk art in embroidery, pottery, and, in Transylvania, woodcarving. Romanesque, Gothic, and Renaissance styles penetrated Hungary, and impressive examples have survived the centuries. The baroque, then neo-classicism, influenced later Hungarian architects and artists. From nineteenth-century painter Mihály Munkácsy to Bauhaus founder László Moholy-Nagy and to the father of op-art, Victor Vasarely, Hungarians have been in the mainstream and often at the forefront of artistic expression.

Nor has excellence eluded Hungarians in other endeavours from science to sport. A Hungarian physician, Ignác Semmelweiss, was one of the first to identify bacterial infection. Albert Szent-Györgyi's work on Vitamin C earned him one of the eight Nobel prizes won by Hungarian-born scientists. Leo Szilárd, Edward Teller, and John von Neumann were among the pathfinders of atomic fission, and Todor Kármán of rocket research. Hollywood has benefited from a number of Hungarian actors, directors, and composers, and modern Hungarian cinema boasts of such internationally recognized directors as Miklós Jancsó. The Olympic revival was enthusiastically supported in Hungary, and at several Olympic Games Hungary has won the most medals per capita of any participating country.

Through the centuries Hungarians have scattered over the globe to explore, to fight for new causes, or simply to escape oppression or poverty. The young explorer-poet Stephen Parmenius reached Canada's shores in 1583.* Hungarians fought in the army of George Washington and for the Union in the American Civil War. Sándor Körösi-Csoma explored Tibet and became a renowned scholar of its culture in the early nineteenth century. Countless others settled in new lands, including Canada, the subject of this study. This brief compendium of their background and achievements may suggest that, despite the vicissitudes of history, Hungarians have stood their ground to earn a respectable place in Western civilization.

---

* On Parmenius and his voyage to Canada, see David B. Quinn and Neil M. Cheshire, *The New Found Land of Stephen Parmenius: The Life and Writings of a Hungarian Poet, Drowned on a Voyage from Newfoundland 1583* (Toronto: University of Toronto Press, 1972). In 1831, almost two-and-a-half centuries after Parmenius, another Hungarian visited Canada and recorded his impressions. These have recently been translated into English. See Alexander Bölöni Farkas, *Journey in North America*, translated and edited by Theodore and Helen Benedek Schoenman (Philadelphia: American Philosophical Society, 1977), Chapters 14-16. Also, Sándor Bölöni Farkas, *Journey in North America, 1831*, translated and edited by Arpad Kadarkay (Santa Barbara, California: Clio Press, 1978). There is some inconclusive evidence suggesting that one member of Leif Ericson's expedition to Vinland around the year 1000 was a Hungarian. See E. Piványi, *Hungarian-American Historical Connections from Pre-Columbian Times to the End of the American Civil War* (Budapest, 1927), 4-8.

TWO

Emigration from Hungary, 1880-1956

Paul Bődy

Hungarian emigration represents one particular component of that vast movement of peoples which resulted in the settlement of more than fifty million Europeans in North America since 1800. This migration across the Atlantic is undoubtedly the most spectacular example of a population transfer in modern history. As such, it helped to settle the fertile Plains of the United States and Canada, made possible the rapid growth of American and Canadian cities, and contributed heavily to the economic, social, and cultural development of these two North American nations.

Hungarians were late in joining this great migration. Throughout the eighteenth century, and as late as the mid-nineteenth century, Hungary was a country of immigration, attracting settlers from the German lands and southeastern Europe. Immigrants to Hungary settled mainly in the central and southern areas of the country, which had been depopulated as a result of over a century of Turkish rule. But it was not only destruction and depopulation which Ottoman rule bequeathed to Hungary. Turkish domination caused economic and social backwardness, as well as exacerbated a nationalities problem that remained unresolved until the breakup of historic Hungary in 1918. These and other economic, social, and ethnic factors played important roles in emigration from pre-1918 Hungary.

The beginning of overseas emigration from Hungary was preceded by large-scale internal migrations. Starting with the mid-eighteenth century, people from the mountainous northern regions of Hungary began settling on the southern fertile plains. Others left their often over-crowded villages and settled on isolated homesteads of the central lowlands. These migrations suggest the presence of imbalances in population distribution and economic productivity in Hungary. During the three decades prior to World War I these same problems helped to promote the growth of overseas emigration from the lands of the Holy Crown of St. Stephen.

Among the more specific historical developments that had a definite, although probably limited impact on Hungarian emigration to North

27

America was the Revolution of 1848-49. In the wake of this unsuccessful struggle against Habsburg rule, many Hungarians emigrated to the United States. Their experience helped to create an image of the American republic as a land of opportunity as well as a place of refuge from political oppression.[1]

Large-scale overseas emigration from Hungary started in the 1880's. In the preceding decade the annual number of emigrants fluctuated between 294 and 1,759. In 1880, that number leaped to 8,766. By 1900, it had reached 54,767,[2] and continued to grow thereafter. Directly related to this marked increase in emigration were certain economic and social developments in the Hungarian countryside. Increasing industrialization posed a threat to craft occupations, while the growing mechanization of agriculture reduced the need for agricultural labour. Large estates were expanding at the expense of small-scale peasant proprietors. It was becoming clear that the peasant – with small parcels of land, using antiquated methods of cultivation, and faced with the decline of other sources of employment – could not compete with the big estates. A short-term solution to the problem was provided by various types of migrant labour: seasonal work on large estates, migrant artisan employment, and public works construction projects. Increasingly, however, emigration to other European countries became the preferred alternative. By 1880 the number of Hungarian subjects who had settled in Austria had reached 183,000, while other thousands had settled in Germany and Romania.[3] In 1879 very poor harvests, natural disasters, and a general economic recession affecting primarily the peasant proprietors and merchants brought the crisis to a head. The obvious way out, taken by over 160,000 during the next decade, was emigration to the New World.[4]

In the hundred years since 1880, many thousands of Hungarian emigrants have come to the United States and Canada. Some general

TABLE 1

Hungarian Emigration, 1870-1970*			
Periods of Emigration	Total Number of Emigrants	Emigration to U.S.	Emigration to Canada
1870-1914	639,541	556,439	8,000
1921-1941	150,000	38,541	33,000
1945-1970	300,000	67,869	49,566
1870-1970	1,089,541	662,849	90,566

* An estimated tabulation of emigrants of Hungarian ethnic origin since 1870. For explanatory notes, see Appendix to this chapter.

observations on the nature and timing of this century of emigration may be useful (see Table 1, Hungarian Emigration, 1870-1970).

The first noteworthy fact is a drastic change in the destination of Hungarian immigrants to North America with the passage of time. Before the First World War, over 90 per cent of overseas emigrants from Hungary went to the United States. In the same period Canada received less than two per cent. After the war, the situation changed. Hungarian emigration to the United States declined considerably, while Canada increased her share of Hungarian emigration substantially. In the interwar years, over 20 per cent of Hungarian emigrants came to Canada.[5] Another striking fact about Hungarian emigration in the past hundred years is its quantitative distribution by time periods. Over 60 per cent of this emigration occurred in the pre-1914 era. The flow of emigrants was low in the interwar years but rose again after World War II.

The third general observation that can be made about emigration from Hungary since 1880 is that each phase of it took place in a different context. The pre-1914 emigration was part of a migration of peoples in which almost all European nations participated. Hungarian emigration in this period clearly reflected the general patterns of European emigration. The quantitative scale of emigrants, the continuous increase in the numbers to 1914, and the preference of the United States as the destination are just some of the tendencies common to Hungarian and general European emigration in this period. Hungarian emigration in the second period, the interwar decades, was a different movement. Its main determinants were the specific post-war changes affecting Hungary. These developments largely explain the reduced rate of emigration as well as the changing social background and destination preferences of emigrants. The third major emigration period shows the pronounced impact of World War II and the political upheavals of its aftermath as primary determinants of the process, rate, and destination of emigrants.[6]

In view of these differences among the three emigration periods, it appears justified to discuss post-1880 emigration from Hungary in terms of the three periods identified.

THE PRE-1914 EMIGRANTS

Perhaps the most important fact about the Kingdom of Hungary in the immediate pre-1914 era was its multi-ethnic compostion. In addition to ethnic Hungarians (or Magyars) there were Slovaks, Germans, Romanians, Ruthenians, Jews, Serbs, and Croats living in Hungary. In certain regions one particular ethnic group predominated, while in others, particularly certain urban areas, the population was often intermingled. Ethnic Hungarians constituted about half of the total population. While the discussion in this study concerns mainly the emigration of ethnic Hungarians, in some cases reference will be made to other ethnic groups or to Hungarian subjects in general. This practice is often made inevitable by the absence of reliable statistical data that distinguish between emigrants of various backgrounds coming from Hungary.

Hungary was a predominatly agrarian country even as late as 1910. Her social and economic problems were those of an agrarian society undergoing gradual industrialization. Ownership of land was concentrated in the hands of the historic nobility. At the bottom of the class structure stood the country's poor peasantry, agricultural labourers, and seasonal or migrant workers. As industrialization proceeded, the position of Hungary's lower classes became worse for a variety of reasons. Two of these reasons appear particularly important from the point of view of emigration. First was the fact that Hungary's growing industrial sector did not provide employment opportunities for the masses of unskilled agricultural wage-earners. The result was that these people had to consider and often to accept emigration as a temporary solution to their increasingly precarious economic position. The second fact was that industrialization, while improving the economy of certain regions, had an adverse effect on economic and social conditions in areas lacking the potential for rapid economic development. The lower classes of these less fortunate districts, seeing their position declining especially when compared with that of people in more prosperous regions, frequently chose migration as a solution to their disadvantaged situation. The destination of these migrants could be another part of Hungary or another country in Europe, but as time went on it became most frequently the New World.

Social Characteristics of Emigrants

The emigrants of the pre-1914 era originated predominantly from among Hungary's rural population. They belonged to a social class which for centuries had been tied to the soil, to the village, and to the church. It had always exhibited traditional moral and religious patterns of belief and behaviour. Yet it was this least mobile class that initiated the migration to the New World.

Available statistics show that the vast majority of emigrants in this period were of peasant origin. Several occupational groups are identified in the official Hungarian emigration counts. These include peasants with dwarf holdings, agricultural wage-earners, unspecified labourers on farms, and domestic servants. All of these groups can be considered predominantly peasant or agricultural wage-earning categories. Taken together, they constituted 84 per cent of emigrants who left Hungary from 1899 to 1913, the period for which emigration statistics are available.[7] Only 16 per cent of emigrants can be regarded as non-agricultural in occupational origin. In this composite group we find 3 per cent artisans, 8 per cent industrial workers, one per cent miners, and only 0.5 per cent merchants.[8]

Since these data pertain to all emigrants from the Kingdom of Hungary they do not reveal regional, ethnic, and occupational variations. We can obtain more specific information on the patterns of emigrant occupational groups by considering a series of correlations, between major occupational categories and ethnic groups, provided in the official Hungarian statistical sources. It appears that the occupational category, peasants with landholdings, constituted the lowest percentage among ethnic Hungarians (7-10 per cent) and Germans (6-10 per cent). The highest percentages of peasants with landholdings were among Croatians (50-54 per cent) and Serbs (39-53 per cent). Ruthenians, Romanians, and Slovaks registered between these two extremes. The agricultural wage-earner category showed the highest percentage among Romanians (76-83 per cent), Slovaks (69-75 per cent), Ruthenians (69-70 per cent), and Hungarians (65-70 per cent). The lowest proportions of agricultural wage-earners appeared among Croatians (25-37 per cent), Serbians (35-52 per cent), and Germans (62-64 per cent). Non-agricultural occupations were represented most frequently among Germans (22-26 per cent) and least among Ruthenians (3-6 per cent) and Romanians (5-6 per cent).[9]

These more specific indicators give us a better understanding of the social differences among the emigrants of various ethnic origins, and particularly of the social characteristics of the ethnic Hungarian emigrants. It is clear, for example, that considerable social and economic differences existed among the three principal occupational categories surveyed. The most important quantitative differences occur between the categories of peasants and agricultural wage-earners. Croatians and Serbs were primarily peasants with land, while Hungarians, Slovaks, and Romanians represented predominantly the agricultural wage-earner group. This distribution is reflected in the social and economic circumstances of different regions in Hungary: the high incidence of small peasant land parcels in Croatia and the scarcity of peasant holdings in central and northern Hungary.[10]

It is difficult to define, however, the specific impact of such differences on emigration. The predominance of small landholdings among Croatians did not deter Croatian emigration, while the absence of land among Hungarians and Slovaks seems to have stimulated emigration. It appears evident, therefore, that emigration cannot be explained by one specific element, such as landholding or occupational category, but only by considering a wide range of social and economic factors related to specific time periods of emigration. This is what we shall attempt to do with respect to each period of emigration studied.

With respect to the period under review, the most important determinants of emigration can be found in agricultural unemployment and its relationships to rates of industrialization. Recent studies show that highly differentiated rates of industrialization evolved in various regions of Hungary. While in the central and north-central regions industrial employment fluctuated between 29 and 22 per cent of total employment by 1900, such a region as Croatia attained only 11 per cent, constituting the lowest rate of industrial employment in any region of Hungary.[11] These relationships, in combination with our information on regional emigration rates, do show that while emigration cannot be attributed to any one set of social-economic indicators, it appears likely that agricultural unemployment coupled with retarded industrial development constituted a major determinant of emigration.

The peasants and agricultural wage-earners who left Hungary had a particular perception of the purpose of their emigration. They did not intend to leave their ancestral lands permanently. Their primary aim was to save sufficient funds in America to invest in land and property after their return home. This was clearly the outlook of Hungarian and Slovak, Ruthenian, Croatian, and other ethnic emigrants who left the Kingdom of Hungary.

This perception of emigration is suggested by the general pattern of emigration. Young men in their twenties were the most likely emigrants from Hungary. As a rule, they travelled in groups from a particular village and had a particular destination. In Canada or in the United States, relatives or friends had arranged for lodging and employment in advance. On their arrival in the New World, they entered a familiar Hungarian social milieu consisting of relatives and kinsfolk from their village or country. This network provided advice on American conditions, assisted them in finding employment, and recruited others from Hungary to emigrate. After the young emigrant had earned and saved sufficient funds, he would return home and assist others to follow his example.[12]

The same perception of emigration emerges from a review of the age and sex distributions of emigrants and from remigration data. The predominant age distribution of emigrants was concentrated in the twenty-year-old to forty-nine-year-old group. Hungarian emigration statistics indicate that 92-94 per cent of emigrants were in this category, while only 3-5 per cent of emigrants were fifty or over. The majority of emigrants were single men. Official emigration records for the period 1899 to 1913 show that 68.2 per cent of emigrants were men, and 31.8 per cent were women.[13] Only exceptionally did families migrate to the New World. Such cases indicate either a deep sense of despair with conditions in Hungary or the decision to establish group settlements in Canada or South America. Remigration data substantiate the familiar pattern of emigration and return. For the period up to 1913, an average remigration rate of 20-25 per cent is indicated.[14]

Though it is true that the majority of emigrants remained in the New World, it is highly important to relate the original perception of emigration held by peasant immigrants to their attitudes and behaviour in the country of destination. Our subsequent analysis of Hungarian immigrant adjustment to Canadian society will attempt to show that this original perception determined the values and goals of many Hungarians long after they had settled in Canada.

Emigrant Motivation: Social and Individual Determinants

International migration research has centred increasingly on the question of the motives of emigration. As a result of a series of studies and interpretations, two distinct views have emerged. One seeks to show that an assessment of complex social, economic, and migration processes in the country of origin, if correlated with economic cycles in the country of destination, will explain the primary motives of emigration. This approach is popularly known as the "push and pull" theory. The second viewpoint, a result of studies emphasizing the individual and family components of the emigration decision, points out that the motives of emigrants can be understood not so much in terms of economic processes, but primarily through a study of regional, community, and family environments. Both views contribute to our understanding of emigration determinants. The first view defines the major economic and social transformations affecting the life of the emigrant, while the second considers the relationships between the community environment and the formation of the decision to emigrate.[15]

The starting point for both types of analysis is the transformation of the European social and economic scene since the middle of the nineteenth century. In Hungary, this transformation began with the Revolution of 1848, which resulted in important social and political reforms. Serfdom was abolished, personal, civil, and political rights were guaranteed, and a parliamentary form of government was introduced. These reforms established guidelines for a modernized political system, but they failed to resolve the most important social issue – the question of land tenure – for the vast majority of the population. The general result of this failure was the gradual acquisition of land by wealthy landowners and the decline of peasant landholdings by the early twentieth century.[16]

The impoverishment of peasants and the gradual decline of peasant landholdings were obviously important causes of agrarian discontent and of emigration. But in fact there were other, equally serious agrarian and social issues. One was the rapid growth of an agrarian wage labour class, consisting of landless peasants or of those with very small plots, who earned their living by seasonal agrarian labour. By 1900, this class constituted 52.3 per cent of the total agrarian employment.[17] Simultaneously, the number of peasants with dwarf holdings steadily increased. In order to keep their very small plots, these peasants became increasingly dependent on seasonal agrarian or semi-industrial employment. The general result of these developments was the emergence by 1900 of an extraordinarily large pool of underemployed, impoverished, and dissatisfied agricultural wage-earners.

Why did these conditions emerge only in 1900 and not earlier? Primarily, because only in the 1880's did a mechanized, large-scale system of agricultural production emerge in Hungary. As a result of mechanization, seasonal employment on the large estates was drastically reduced. For a time, public works projects provided employment to large numbers of the agrarian unemployed. These projects were terminated, however, by 1900. The consequence was that the majority of the Hungarian agrarian labour force had no other employment alternative but seasonal work on large estates.

Nor did industrialization offer a remedy. In fact, industrialization had produced substantial dislocations of artisans, craftsmen, merchants, and peasants engaged in occasional service jobs. Where it had been established, the cottage industry declined or disappeared altogether. These dislocations meant economic ruin to such regions as northeastern Hungary (eastern Slovakia), where agricultural employment traditionally had been supplemented by commercial and handicraft activities. The slowly developing Hungarian industrial sector could not absorb the enormous reserves of agrarian labour. Only in the case of Budapest, the primary industrial centre, was urban immigration significant. But those who settled in Budapest constituted only a modest percentage of the available agrarian labour force.[18]

These transformations define the substance of the push factors leading to emigration from Hungary. The pull factors are usually defined in terms of American wages and excellent employment opportunities. While it has been shown by previous studies that these attractions existed and exercised magnetic effects on the impoverished Hungarian peasantry, it is still necessary to explain how, when, and why there emerged an actual linkage between dissatisfied peasants and American employment opportunities.[19]

This question involves at least three types of analysis. First, it is necessary to inquire into the process by which agrarian wage-earners gained information and certainty about the advantages of travelling to an unknown land, where so much wealth was to be obtained. Second, we need to explain how they became participants in a complex migration chain linking obscure villages in Hungary with North American industrial centres or agricultural regions. Third, propensity to migrate played a role. Regional, local, ethnographic, family, and personal motives frequently interacted to produce emigration in some cases, but not in others.

Sources of Information and Communication

An overwhelming body of evidence indicates that Hungarian emigrants obtained their information concerning emigration from three types of communication: personal letters of emigrants, the savings transmitted to Hungary by emigrants, and personal testimonies related by emigrants on their visits home. These types of communication exercised an extraordinary impact on those who for one reason or another considered emigration to the New World.[20]

The following account demonstrates the singular effect produced by the arrival of an emigrant letter in a Hungarian village:

> Arrival of an emigrant letter was an event of the first order, causing considerable excitement. It is read aloud in a dignified manner to a large audience. The whole village learns of its contents. The money transmitted, photographs showing emigrants in new clothes, portrayals of American life have the effect of creating a general desire, particularly among less industrious and impoverished peasants, to travel to that miraculous land of promise.[21]

The two other types of information concerning American emigration were equally effective. The regular transmittal of savings to the family of the emigrant made the case for American emigration by demonstrating the practical impact of the emigrant's labour. The savings received by the family were used to pay off debts, to purchase additional land, and in some cases to build new homes. All of this became highly visible and created an impact on the community as a whole. Above all, American savings and their investment demonstrated the possibility of improving life in Hungary through emigration. The third form of communication was the returned emigrant himself. He was usually received in the village as a famous person. In the course of his visits to family, friends, and relatives, he dramatized his experiences, magnified the successes achieved, and attempted to persuade others to return with him to America.

Contemporary accounts suggest that the personal dramatizations of returned emigrants were the most effective persuasions for others to attempt emigration. This is also the view of Sándor Tonelli, a young economist who travelled on emigrant ships to America. In the course of his passage he interviewed several hundred emigrants from Hungary. He was primarily interested in collecting information on emigrant motives, attitudes, and perceptions. He reported that the returned emigrant was in fact the most important influence on the prospective emigrant for two reasons: first, because the returnee provided detailed information on American employment opportunities and on specific persons prepared to assist the emigrant; and second, because it was a frequent practice for returnees to accompany novice emigrants on their first journey. Tonelli's views constitute credible and persuasive evidence of the predominant influence of returned emigrants on subsequent emigration in view of his documentation of interviews, but even more importantly because his statements are fully confirmed by other contemporary sources to be discussed later in this chapter.[22]

We have an interesting confirmation of the effectiveness of the returned emigrant in recruiting others to emigrate in the documented efforts of the early Hungarian settlers of Saskatchewan to recruit new emigrants. One of these settlers, Mrs. Steven Gyuricska, visited her native village in 1901 and spread the message of emigration to Canada. A contemporary witness relates the impact of her activities:

by her vivid accounts of the way of life in the Great West (she) made a lasting impression on her listeners in the neighboring villages. . . . To these land-hungry people she spoke about the free homesteads of 160 acres with their fertile black soil. She described the grazing fattened cattle, the groves of poplars providing building material and ready fuel, the low level of taxation, the great freedom enjoyed by all, the great open spaces for hunting, the lakes for fishing, the abundance of meat and white bread even on weekdays, making each day of the year like Easter Sunday in Hungary.[23]

In view of the strong impact of the returned emigrant on the emigration of others, the question arises as to what role emigration propaganda, in the form of published materials, travel agents, and other forms of persuasion, played in inducing emigration from Hungary. There is no question that emigration literature circulated widely in Hungary and emigration agents were active in many areas of Hungary.[24] After a review of available evidence and documentation, however, both in Hungary and in American sources, it can be stated conclusively that emigration propaganda played a limited role in persuading peasants from Hungary to emigrate. Several sources can be cited in support of this conclusion. An important one is Sándor Tonelli, cited earlier.[25] Tonelli studied over a hundred life histories and statements of prospective emigrants and developed a composite pattern of the decision made to emigrate. According to this pattern, emigrants returning from America would visit their native villages, relate their experiences to family and friends, and then return to America accompanied by several novice emigrants from their villages. Those who travelled without such an emigrant guide usually had in their possession the addresses of relatives or friends living in America. Of over 1,000 emigrants Tonelli talked to, only one did not have an address of destination.

Another source stating the same conclusion can be found in contemporary Hungarian police reports on emigration. These reports are based on intensive and confidential investigations of emigration propaganda and of persons suspected of distributing emigration literature. They confirm the conclusion that emigration propaganda played a minimal role in inducing people to emigrate. One of the representative statements of a police official, contained in the report of the Torontál county administrator to the Hungarian central government, makes the following points:

> According to my information, the massive scale of emigration is not caused by secret emigration agents, but exclusively by the prevailing social and economic conditions. For the most part, the primary inducements to emigration are the payments sent home by emigrants and the letters of relatives from America promising employment opportunities.[26]

A selection of life histories of emigrants, included in this chapter, generally confirms the pattern of the emigration decision stated by Tonelli: the inducement to emigrate was most effective when transmitted by personal testimonies of relatives and friends in America.[27] It may be of interest to note as well that comparative studies of emigration, particularly those relating to English, Greek, and Swiss emigration, have confirmed the primary importance of personal influences on emigration decisions.[28]

In view of the predominant role of personal information in the decision to emigrate, the question arises as to what was the specific impact of emigration publicity. Undoubtedly, these publications played a limited but at the same time useful role in the emigration process. Maldwyn Jones, the noted British historian of emigration, has defined that role accurately: "most emigrant guidebooks were devised not so much to stimulate emigration as to provide those already disposed to emigrate with the kind of information which would be helpful in deciding where precisely to settle."[29] This statement seems to apply to much of the emigration literature circulated in Hungary.

It is worth noting that the Hungarian government tried to restrict the distribution of emigration propaganda in Hungary. In 1881 it enacted a law dealing with emigration that prohibited the operation of emigration agencies in Hungary. Until 1900 this legislation was the primary legal means of discouraging emigration from Hungary. The adoption of this law can be explained by the contemporary view that emigration resulted from false claims of emigration agents who misled the uneducated masses. Whatever the merits of this argument, the law adopted had a very limited impact on emigration. In fact, Hungary experienced successively larger rates of emigration throughout the period from 1881 to 1900. Another somewhat more stringent law was passed in 1903, requiring strict controls at border crossings and limiting the emigration of persons of military conscription age. A third law was enacted in 1909, imposing penalties for illegal emigrants and requiring the payment of a fee for emigration permits issued to persons liable for military service. Neither law could be enforced. Extensive travel between Hungary and Austria and Germany, the ease of border crossings, and the vast experience available to prospective emigrants on ways to elude detection made the identification of illegal emigrants very difficult. Police reports and other contemporary accounts testify that these laws had no significant impact on the continuously increasing rates of emigration.[30]

The Migration Chain

The second crucial element of emigration as a social process was the formation of an intercontinental migration chain linking the emigrant in America with his community in Hungary. This highly important social practice can be understood as the response of the emigrant to the innate need for contact with his family, village, and the wider ethnic community. The letter home and the personal return represented a primary ex-

37

pression of that response. But, in addition, the emigrant established in North America also maintained a lively and continuous relationship with his family and relatives. He encouraged them to join him in the New World. He assisted prospective emigrants by securing them jobs, paying the passage, transmitting savings. As a result of the pervasiveness of this migration chain, practically all peasant emigrants could count on the support of relatives and friends established in America. A local Hungarian government report on this practice is one of many that confirms the importance and effectiveness of this communication network:

> There is no village in this district without American emigrants. Those who have left constantly encourage their relatives and friends to join them and to accept pre-arranged jobs. They also send pre-paid ship's passage. In view of the substantial quantity of money transmitted to those still here, there seems no way to counteract the desire to emigrate.[31]

The migration chain consisted of yet another link. As noted earlier, the original intent of the peasant emigrant was to earn funds abroad for the payment of debts and the purchase of additional land. Therefore, he needed a reliable intermediary in his village, someone who could be trusted to act in his place in investing his savings. This person could be a family member, but frequently a member of the village elite was selected, such as the teacher, priest, or alderman. The intermediary took care of the emigrant's finances, made regular reports to the emigrant, and generally provided a vital link between the emigrant and the home community. It is clear that both parties benefited from the arrangement. While the emigrant retained contact with his community, the intermediary profited generously from emigrant earnings in a variety of ways.[32]

Migration Propensity

The third element of emigration, migration propensity, is an intricate but quite influential aspect of the decision to emigrate. Its most visible form is expressed in the regional differentiation of emigrants. In the first two decades of emigration from Hungary, emigrants originated predominantly from the northeastern region of the kingdom, primarily the counties of Sáros and Zemplén.[33] Only after 1900 did emigrants from other regions join the great migration. But throughout the pre-1914 period, emigration from the northeastern region continued and surpassed in intensity and quantity all other regional emigration streams.[34]

The migration propensity of the Hungarian northeast has been analysed from several viewpoints. The best known is the economic and social analysis demonstrating the region's underdevelopment and inaccessibility in an age of industrialization.[35] But equally significant is the recently developed approach, by which interregional development is compared and evaluated in terms of national development. The main conclusion of this approach is that certain regions, because of economic and social circumstances, were able to adjust successfully to the emerging industrial system, while others, such as the northeast, failed to make a successful adjustment, resulting in severe economic underdevelopment.[36] Still another view is that migration had been a long-standing social process characteristic of the northeast. From the eighteenth century on, many communities of peasants had migrated from the northeast to parts of southern Hungary. Annual seasonal migrations to agricultural regions of central Hungary, Romania, Bohemia, and Austria were commonplace and, in fact, were vital sources of livelihood. Another recent migration was to the Budapest industrial zone. Finally, migrant artisans and tradesmen from the northeast provided their expert services to many regions of the Habsburg Monarchy. The prevalence and acceptance of migration as a means of livelihood certainly had an impact on the subsequent decision to emigrate to the New World.[37]

The Decision to Emigrate

Migration propensity may include all of these considerations, but it refers also to still another action: the individual decision to emigrate. While overall economic forces may predispose many to consider emigration, the specific decision to emigrate results from an individual judgement that weighs, calculates, but eventually chooses to remain or leave. Such a judgement must be seen as the result, in many cases, of personal attitudes, family and social ties, perceptions of the old country and the new, and countless imponderables. We present a selection of available emigrant life histories as illustrations of the interaction between social influences and individual decisions. But they exemplify in particular the crucial role of the individual decision as the climax to a long series of influences and persuasions affecting the individual emigrant.[38]

The case of József shows a combination of family circumstances and the desire for economic independence as important emigration motives. József, a young peasant, lived with his wife and two children in his parents' home in the village of Ricse. His father owned six acres of fertile farmland in the northeastern lowlands. József helped his father in cultivation and undertook seasonal employment on large estates. He earned enough to provide for himself and his family while living in his parents' household, but not enough to establish himself on his own plot of land and home. His goal was to obtain a sizable piece of land and to build a home. He explained his decision to emigrate in 1912:

> I received information about conditions in America from villagers who had emigrated. I had learned from letters received in the village and from conversations with returnees that one had to work hard in America, but equally that it was possible to save money by honest work and frugality.
>
> I emigrated not so much because of economic hardship, but primarily as a result of family circumstances. My father drank too

much, my stepmother interfered in my private life, and I was unable to establish an independent household. I decided to emigrate in order to save money sufficient for financing a plot of land and a home for my own family.

The case of Benjamin illustrates strong economic motivation. The family owned no land. The main source of income for five brothers was employment on large estates. Their income and payments in kind provided them bare subsistence but no hope that they would be able to secure a comfortable livelihood. His decision to emigrate is given in this explanation:

> Family discussions had considered the possibility of emigration for several years. We felt that it would be a good way for one son to save money and assist the others. In 1906 an emigrant returned to the village. The family decided that Benjamin would accompany . him when he returned to America.

Károly was a boy of fifteen when his father made the decision to emigrate. His father, a sharecropper, faced the same problems of livelihood as Benjamin and his brothers. The pattern of emigration was a familiar one: the head of the family emigrated alone and the male family members followed him as soon as employment and living accommodations were available. In this particular case, however, Károly emigrated contrary to his own wishes and eventually returned to Hungary. Károly made the following comment:

> I would not have emigrated on my own. The decision was influenced by my father. He wrote to me from America that he wished to make possible an easier life for me. This could be realized only if I joined him in America and both of us worked to save money for purchasing land at home.

Béla represented still another case. His family owned eight acres of fertile land in the northeastern lowlands. He was the only child. The family had no economic problems. The decision to emigrate is explained primarily by family and personal considerations:

> I feel that the decision was not influenced primarily by economic needs, since my family was well off. A minor motivation was the occurrence of disagreements with my stepfather. The primary reason was my wish to see the world. I was curious about life in America and I wanted to be on my own. I stayed in America for a period of three years. That was sufficient to observe life and to decide whether to stay or leave.

These case studies show that the individual decision to emigrate arises from multiple personal as well as social and economic influences. Admittedly, it is difficult to define the great variablility of motivation, given the size and scale of emigration. But a selective and illustrative analysis of immigrant life histories does suggest that the great masses of data are in reality human beings who made highly personal decisions to leave their native land and to emigrate to an unknown world.

THE INTERWAR EMIGRATION, 1921-1940

Hungarian emigrants of the interwar period were deeply affected by the social and political changes that took place in Central Europe in the wake of World War I. The motivation to emigrate, attitudes toward Hungary, the social composition of the emigrants, and what might be called the restlessness of these emigrants were all influenced by the transformations following the war. In fact, to the extent that the interwar emigrants were different from their pre-war predecessors, much of the difference can be related to the radically altered society that emerged after the war.

World War I profoundly changed Hungary's international position as well as her internal structure. The country lost the significant political influence she used to have as a privileged member of the Austro-Hungarian Monarchy. She became a small nation-state in Central Europe. Her internal transformation had been painful. Her first post-war revolution, associated with the person of Count Mihály Károlyi, had been relatively violence-free. This regime, however, was crushed under the weight of external pressures and internal problems, and was replaced in March of 1919 by the Communist dictatorship of Béla Kun. The new government embarked on a violent class struggle against both the former ruling classes and the basically conservative peasantry. Some six months later the period of revolutionary experimentation was brought to an end by conservative forces headed by Admiral Miklós Horthy. The new regime was able to achieve acceptance by putting an end to unrest and turmoil and by capitalizing on the universal resentment that developed in Hungary against the Treaty of Trianon, the peace settlement which deprived Hungary of over two-thirds of her pre-war territory and assigned large Hungarian minorities to Romania, Czechoslovakia, and Yugoslavia.

These events had important consequences for Hungarian emigration in the interwar years. First, both participants and victims of the 1918 and 1919 revolutions appeared among Hungarian immigrants to North America in the 1920's. Second, as popular expectations of social reform were dashed by 1920, more of Hungary's poor became interested in emigration. Third, there were the economic setbacks caused by the war, the post-war civil strife, and the peace settlement. The Treaty of Trianon, in particular, deprived Hungary of a large portion of her natural resources and much of her transportation system and disrupted her trade patterns. The resulting economic chaos, manifested in unemployment, inflation, and poverty, made emigration a preferred alternative for many. Fourth, the Hungarian minorities in Romania, Czechoslovakia, and Yugoslavia became subject to hostile treatment on account of their

41

national origin. Many of them resorted to emigration, both to Hungary and to the New World, as a solution to their difficulties. Last, there was the old question of land tenure. The post-war revolutionaries talked of land reform but could not or would not affect suitable and lasting change. The Horthy regime did sponsor a limited land-allotment program, but this did not meet the essential need to provide basic livelihood to millions of poor peasants and landless agrarian wage-earners. The failure to implement effective land reform contributed to widespread disaffection and stimulated interest in emigration from the Hungarian countryside.

Motives of Emigration

It has been shown above that emigration motives can be explained by three principal considerations: accessible information on emigration, an international migration chain as a social network, and the propensity to emigrate. These factors also played a role in interwar emigration, but with important differences.

There is little doubt that by 1921 prospective Hungarian emigrants had access to considerable information and were able to utilize well-established migration chains to America. We have detailed testimonies regarding the availability of these resources in the interwar period. Francis Hoffmann, the Canadian immigration agent who travelled in Eastern Europe extensively in the 1920's, for example made the following observation:

> There is, of course, a fairly good knowledge amongst them (Hungarian peasants) about Canada. . . . and you very seldom go into a hamlet where there are not some members of Hungarian families in Canada and they write letters home and exercise a propaganda influence in that way.[39]

Another interesting contemporary account confirming the prevalence of information concerning emigration and the availability of migration networks can be found in the interviews of Linda Dégh with several Hungarian emigrants to Canada. The following is one emigrant's recollection:

> So, I heard one day that several people from the neighboring villages had gone to Canada. Then I said to a friend, "Hey, András" – he was my age, a year younger than I, my neighbor, András Borsi – "hey, you," I said, "how many people have left already for Canada from the neighborhood? Let's go and ask around; maybe some have sent letters back; maybe we can hear something? Let's find out about the situation." So we went over to the neighbor village. And yes, they were telling that "My son also," and "My husband, too," and this and that; they were already there and how much they were earning. So the two of us decided that in the fall of '26 that we would go to Canada.[40]

In view of the widespread availability of information concerning emigration and the existence of established migration chains, our discussion will concentrate on personal motives characteristic of interwar emigrants. These personal motives are different on several counts from the pre-war emigrant motivation. One of these can be seen in the frequency of a combination of personal, political, ideological, and economic influences. Another is the complexity of personal motivation reflected in the articulation of a high level of political and ethnic consciousness. It is also observable that the interwar emigrants related their decision to emigrate much more to political and social dissatisfaction, perceived injustices, and specific grievances than did their pre-war predecessors. Several life histories illustrate these tendencies and patterns of motivation. The following case studies are particularly interesting examples of interwar emigrant motivation.[41]

Imre emigrated to Canada in 1925. The decision to leave arose from two main influences: extreme economic hardship as a smallholder and teamster, and strong encouragement from his wife and friends. His interviewer made the following assessment of his decision to emigrate: "He had many friends who were living in America. His wife had been born in Ohio. His friends encouraged him to emigrate. His wife also encouraged him and frequently recalled her childhood experiences in the United States. He hesitated for a long time, but finally decided to leave." While Imre's case is strongly reminiscent of the pattern of pre-war motivation, it does illustrate a combination of influences at work, including accessibility of information, family persuasion, and a general form of dissatisfaction with existing conditions.

The impact of political events on emigration is shown particularly well in the published autobiography of Bernát Hoo, who emigrated from Hungary in 1925.[42] Born in Bereg county in northeastern Hungary in 1891, Hoo was the son of a smallholder who owned a ten-acre farm. His father owned and used several agricultural machines, an indication of his economic standing as well as his modern attitude. Young Hoo was employed as a farm hand, wood cutter, logger, and teamster. He saw service in World War I. Following the war, he became involved in agrarian movements seeking to carry out land distribution to smallholders and landless agrarian wage-earners. He participated in a local demonstration to secure land for distribution. The action failed and he was viewed with extreme disfavour by the authorities. He continued to participate, however, in several organizations devoted to the land distribution issue. A sense of deep disappointment with the prospects for social improvement led to his decision to emigrate:

> As we approached, a group of gendarmes ordered us to stop. They were armed with bayonets and loaded rifles. They threatened to shoot if we disobeyed their orders. We did not want to oppose the show of force. Our purpose was to gain information on land distribution. After a while we left and went home. As we returned

43

home, we considered and discussed emigration as a way out. Fifteen of those present made the decision to emigrate to Canada in the hope that we shall fare better in the New World.[43]

A different type of post-war emigrant motivation is exemplified by the story of Joseph Kéri.[44] Kéri was born in 1898 as the son of a well-to-do farmer in Szatmár county who had emigrated to America in 1908. Young Kéri served as a combatant in World War I on the Russian, Serbian, and Italian fronts. Following his return to Hungary, he lived through times of revolution, turmoil, and confusion. His native village was annexed to Romania, but many of his relatives continued to live in Hungary, on the other side of the new frontier. He tried to make a living in Hungary, but all his efforts to establish a satisfactory livelihood failed. He returned to his village in Romania. Meanwhile, one of his brothers died. A series of post-war political changes and personal failures and, above all, a sense of dislocation from his community explain to a large extent Kéri's emigration. Of these causes the most significant was the annexation of his village to Romania and the resulting sense of disorientation:

> We belonged to Hungary before the First World War. But when the War of 1914 came, they partitioned the country. I belonged to Romania, all my village. The borderline was half a kilometer from our village, Kispeleske, in Szatmár County. Now it is called Pelisor in Romanian.
>
> I came back home to Hungary. But then our country was already chopped up. In Hungary at that time there were no more than three counties free from the enemy.
>
> In a way there was no trouble. We had our land. We also had cattle as much as we had. Then we bought more stock and we began to farm. We were under Romanian occupation, I did not like this situation very much.[45]

Ambrus Lörincz is representative of a substantial group of interwar Hungarian emigrants known as the Székelys whose lands were also annexed to Romania following World War I.[46] Lörincz emigrated to Canada at the age of twenty. His father had died in the war, leaving his mother to care for three boys. The two oldest dropped out of school to help support the family. The main motive of emigration was the hostile treatment given to Székely conscripts by the officers of Romania's armed forces. As Lörincz told the story, he fled from Romania in order to escape oppression on account of his Hungarian national origin:

> You were asking: why did we come here from Transylvania? Because the Romanians treated us abominably. I mean then, it was hard on young people. And they ran away so that they could dodge the draft. . . . There were 320 of us on the same boat. . . . The same spring they would have been summoned before the recruiting commission; that's why we came in February. They mistreated us in the

Romanian army and of those who came to our village after discharge, one became deaf, they broke the nose of the other. They made them work hard; in six weeks their clothing became rags and tatters. At that time they didn't dress them up in soldier's uniforms. They weren't really soldiers; they had them only to work. Once they drafted them, they made them work for three years. There were three from our village whom they gave a beating with the gun-stock, their eardrums ruptured during military service. So we fled.[47]

From these emigrant life histories we can conclude that, following World War I, many prospective emigrants came to consider emigration as a means of resolving political dissatisfaction and social dislocation as well as economic and personal troubles. Another definite factor is the exposure of many emigrants to information concerning emigration to America, as a result of prior emigration by family members and relatives.

Emigrant Social Characteristics

We have no accurate estimates of the number of Hungarian emigrants in the interwar period. On the basis of calculations derived from several reliable sources, however, we can place the maximum number of Hungarians who emigrated at 150,000.[48]

Compared with the pre-war emigration movement, this number is insignificant. Several reasons can be cited to explain the low rate of emigration following World War I. One of these was the drastic change of the European international migration flow. While prior to the war a comparatively unhindered movement of migrants across national boundaries was prevalent, the post-war system of small nation-states effectively restricted emigration. A strict policy of surveillance at border crossings was established by the Central European nation-states. National jealousies, rivalries, and fears dictated such policies. Therefore, it was no longer possible for emigrants to board a train in Hungary and travel to Atlantic ports without being subjected to stringent police questioning and examination of travel documents. Another new factor was the immigration policy of the United States. Under the new immigration laws, the admission of East Europeans was strictly limited. As a result of this policy a substantial share of the total Hungarian emigrant group chose Canada as a land of settlement.

A survey of the social composition of interwar emigrants shows some interesting results. Most striking is the fact that a cross-section of all Hungarian social classes participated in emigration. Among the first post-war emigrants were several members of the Hungarian nobility, who escaped from the post-war revolutionary disturbances.[49] At the same time a number of artists, musicians, businessmen, and professionals also emigrated from Hungary. But it is important to point out that the large majority of interwar emigrants consisted of the agrarian wage-earning and peasant groups who had dominated pre-war emigration as well. Again, we do not have accurate data on the proportion of these groups, but it has been estimated that 75 to 80 per cent of all emigrants were agricultural wage-earners.[50]

The largest group of interwar emigrants consisted of those who emigrated from post-war Hungary in the decade 1920 to 1930. Their number has been estimated at 85,000 or almost 60 per cent of all emigrants for the period.[51] Another group emigrated from Romania, Czechoslovakia, and Yugoslavia, states which had received sizable Hungarian minorities as a result of post-war territorial settlements. It can be suggested that this group numbered approximately 37,000 emigrants or about 25 per cent of all Hungarian emigrants. A third very small group consisted of those who left Hungary in the 1930's. A derived estimate places the number of these at just over 19,000 or about 15 per cent of the total of interwar emigrants.[52]

Several comments can be made concerning the quantitative and social characteristics of this emigrant stream. Perhaps the most significant point to be made concerns the small size of the interwar emigration. It was slightly less than a quarter of the pre-war exodus. In addition, it should be noted that interwar emigrants had a great variety of troubles to prompt them to consider emigration. Economic conditions were clearly important, but other reasons for emigrating ranged from the conservative political order in Hungary to various forms of minority repression in Romania, Yugoslavia, and Czechoslovakia. Therefore it is a matter of surprise that emigration was held to such an insignificant movement, given the substantial motives to emigrate.

THE POST-WORLD WAR II EMIGRATION

With the coming of the Second World War, emigration from Hungary effectively ceased. But the war produced conditions that made the resumption of emigration certain, even before the conclusion of hostilities.

In March, 1944, German forces occupied Hungary. Six months later followed the installation of Ferenc Szálasi's Arrow Cross government. The new regime's policies included heightened loyalty to Germany, ruthless persecution of Jews, and repression of anti-Nazi elements. Not surprisingly, civilian and military personnel serving under the new government felt "compromised" and fled the country as the German armies retreated. By April of 1945, all of Hungary had been occupied by Soviet forces. The task of economic reconstruction and social reform was entrusted to a coalition government representing Hungary's left-of-centre parties. Soon, however, progressive democracy was replaced by the rule of the Communist Party, backed by Soviet power.

With Communist rule came the persecution of everyone opposed or suspected of opposition to Hungary's transformation into a Soviet-style dictatorship. The reign of police terror, show trials, imprisonments, and deportations lasted well into the mid-1950's. To prevent the new regime's victims from escaping to the West, Hungary's borders were sealed. When the frontiers were opened during the abortive anti-Communist uprising in 1956, thousands of Hungarians made use of the opportunity and fled to neighbouring Austria and Yugoslavia. By then, the number of people who had left the country for good since the last phase of the war had exceeded 300,000.

The complex events which took place in Hungary after 1944 had driven from the country groups with widely divergent social and ideological backgrounds. The members of each of these groups had different motives for emigration and brought different social values and political attitudes to their new homelands. For these reasons it is important to discuss each of these groups in some detail.

The Post-war Emigrant Groups

For the purposes of more detailed analysis, it may be said that five distinct groups of people had left Hungary since 1944. The first were those forcibly removed from Hungary during the war; the second was the group which left the country with the retreating German armies early in 1945; the third was made up of the people who fled during the Communist reign of terror; the fourth were the 1956 refugees; and the fifth, the emigrants who succeeded in leaving Hungary either legally or illegally since the Revolution.

The first of these groups was made up mainly of members of Hungary's Jewish population. They were interned in Nazi concentration camps or were employed as forced labour. Many perished before the end of the war. The total number of those who had survived the war and later emigrated overseas has been estimated at 25,000.[53]

The second, and probably the largest group to have left Hungary after 1944, was made up of those groups who fled the country during the collapse of the Axis war effort in the winter of 1944-45. These emigrants have been often labelled as "fascists" or "Nazi sympathizers," but in fact they consisted of at least three distinct elements. There were the members and followers of Szálasi's Arrow Cross movement. Then there were government bureaucrats and members of the officer corps who may not have approved of Szálasi's programs and policies, but who had continued to serve in their positions during his government. A third group consisted generally of middle-class and professional people who feared Soviet occupation and its consequences for personal reasons.

Taken as a whole, this emigrant group can be characterized as one with rather high social status in Hungary. By emigrating, it lost its wealth and social standing. This fact helps to explain this group's social psychology as emigrants. As a result of their loss of social standing, they encountered unusually great difficulties in adjusting to new social systems in Western countries.[54] The emigrant writer, Kázmér Nagy, suggests that

47

certain dominant psychological and mental attitudes characterize many members of this group. These include an extremely self-centred nationalism, psychopathic preoccupation with Hungarian history, and erratic forms of religious attachment.[55] The same author offers an interesting comment on some of these emigrants' lifestyles and social attitudes:

> The emigrant middle class, which feels acutely deprived of its social status, displays a particular preference for its traditional way of life. Naively or otherwise, they consider emigration a temporary status. This illusion sustains their existence and leads them to accept the lowest menial jobs.[56]

The size of this group is difficult to estimate. Approximately 800,000 to 1,000,000 people actually left Hungary in this period, but the majority either perished before the end of the war or returned home later. Those that remained abroad can be estimated at 55,000.[57] Their social origin was heavily middle-class. According to data of the International Refugee Organization, 57 per cent of a selected sample belonged to middle-class and 16 per cent to lower-class occupations. This estimate generally agrees with the social and political origins of this group and with the illustrated life histories discussed later in this chapter.[58]

The third post-war emigrant group left Hungary in the period 1946-49. It was made up predominantly of people who opposed the Communist-led transformation of their country. Several types of emigrants can be distinguished among them. The best known were prominent diplomats, government officials, and political leaders who had helped to establish a democratic government in Hungary in the immediate post-war period. Another type of emigrant was the businessman and professional people whose property was confiscated and who faced certain harassment in a Communist society. As Communist control over economic life was being established, more and more industrialists and managers chose to leave Hungary. Another component of this group were those who for a variety of personal and ideological reasons expressed opposition to Communism and fled the country. The size of this emigrant group has been estimated at approximately 40,000.[59] It undoubtedly represented a cross-section of the upper and middle classes, which had been deprived of their social and economic positions by the Communist dictatorship.[60]

The fourth post-war emigrant group is the best known in the Western world: those who fled Hungary after the Hungarian Revolution of 1956. It is somewhat difficult to characterize this group, in view of the dramatic circumstances of their flight, the publicity surrounding their revolutionary role, and the still prevailing preconceptions and controversies concerning their identity. One fact stands out: they were predominantly young people. Of those who came to Canada, 48 per cent were under twenty-nine years of age. Another 38 per cent were between the ages of twenty-nine and forty-five, while only 5,000 were over the age of forty-five.[61] A sample group, used for a study conducted by the Cornell University Medical College, consisted of 66 per cent below the age of twenty-five, and 30 per cent in the twenty-six to forty-five age group.[62] Another established fact is that a predominantly large proportion were highly skilled or university-educated. One study concluded that 58 per cent of emigrants arriving in the United States belonged to groups such as students, professionals, managers, and skilled technicians, while 18 per cent were considered unskilled or semi-skilled.[63] A Canadian survey of a Hungarian emigrant sample points out that 25.9 per cent were skilled workers, 17.7 per cent were vocationally trained, and another 23 per cent were managerial or professional people.[64]

The 1956 emigrant group can be characterized as socially and psychologically distinct from many of its predecessors, primarily because of its unique historical experiences. The 1956 refugees were profoundly affected by the sudden opening up of the Iron Curtain. For over eight years, it had been practically impossible for Hungarians to travel in Western countries, to observe Western social developments, or to join relatives. Now the Hungarian Revolution suddenly made possible all of these things. A Canadian study makes the following striking observation on the impact of this experience:

> The sealed borders and the closed door policies suddenly disappeared with the success of the uprising. The Western boundaries were suddenly opened and . . . large masses of people took the opportunity to escape. The chance to leave Hungary was unexpected and those who probably for many years had given up hope of ever leaving suddenly found themselves one week later walking the streets of Montreal, Toronto or some other large Canadian city.[65]

Life behind the Iron Curtain not only meant being sealed off from Western countries, but it also fostered a strong dependency on the Communist state in the most important matters of daily life, including employment, housing, social services, and education. The totalitarian system was clearly rejected by most Hungarians, yet it is unquestionable that it accustomed many to receiving the necessities of life from the state. This sense of dependency influenced the expectations of many young immigrants and inhibited temporarily their independent and responsible functioning in the receiving countries.

Experiences and educational influences in Communist Hungary did exert an impact on the social awareness, value systems, and ethnic consciousness of the 1956 emigrants. Their concepts of freedom, nationality, and morals were shaped in a period of social upheaval and violent conflict. No generalizations valid for the 1956 emigrants as a whole are possible, but certain recurring characteristics can be singled out. It is well-known, for example, that the majority shared strong national feelings against the Soviet Union. But it has also become evident that many failed to develop loyalty to the Hungarian ethnic communities of Western countries. The primary interests of these young emigrants were individual effort and advancement.[66] Furthermore, experiences of these people in Hungary predisposed them to question established social and moral ideals. This does not mean that they had abandoned moral and social commitments, but it suggests that as emigrants they reconsidered such commitments in the light of their painful disillusionment with ideological systems. When they settled in Western societies, they sustained deep skepticism toward traditional values. In many cases, their search for new values did lead to the rejection of ethnic, community, and religious relationships and to the pursuit of predominantly individual career goals.[67]

CONCLUDING OBSERVATIONS

For over a hundred years Hungarians have been leaving their country to try their luck in the New World. At first the vast majority of Hungarian emigrants to the Americas went to the United States. Since the 1920's, however, Canada has played an increasingly important role in this movement. Our survey of Hungarian emigration to North America has led to two main conclusions. The first is that the most crucial act of the emigration process is the decision to exchange the familiar native community for a strange and unknown environment. The second main conclusion is that a proper understanding of this momentous decision helps to clarify the self-perception, attitudes, and behaviour of emigrants in their new homeland.

The human context for the emigrant's decision to leave his country is defined by a variety of complex social, economic, and political circumstances, as well as personal, psychological factors to which our study has given considerable attention. Prominent among these factors is the social, political, and economic status of emigrants prior to the process of emigration. It is unquestionable that these influences have helped to shape in divergent ways the perceptions, attitudes, and patterns of behaviour of all emigrants. In the case of the early peasant emigrants, for example, there was a strong tendency to maintain the traditional ties to the family, the village, and the church, and to the ethnic community long after emigration. Mid-century emigrants, on the other hand, disillusioned by wars and political strife, displayed less interest in community life and more in the pursuit of personal fulfilment.

The decision to emigrate can be viewed also from the perspective of the so-called "push and pull" factors. The differing social, political, and economic conditions prevalent in the country of origin and country of destination undoubtedly played important roles in most Hungarians' decision to emigrate. In the case of the pre-1914 emigrants, the vital influences were economic and social distress in their homeland. Later emigrants, especially the post-1945 ones, were affected primarily by factors such as wars, ideological strife, and political persecutions. At the same time, the pull factors of economic prosperity and political security in North America also exerted their influence.

There can be little doubt that the push and pull factors contributed to shape the emigrants' attitudes in a variety of ways. A good example is the perception of early and later emigrants concerning the purpose of emigration. Most early emigrants had every intention of returning to their homeland after accumulating substantial savings. Many of them persisted in their plans for several decades. In contrast, more recent emigrants from Hungary rarely entertained such ideas. Their decision to leave had resulted from a profound disenchantment with the prevailing political and ideological order in Hungary.

Each emigrant's decision to leave his homeland and start life anew in North America was induced also by personal and family circumstances. The importance of the personal element in this decision is illustrated by the frequency of highly personal considerations that prompted people to emigrate. In the case of many emigrants, restlessness or curiosity, family disputes or other personal disappointments were as important as the more general social, economic, or political factors.

Whether influenced by personal motives, larger forces at work within Hungarian society, or a combination of both, an individual's decision to emigrate came as a result of a sense of dissatisfaction with life in his native country. That sense of discontent, combined with a hope for a better future abroad, produced the decision to emigrate. The circumstances and motives of this fateful act in turn became important determinants of emigrant lives and influenced even the lives of the emigrants' North American descendants.

APPENDIX: METHODOLOGY OF ESTIMATES AND SOURCES USED FOR TABLE 1

The following procedures were used in estimating the data provided in Table 1. In cases where available data were obviously inadequate, consistent methods of estimates were employed to supplement existing sources. In all other cases source data were used as indicated.

1. Estimate for total number of emigrants, 1870-1914. Available data for the emigration of this period are incomplete. The three main sources are the Hungarian passport counts, U.S. immigration data, and West European port statistics. Each of these sources is deficient for estimating Hungarian ethnic emigration. None of them provide accurate counts for Hungarian ethnic emigrants for the period under review and the data provided are inconsistent with each other. In order to estimate the total emigration of ethnic Hungarians in this period, the following procedures were used:

    a) Total Hungarian emigrants according to Hungarian passport counts, 1899-1913   401,123[68]

    b) Estimate of illegal emigrants, 1899-1913, reflected in West European port statistics   160,448[69]

c) Estimate of pre-1899 emigrants   77,970[70]
d) Total Hungarian emigrants, 1870-1914   639,541

2. Estimate for emigrants to U.S., 1870-1914. The two main sources used for estimating emigration to the U.S. in this period were the Hungarian passport counts and the West European port statistics. The U.S. immigration figures do not specify emigrants by ethnic origin. The two sources used are also incomplete. Their data were supplemented by adjustments and calculations.

a) Total Hungarian emigrants to U.S., 1905-1913, according to Hungarian passport counts   287,165[71]
b) Estimate of illegal emigrants to U.S., 1905-1913, indicated by West European port statistics and other sources   114,864[72]
c) Estimate of pre-1905 Hungarian emigrants to U.S.   154,410[73]
d) Total Hungarian emigrants to U.S., 1870-1914   556,439

3. Estimate for emigrants to Canada, 1870-1914. No accurate data exist for estimating the number of Hungarian emigrants to Canada in this period. Canadian census information, used with caution and adjustments, provides the most reliable basis for making an acceptable estimate.

a) Hungarian emigrants to Canada, before 1901   1,000[74]
b) Hungarian emigrants to Canada, 1901-1911   5,300[75]
c) Hungarian emigrants to Canada, 1911-1915   1,700[76]
d) Hungarian emigrants to Canada, 1870-1914   8,000

4. Estimate for total emigrants, 1921-1941. It is extremely difficult to give an accurate number for this period, due to several complicating factors. One is the lack of reliable information on the emigrants of Hungarian origin who emigrated from Romania, Czechoslovakia, and Yugoslavia. Another is the absence of consistent statistics on emigration in the 1930's. Our estimate is based on the following calculations:

a) Authorized emigrants from post-war Hungary, 1921-1930   42,591
b) Estimated illegal emigration from post-war Hungary, 1921-1930   40,000
c) Estimated emigration from succession states, 1921-1941   37,000[77]
d) Estimated emigration from post-war Hungary, 1930-1941   19,254[78]
e) Total emigration, 1921-1941, estimated   138,845
f) Total emigration, 1921-1941, adjusted   150,000

5. Estimate for emigrants to U.S., 1921-1941. Official U.S. immigration data have been used to derive Hungarian emigrants to the U.S. in this period.[79]

6. Estimate for emigrants to Canada, 1921-1941. This estimate was based on Canadian census information and additional adjustments, as outlined in the following:

a) Hungarian emigration to Canada, 1923-1929   27,600[80]
b) Hungarian emigration to Canada, 1931-1941   4,700[81]
c) Estimated emigration to Canada, 1921-1941, adjusted   33,000

7. Estimate for total emigrants, 1945-1970. See the sources cited in notes 53, 57, 59, and Report of the Intergovernmental Committee for European Migration, *Record Admission of Certain Hungarian Refugees,* December 31, 1957, U.S. Congress, House of Representatives, Report No. 1661, 85th Congress, 2nd Session.

8. Estimate for emigrants to U.S., 1945-1970. Official U.S. immigration data have been used for this estimate.[82]

9. Estimate for emigrants to Canada, 1945-1970. Official Canadian immigration data have been used for this estimate.[83]

NOTES

1. Emil Lengyel, *Americans from Hungary* (Philadelphia, 1947), pp. 47-64.
2. Julianna Puskás, *Emigration from Hungary to the United States before 1914* (Budapest, 1975), Table 1a.
3. Hungarian Bureau of Statistics, *Emigration et Retour des Émigrés des Pays de la Sainte Couronne Hongroise de 1899 à 1913* (Budapest, 1918). Publications Statistiques Hongroises, Nouvelle Serie, v. 67, pp. 97, 106. This source presents the official Hungarian passport count statistics from 1899 to 1914. It will be referred to hereafter as HBS.
4. The figure is given by Puskás, *Emigration from Hungary,* Table 1a. The most interesting recent analysis of the social and economic background is István Rácz's study: "A parasztok elvándorlása a faluból" [Migration of Peasants from the Village], in *A parasztság Magyarországon a kapitalizmus korában, 1848-1914* [The Peasantry in Hungary in the Age of Capitalism], II, pp. 433-83.
5. It is interesting to note that, prior to World War I, the overwhelming proportion of emigrants from Hungary went to North America. After the war, this trend was changed greatly. In the period since 1945, for example, only 40 per cent of the Hungarian emigrants have come to North America.
6. For further details and documentation see the subsequent sections of this chapter discussing each emigration movement in detail.
7. HBS, Table 19.
8. HBS, Table 19.
9. HBS, Table 20.
10. The best study of the agrarian social and economic structure is Tibor

53

Kolossa, "Statistische Untersuchung der sozialen Struktur der Agrarbevölkerung in den Ländern der Österreichisch-Ungarischen Monarchie (um 1900)," in *Die Agrarfrage in der Österreichisch-Ungarischen Monarchie, 1900-1918* (Bukarest, 1965), p. 168.

11. *Ibid.*, p. 139.

12. This pattern of migration has been analysed in John Kósa, *Land of Choice: The Hungarians in Canada* (Toronto, 1957). The recent collection of Hungarian emigrant life histories by Linda Dégh documents the same process: Linda Dégh, *People in the Tobacco Belt: Four Lives* (Ottawa, 1975). Unfortunately, no comparable studies are available for Hungarian immigrants in the United States.

13. HBS, p. 42.

14. Puskás, *Emigration from Hungary*, p. 26.

15. For a full discussion of this controversy and the issues, see Kristian Hvidt, *Flight to America* (New York, 1975), pp. 29-36.

16. Puskás, *Emigration from Hungary*, p. 11.

17. Kolassa, "Statistische Untersuchung," p. 168.

18. For data on migration to Budapest a good source is Gusztáv Thirring, *Budapest félszázados fejlödése 1873-1923* [Half a Century of the Development of Budapest] (Budapest, 1925), Table 53.

19. The basic study of the pull factor for Europe generally is Brinley Thomas, *Migration and Economic Growth: A Study of Great Britain and the Atlantic Economy* (Cambridge, 1954).

20. These conclusions are based on studies recently conducted in Hungarian, American, and Canadian collections. Detailed documentation of the specific points developed can be found in the subsequent discussions.

21. Sándor Bujanovics, "A felvidéki, különösen a sárosmegyei kivándorlásról" [Concerning Emigration from Upper Hungary, Particularly Sáros County], *Nemzetgazdasági Szemle (1881)*, v, no. 3, pp. 52-3.

22. Sándor Tonelli, "Utazás a magyar kivándorlókkal Amerikába" [With Hungarian Emigrants to America], *Közgazdasági Szemle*, XXXII, 40, No. 1 (1908), pp. 427-44. Also Sándor Tonelli, *Ultonia. Egy kivándorló hajó története* [Ultonia, History of an Emigrant Ship] (Budapest, 1929); Paul Farkas, *Az amerikai kivándorlás* [American Emigration] (Budapest, 1907). Numerous government reports confirm the influence of the emigrant and his letters in encouraging emigration. See, for example, the report of the administrator of Sáros County, dated March 5, 1882, to the Hungarian prime minister, in Hungarian National Archives, BM, K-150, 1882-III, 17, 6078.

23. Paul Sántha, *Three Generations, 1901-1957: The Hungarian Colony at Stockholm, Saskatchewan* (Stockholm, 1959), pp. 14-15.

24. There are indications of the widespread circulation of emigration literature in Hungary. Examples are several emigration pamphlets advertising emigrant settlements in Manitoba, reported in police reports, Hungarian National Archives, I-150-1885. A pamphlet of the "Western Canada

Farm Lands and Colonization Bureau" was noted in the provincial journal, *Somogyi Hirlap*, April 8, 1906. The North Atlantic shipping lines sent great quantities of their literature to Hungary.

25. Tonelli, "Utazás."
26. Hungarian National Archives, Report of the Torontál County Administrator dated July 12, 1910, BM-eln-K-148, 1910-26-3291.
27. For further details see the emigrant life histories discussed in this chapter.
28. *Dislocation and Emigration: The Social Background of American Immigration* (Harvard, 1974). The studies by Maldwyn Jones, Leo Schelbert, and Theodore Saloutos are particularly pertinent.
29. Maldwyn A. Jones, "The Background to Emigration from Great Britain in the Nineteenth Century," *ibid.*, p. 19.
30. An excellent analysis of emigration legislation can be found in István Rácz, "Kísérletek az Egyesült Államokba irányuló magyarországi kivándorlás korlátozására" [Attempts to Limit Emigration from Hungary to the United States], *Egyetemes Történeti Tanulmányok*, v (Debrecen, 1971), pp. 53-88,
31. Report of the administrator of the Tisza district, Szabolcs county, January 9, 1902, in Archives of Szabolcs-Szatmár, Alispáni Iratok, I-1900-236. No. 932.
32. Farkas, *Az amerikai Kivándorlás*, pp. 38-42; and I. József Gerényi, *Az amerikai kivándorlás oka és hatása* [Origin and Impact of American Emigration] (Bartfa, 1913), pp. 22-3, 35-41.
33. Numerous studies have discussed the regional patterns of emigration. A convenient English-language summary is available in Puskás, *Emigration from Hungary*.
34. These data are available in HBS, p. 49.
35. For a recent summary of this view, see Jan Sveton, "Slovenske vystahovalectvo v obdobi Uhorskeho kapitalizmus," *Ekonomicky Casopis*, IV (1956), p. 173.
36. Several studies by Hungarian scholars which deal extensively with this approach have been published in *Die Agrarfrage in der Österreichisch-Ungarischen Monarchie, 1900-1918*.
37. A basic study of this question is Manó Somogyi, *A hazai vándoripar és vándorkereskedés* [Domestic Itinerant Industry and Trade] (Budapest, 1905).
38. These case histories are in the ethnographic collections of the Church Archives of Sárospatak, Hungary.
39. Records of the Royal Commission on Immigration and Settlement of Saskatchewan, 1930, II, p. 125. Provincial Archives of Saskatchewan.
40. Dégh, *People in the Tobacco Belt*, p. 58.
41. The following case history is in the ethnographic collections of the Church Archives of Sárospatak, Hungary.
42. Bernát Hoo, *Tiszakerecsenytöl Kanadáig* (Budapest, 1963).
43. *Ibid.*, pp. 181-2.

44. Dégh, *People in the Tobacco Belt.*
45. *Ibid.*, pp. 55-7.
46. *Ibid.*
47. *Ibid.*, pp. 235-6.
48. The estimate is based on calculations derived by John Kósa, "A Century of Hungarian Emigration," *The American Slavic and East European Review,* XVI (December, 1957), p. 513. This result has been compared with incomplete tabulations of the Hungarian Statistical Office, as developed in Tivadar Szél, "A külsö vándormozgalom ujabb alakulása," *Magyar Statisztikai Szemle,* XXI, I. 2-3 sz. (1943), pp. 83-102. The two sources confirm that the estimate is reasonable.
49. Ödön Paizs, *Magyarok Kanadában* [Hungarians in Canada] (Budapest, 1928), pp. 89-97.
50. John Kósa, "Immigration and Adjustment of Hungarians in Canada" (ms, ca. 1955), p. 70. A copy of this work is in the library of the Department of the Secretary of State in Ottawa.
51. Kósa, "A Century," p. 509.
52. Szél, "A külsö vándormozgalom," p. 85.
53. This estimate has been provided by Kósa, "A Century," p. 513. The estimate has been compared with two other calculations: Jacques Vernant, *The Refugee in the Post-War World* (New Haven, 1953), p. 61; and Randolph L. Braham, *The Destruction of Hungarian Jewry* (New York, 1963), II, 970. The comparisons indicate that Kósa's estimate is the best available.
54. These views are stated in Kósa, "A Century," p. 512; and Kázmér Nagy, *Elveszett alkotmány. Vázlat az 1944 és 1964 közötti magyar politikai emigració kialakulásáról* [Lost Constitution. Notes on the Development of the Hungarian Political Emigration between 1944 and 1964] (Munich, 1974), pp. 14-16.
55. *Ibid.*
56. *Ibid.*, p. 18.
57. Kósa, "A Century," p. 513.
58. *Ibid.* A random sample of eight families who had left Hungary in late 1944 and early 1945 was interviewed by this author concerning their social status and motives of emigration. Significantly, all members of the sample group were of middle-class background: a university professor, a teacher, a landowner, a businessman, a judge, and three local government officials. All left Hungary for fear of Soviet occupation and its consequences. The landowner feared the rumoured atrocities of the invading Soviet army. The government officials left because they anticipated reprisals following the Soviet conquest. The teacher had served as a reserve officer in a forced labour camp and was concerned about his and his family's safety following Soviet occupation. The businessman emigrated because he had acquired a formerly Jewish-owned business during the war and feared that he would be imprisoned as a result of his actions. These examples show the predominant emigration motives of

this emigrant group: a general concern for personal safety, and uncertainty regarding the future following Soviet occupation and a Soviet-inspired political transformation of Hungary.

59. Kósa, "A Century," p. 513.
60. *Ibid.*, p. 512; Nagy, *Elveszett alkotmány*, pp. 18-20. A random sample of five persons, interviewed by the author, illustrates the motives of emigration of this group. One respondent, a well-to-do attorney, left Hungary in 1947 because he feared imprisonment after his properties were confiscated. Two tradesmen left because they feared political reprisals after arguments with superiors. Another person, a veterinarian, was forced to leave Hungary in 1946 because of his German ethnic origin. And the last of the group, a businessman, left to escape probable imprisonment as a capitalist "class enemy."
61. Gerald E. Dirks, *Canada's Refugee Policy* (Montreal, 1977), p. 203.
62. S. Alexander Weinstock, *Acculturation and Occupation: A Study of the 1956 Hungarian Refugees in the United States* (The Hague, 1969), p. 46.
63. *Ibid.*, p. 47.
64. Klaus Weiermair, "Economic Adjustment of Refugees in Canada: A Case Study," *Migration News*, 83 (1972), pp. 7ff.
65. E.K. Koranyi, A. Kerenyi, and G.J. Sarwer-Foner, "On Adaptive Difficulties of Some Hungarian Immigrants," *Medical Services Journal*, XIV (June, 1958), p. 392.

The deep sense of disillusionment in socialist Hungary and the revulsion against the excesses of the Communist system that many of the refugees experienced can be gauged by reading some of the life stories of the revolution's participants as told in James Michener, *Bridge at Andau* (New York, 1957), pp. 8, 27-34, 157:

József Tóth, an eighteen-year-old factory worker, had lived the years prior to the Revolution in fear of the powerful secret police. He was an average youth, trying to do his job well and trying to stay out of political difficulty. When the Revolution came, however, he was swept along with its momentum and took an active role in disarming policemen, collecting arms, and engaging a tank in battle. He left Hungary as it became evident that the Revolution would be defeated.

Péter Szigeti had accepted Communism on the basis of intellectual conviction. He believed fervently in the mission of Communism. He served in highly placed positions in the Communist Youth Movement. He repudiated Communism prior to the Revolution as a result of his perception of the gap between official promises and reality. He was turned off particularly by Soviet domination of Hungary, the police terror, and the poor economic performance. He participated in the movements and demonstrations of the Revolution. He left Hungary in protest against the Communist system of terror and deception.

György Szabó was a skilled industrial worker in the large industrial centre of Csepel, a show-piece of Communist industrial management. Although a supporter of Communism from his youth, he became disillusioned with the Communist system to improve the economic position of workers and the repression of free expression. He came to realize in fact that workers were not better off under Communism and that the oppressive system under which it operated enslaved the worker.

66. Nagy, *Elveszett alkotmány*, p. 68; Joshua Fishman, *Hungarian Language Maintenance in the United States* (Bloomington, 1966).

67. See the comments in Koranyi *et al.*, "On Adaptive Difficulties"; and sources cited in note 66.

68. HBS, p. 53.

69. The Western European port statistics are presented in Walter F. Willcox (ed.), *International Migrations* (New York, 1969), v. I, Statistics, Tables V-VIII, pp. 716-18. Illegal emigrants have been estimated by assuming that they constituted an additional 40 per cent of those who emigrated legally. This assumption is supported by port statistics tabulations and Hungarian governmental reports. One of many such reports estimated that illegal emigration amounted to at least 57 per cent of passport emigrants. Cf. Hungarian National Archives, K-26, M.E. 1905, XVI, 1450.

70. This estimate is based on an analysis of the ethnic composition of emigrants as recorded in Hungarian passport counts. It has been assumed that in this period Hungarian ethnic emigrants constituted 20 per cent of the total emigrant stream from the Kingdom of Hungary. This assumption is supported by a detailed trend analysis of Hungarian passport counts after 1899 and the testimony of Hungarian governmental reports stating that over 20 per cent of emigration represented ethnic Hungarians. Cf. Hungarian National Archives, K-26, M.E. 1905, XVI, 1450. The calculations are based on the Western European passport statistics, as published in Willcox, I, Tables V-VIII, pp. 716-18.

71. HBS, pp. 26-7.

72. Illegal emigrants have been estimated by assuming that they constituted 40 per cent of passport emigrants. This assumption is confirmed by contemporary sources, as specified in note 69.

73. This estimate was derived by assuming the following percentages for Hungarian emigrants in the following periods of emigration: 1870 to 1899: 20 per cent, 1899 to 1905: 25 per cent. A trend analysis of emigration statistics and contemporary reports as specified in note 70 support these assumptions. The Western European port statistics were used as the basis of the estimate. Cf. Willcox, I, Tables V-VIII, pp. 716-18.

74. A separate entry for Hungarians appeared in Canadian census records for the first time in 1901. Their number was given as 1,549. According to official information, this figure included Lithuanians and Moravians (presumably Czechs), two completely unrelated groups. The figure undoubtedly also included non-Magyar nationalities, especially Slovaks, who were not distinguished from ethnic Hungarians in the census records until 1921. In that year Moravians (and Lithuanians) were no longer included with Hungarians, but there was a new entry, "Czechs

and Slovaks." (*Census of Canada*, 1961, Bulletin 1.2-5, *Population: Ethnic Groups*, Table 34).

Immigration statistics for this period are equally incomplete and unreliable. Immigrant arrival statistics are available for major ports of entry such as Quebec and Halifax, but port officials did not distinguish Hungarians from Austrians until the late 1890's. No attempt was made to differentiate among the various nationalities coming from Hungary until several years later. In 1898 Canadian immigration officials estimated the number of Hungarian arrivals to that date at "about 1,000." Later, they gave the number of those who landed in 1899 as 176. (Report of the Department of the Interior on Immigration for 1902, p. 120, printed in Sessional Paper no. 25 for 1902, Canada, Parliament, *Sessional Papers*, Vol. 10, 1902). There is every reason to believe that these figures included Hungarians of non-Magyar ethnic background.

The 1921 census gave the number of Hungarians who came to Canada before 1901 and were still living in the country in 1921 as 846. (*Census of Canada*, 1921, II, Table 61.) Based on this mass of unreliable information, 1,000 is probably a reasonable estimate of the total Magyar emigrants to Canada before 1901.

75.   The 1911 census gave the number of Hungarians as 11,648. This figure, also, included Lithuanians and Moravians, and undoubtedly, Slovaks and other non-Magyar nationalities as well. Immigration statistics for the 1901-1911 period are particularly confusing. By the middle of the decade, figures were entered in the statistics for not only Hungarians, but Slovaks, Croatians and Magyars as well. According to the statistics, 1,400 Magyars came to Canada between 1904 and 1911. For the same period the number of Hungarians is given as 4,260. (Statistics provided in the annual reports of the Department of the Interior, printed in the Sessional Papers for these years.) Since the number of Slovak immigrants is also rather small, these figures suggest either that most immigrants from Hungary were neither Magyar nor Slovak, or that the statistics are very unreliable. The available evidence suggests that the latter is the case. Accordingly, we are forced to rely on 1921 census data giving the number of ethnic Hungarians living in Canada at that time who came to this country between 1901 and 1911. This figure is 4,850 (*Census of Canada*, 1921, II, Table 61). Assuming, rather arbitrarily, that about nine out of every ten of these immigrants were still alive and living in Canada in 1921, we arrive at the approximate figure of 5,300.

76.   The 1921 census gives 1,528 as the figure for Hungarian immigrants still living in Canada in 1921 who arrived here in 1911-1914 (*Census of Canada*, 1921, II, Table 61). Using the method of calculation outlined in the above footnote, we arrive at the approximate figure of 1,700. Estimates for Section 3 of Appendix were provided by N.F. Dreisziger.

77.   Kósa, "A Century," p. 508.

78.   Szél, "A külsö vándormozgalom," pp. 83-102.

79. U.S. Department of Justice, Immigration and Naturalization Service, *1976 Annual Report* (Washington, D.C., 1976), Table 13, p. 87.

80. Report of the Department of Immigration and Colonization for the Fiscal Year Ended 31 March 1930, Table 5 (p. 12), in *Annual Departmental Report, 1929-30*, Vol. II (Ottawa, 1931).

81. *Census of Canada*, 1941, II, Table 32, pp. 424-26. According to official Hungarian statistics, 2,800 of these emigrants came from Hungary proper. See Egon Szabady *et al. Magyarország népesedése a két világháboru között* [Hungary's Population between the Two World Wars] (Budapest, 1965), p. 327. Presumably, the remaining 1,900 came mainly from the three other East Central European states with large Hungarian populations: Romania, Yugoslavia, and Czechoslovakia.

82. Official U.S. immigration data pertaining to Hungarian immigrants to the United States from 1946 to 1973 are available in U.S. Department of Justice, Immigration and Naturalization Service, *1973 Annual Report of the Commissioner of Immigration and Naturalization* (Washington, D.C., 1973), Table 6E, p. 35.

83. Immigration statistics published annually by the Department of Citizenship and Immigration in Ottawa. Also, Vernant, *The Refugee*, p. 72.

THREE

The Saskatchewan Era, 1885-1914

M.L. Kovacs

IMMIGRATION AND SETTLEMENT

The first settlements of Hungarians in Canada were established, almost without exception, in regions which later become parts of the province of Saskatchewan. Although Saskatchewan's Magyars constitute today only a small fraction of Canada's total Hungarian population, the province was often looked upon as Canada's "Little Hungary" before 1914. A large majority of Hungarian Canadians lived there, and Saskatchewan was the home of nearly all important Hungarian-Canadian communities. Hungarian life in the province often served as inspiration and model to Magyars living in the rest of the country. It is the purpose of this chapter to outline the early history of Saskatchewan's Hungarian settlements as well as to show how Hungarian-Canadian "ethnocultural islands" on the Prairies were affected until about 1914 by the interplay between the agencies of cultural continuity and the forces of modernization and change.

The coming of Hungarian immigrants to the Canadian West was the coincidence of two historical developments: the presence of factors in Hungary after 1880 prompting the emigration of a large number of people, and the desire of Canada's leaders to populate the vast and largely empty lands west of Ontario. In Hungary, the idea of emigration to distant North America was grafted onto the public's consciousness by the example of the post-1849 Hungarian refugees who had gone to the United States. The process of the post-1880 emigration was then facilitated by such members of this group as Paul Oscar Esterhazy, who in the 1880's became one of the most effective promoters of Hungarian immigration to the United States and Canada. Esterhazy, with his aristocratic appearance and military bearing, was able to impress and influence people; nevertheless, it is obvious that even the most persuasive immigration agent could not have been successful in his work without social, economic, and psychological factors in Hungary favouring a major population movement.

On the northern half of the North American continent, developments such as the acquisition of Alaska by the United States in 1867 and the rapid advance of the American frontier toward the forty-ninth parallel helped to prompt the leaders of the newly established Dominion of Canada to take steps to prepare for the peopling of the immense tract of land stretching from Ontario to the Pacific Coast. These measures included the securing of the vast areas known as "Rupert's Land," the surveying of the Prairies, the start of construction of the Canadian Pacific Railway, and the recruiting of immigrants in Europe and elsewhere. The Canadian government would have preferred farmers from the United Kingdom, but these people were reluctant to come to Canada in the 1880's and 1890's. Thus, the tough, hard-working, and unassuming peasants of Central and Eastern Europe were sought after as pioneers for the virgin lands of the Canadian Plains.[1]

Hungarian peasants were among the first to come. Although their way of life was closely associated with farming and animal husbandry, they could not be equated with what North Americans called farmers. Socially, they stood somewhere between the propertyless day labourers and the smallholders who owned a dozen or so acres of land. They rarely had any greater economic ambition than to produce food for their families and market enough of it to obtain cash to pay taxes and buy goods that could not be made by hand at home. By tradition, peasants did not always till the land individually as farmers today do. Moreover, they were members of the village, the peasant community which formed in many ways a uniform style of life.[2]

One of the basic facts of Hungarian immigration to Canada is that most of the first and many of the later Hungarian newcomers came via the United States. Hungarians began arriving in American industrial and mining centres in the early 1880's. But life in such places as Pennsylvania's mines and iron foundries was not easy. Owing to their lack of skills, technical and linguistic alike, most Hungarians and other Central and East Europeans were hired for the most undesirable, most dangerous, and worst paying jobs. They were likely also to be caught up in battles between management and employees, either as strikers or, more often, as strike-breakers. They often became the object of public hostility and ridicule.[3] Life in the cities was unpleasant for these ex-peasants, and the particular conditions they encountered in Pennsylvania of the 1880's made them especially anxious to return to the land. The fact that many of the early transmigrants became successful and contented homesteaders in Canada made the idea of relocation all the more attractive to Hungarians who remained in American industrial and mining centres.[4]

The Settlement Process

When Hungarian newcomers from the United States or, as became increasingly the case in the 1890's, directly from Hungary arrived in the Canadian West, they were detrained at the railroad station nearest to their ultimate destination. From there they were directed to the township where land was available for them.[5] Despite the existence of an ingenious system for the location of townships and of "sections" within them, newcomers often found it very difficult to find the allotted homesteads or "quarter sections." They were usually helped in this task, as well as others awaiting the would-be homesteaders, by a settling agent. This person was usually an enterprising Hungarian peasant who had settled on the Prairies earlier, but in some cases it was a member of the Hungarian intelligentsia imbued with the idea of establishing prosperous Hungarian settlements in Canada. In fact, Esterhazy, the most notable of this latter type of settling agents, had hoped to create a "New Hungary" on the Canadian Prairies.[6]

Esterhazy's dream of a region populated by Hungarian settlers was never realized. Instead, what took place was the establishment of scattered Hungarian colonies in the area bounded by the present-day communities of Whitewood, Kipling, and Wakaw.

The Early Colonies

The first "Hungarian" settlement in the Canadian West was Hunsvalley (originally Hungarian-Valley), in Manitoba. It was established in August of 1885 near the village of Minnedosa by Magyar and Slovak settlers under the leadership of Géza de Dóry.[7] But Hunsvalley did not become a Hungarian colony of any consequence: after the premature death of Dóry, most of the Magyar homesteaders drifted away. More permanent was the colony established by Esterhazy near the city that bears his name today.

Esterhazy's dream of a "New Hungary" in Canada has been mentioned. He had taken the first substantial step for the realization of his plans in June of 1885 when he and Dóry visited the Whitewood region of the district of Assiniboia. Esterhazy planned to bring a large number of Hungarians from Pennsylvania to this part of the Canadian Prairies in 1886, but only a few of those who had put down their names as prospects for the intended settlement actually undertook the long journey. Nevertheless, by June 8, 1886, Esterhazy's advance party had reached Winnipeg, and it was followed in a few days by a group made up of thirty families. By the end of the month the newcomers had been located on their lands near Whitewood, were put up in tents, and had started to break up some land to plant potatoes.[8]

The settlers of what became known for many years as Esterhaz received help from Sir George Stephens, the president of the Canadian Pacific Railway Company, in the form of a loan of $15,000 which was handled by the Canadian North-West Land Company. The money was used to buy implements and oxen for each family, and to have a sizable farmhouse built for them. The settlers did not realize the magnitude of the debts they incurred, otherwise they might have preferred to erect inexpensive log cabins for themselves.[9] After a while, most newcomers fell behind in the repayment of their portion of the loan. This fact proved an embarrassment for Esterhazy and contributed to his dismissal by Ottawa as an official immigration agent. In Esterhaz itself, prairie fires, an extremely cold winter in 1886-87, and discord among the homesteaders led to the drifting away of all but a few of the original pioneers. Fortunately, the colony was saved when new settlers arrived in 1888 from Hungary as well as from the United States.[10] It should be added that Esterhazy himself never settled in the colony but maintained cordial contacts with its people. When the region received a railway station in 1902, it was named after him. The town of Esterhazy was to grow up around this station. In the meantime, the Hungarian settlement in the area became known as Kaposvar, named after a Hungarian city with large Esterhazy estates.[11]

Another Hungarian colony, named Otthon (Home), came into being during the mid-1890's a few miles southwest of Yorkton. It was the fruit of the efforts of the Reverend János (John) Kovács, the founder of the first Hungarian Reform Church of Pittsburgh, Pennsylvania, and an advocate of a "return-to-nature" philosophy among his immigrant countrymen. The first settlers of Otthon consisted of only a handful of people, but soon Kovács and his followers were joined by more than a dozen families from the United States as well as several from Hungary.[12]

A more important settlement of Hungarian Calvinists grew up after the turn of the century near Kipling. The core of the population of Bekevar (correctly, Békevár – Fortress of Peace, or, another possible meaning: Peace Awaits You) came from the village of Botrágy in northeastern Hungary. The real founder of the colony was János (John) Szabó, a man who had first tried his luck in the United States. Just as the Rev. Kovács of Otthon had been inspired by Esterhazy's colonization efforts, Szabó conceived his plans to start homesteading in Canada after reading about Kovács' success in the Hungarian-American press. In 1900, after a visit to his native Botrágy, he came to Canada and, two years later, he and two of his relatives selected their homesteads in what was soon to become Bekevar. Thereafter Szabó acted as an unofficial settling agent who recruited relatives as well as co-villagers as immigrants, and helped them as an *anchorage person* in starting life anew on the Prairies.[13]

The most active Hungarian anchorage person seems to have been Imre (James) Pinke of Whitewood. Pinke, a native of western Hungary, was also a transmigrant from the United States. He attracted settlers to the vicinity of his own farm chiefly by writing about homesteading in Canada in Hungarian-American newspapers. Through such means he became the founder of the colony of St. Luke, which by 1898 had almost 200 residents. But St. Luke was made up of a mixture of nationalities and religious groups and never developed a cohesive Hungarian community

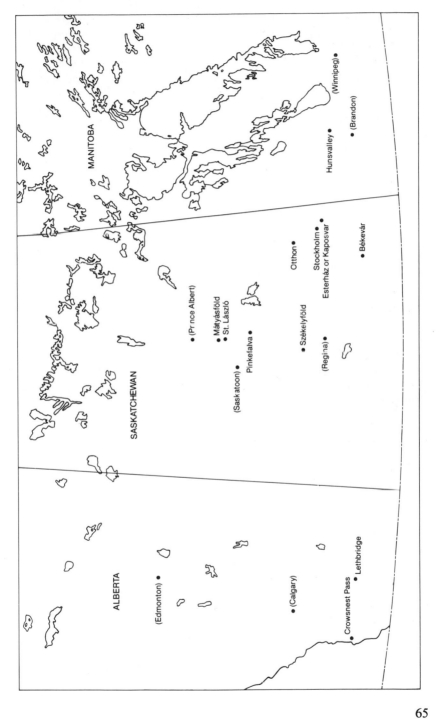

life.[14] Later Pinke became instrumental in the establishment of a more homogeneous Hungarian colony near Plunkett, appropriately called Pinkefalva (Pinke's Village).[15]

Another Hungarian colony was Stockholm. Its name derived from "New Stockholm," a settlement of Swedish immigrants established near Esterhaz in 1886. After the turn of the century, the Reverend Francis Woodcutter, the priest of Esterhaz, began to promote Hungarian Catholic settlement in the Swedish colony's vicinity in order to ensure the future of Catholic influence in the area. By 1903 he had succeeded in settling some fifty Hungarian families in the community they would call Sokhalom (Many Hills). It may be of interest that many of the arrivals were relatives and *földi(s)* (co-regionalists) of the settlers of Esterhaz, and that several of the second-generation Esterhazians also took up homesteads in this area.[16] Throughout the interwar years, and even later, the Stockholm-Kaposvar district was to be one of the foremost centres of Catholic Hungarian influence not only in Sasktachewan but in the whole of Canada.

By the early years of the new century, Hungarian immigrants were also making their appearance on the northern Prairies, in the areas between Saskatoon and Prince Albert. One of the largest Hungarian colonies here became Mátyásföld (the Land of Matthias), established under the leadership of Zoltán Rajcs in what is now the Wakaw-Prud'homme area. Rajcs planned also to establish a Hungarian urban settlement here named Idavár (Ida's Fortress) but failed to realize his plan. The market and shopping facility for the pioneers of this area was to be Wakaw. In time this town acquired a substantial Hungarian population.[17] Those Hungarians who could not receive land in the Wakaw area were directed by Rajcs to a still-vacant township south of present-day Wakaw. Here the newcomers established the colony of St. László, close to Howell (later known as Prud'homme). The Hungarian settlers of this area suffered not only from the severe prairie winters but also from the multitude of mosquitoes, which made the summers miserable for everyone.[18]

The last early settlement of Hungarians that deserves a mention in a brief survey such as this is Székelyföld (the Land of the Székelys). This was the unofficial name of an area about sixty-five miles north of Regina, in the vicinity of Arbury. The settlers of Székelyföld came from southern Bukovina (today part of Romania). The first members of the group arrived in Saskatchewan in 1906 and quickly alerted their co-villagers in Bukovina about the great opportunities offered by Canada. A point of interest about the settlers of Székelyföld is that they built their houses in the old Transylvanian Székely style, after having lived for some time in temporary shelters made of wooden poles and sheaves of grass.[19]

Adjustment to the Environment

Immigrants usually find different physical, social, and cultural conditions in their new homeland. Whether they like it or not, they must adjust, to some extent at least, to the new environment. Adjustment involves both the acquiring of new ways and the discarding of old ones. For Hungarian newcomers to the Prairies the first major task of adjustment was getting used to the climate. Esterhazy had only praise for Canadian winters:

> During the winter months the country is blessed with that peculiarly healthful, elastic, bracing atmosphere so common to the higher latitudes, which gives such a buoyancy and vigour to the mind and body. . . .[20]

But surviving the prairie climate proved to be a trying experience. The newcomers made the adjustment by adopting winter garments worn in Canada and by settling near woodlots, if at all possible, to ensure ample supply of firewood. Canadian house styles and traditions were usually not followed at first; only when the homesteaders replaced their first permanent dwellings with new and usually larger ones did they opt for Canadian-type houses.[21]

In the realm of social conventions, also, Hungarian peasants had to make adjustments. They had to get used to being called "Mister" whereas in the old country members of the higher classes simply addressed them by their first names or turned to them with the proverbial "hey you." This change was welcome, but some other Canadian social conventions or traditions were more difficult to accept. One of these was the higher status of women. Although the wife was the most important worker of the Hungarian immigrant household, working often at least from dawn until well after dusk and partaking in various chores, she was expected to show deference to her menfolk even after years and decades of life in Canada.[22]

One of the great difficulties faced by the settlers in their new environment was their near-total and, in some cases, total inability to communicate in English. It is noteworthy that Esterhazy, who had a superb command of English, was held in very high respect by his Hungarian settlers. Perhaps it is no exaggeration to say that the better a Hungarian immigrant spoke English, the higher his social status was within his community.[23] Unfortunately for the settler, the improvement of his English did not depend entirely, or even to a large extent, on his determination. Yet, even though most Hungarian newcomers acquired only modest language skills and vocabularies, they made sure that their children had a reasonable command of English (as well as Hungarian). Interestingly enough, while progress in the knowledge of English was made from one generation to the next, there was a deterioration in the standard of spoken Hungarian. Often even first-generation Hungarian Canadians were found groping for words to describe some novel aspect of their new lives for which their Hungarian contained no equivalents. The result was the adoption of English terms with Hungarian endings such as boxi (box), káré (car), and the like.

As far as language was concerned, a dual process was taking place in most Hungarian-Canadian colonies throughout the years under discussion in this chapter. The native tongue was taught to the children while both the first and second generation settlers attempted to learn English. And the same dual process went on in regard to aspects of culture other than language, such as value systems, customs, literature, art, and folklore. Sociologists call these processes enculturation and acculturation. The former as a rule refers to the exposure of children to their ancestral culture with the aim of acquiring as many elements of this culture as possible. Cultural transmission of a different kind is implied by the word acculturation. It, too, denotes initiation into a culture, but *not* the ancestral culture. Acculturation refers to the changes in the mind of the immigrant, or a member of an ethnic group, effected by environmental influences coming from the larger society within which he or his particular group is living.[24] Expressed briefly, enculturation works toward cultural continuity while acculturation introduces cultural change.

The coexistence of enculturation and acculturation in early Hungarian-Canadian communities was a normal phenomenon. The efforts to perpetuate the native culture were inevitable. The continued contact between the newcomer and his own culture is one of the essential conditions of his emotional stability. The preference of Hungarian newcomers to settle in groups was motivated by much more than their desire for fraternal economic co-operation. In group settlements they hoped to maximize the prospects of maintaining their ancestral culture. Yet the Hungarian "heritage" had to be adjusted to the new circumstances. Unfortunately for the cause of cultural continuity, every adjustment represented a change that involved a modification or even a disruption of existing practices, customs, and patterns of behaviour. Inevitably, the desire of the settlers for cultural fulfilment in the midst of their own kind conflicted with the pressures of the North American milieu for technological efficiency, conformity, and greater rationality. Rationality itself tended to argue against cultural continuity. The latter rested on *emotional* group solidarity and orientation to the past, while rationality suggested conformity (*rational* group solidarity) and modernization, which was present- and future-directed. Moreover, modernization eroded the bases of cultural continuity by increasing the prospects of quick social mobility – outside the ethnic community – and thereby reducing many individuals' beliefs in the value of ethnocultural integrity. Indeed, it seems that in the contest between the agencies of continuity and change, the forces had been mostly unequal, and the outcome was preordained. This fact may explain why Hungarian (and other) prairie settlements or "ethnic islands" with the passage of time underwent similar stages and patterns of transformation.

THE AGENCIES OF CONTINUITY

An ethnocultural island may be conceived of as a more or less closely settled ethnic community. It can be termed an "island" because it is enclosed by socio-cultural boundaries, with boundaries meaning "criteria of membership." Membership is based on values adopted by the group.[25] Owing to factors such as the peculiar nature of the township-range system, the opening up of railway and homestead lands in various stages, and the arrival of waves of immigrants at irregular intervals, practically no prairie settlement ever attained complete ethnocultural homogeneity. Thus these "islands" can only be theoretical models, which are useful for the purposes of analytical description but reflect reality only in a greater or smaller measure. In any case, the cultural vitality of an "island" is dependent not so much on the ethnic homogeneity of the people living in a geographic area as on the nature and strength of the institutions it possesses. It seems to be the rule that the more an ethnic island can rely on institutions of its own, the stronger and stabler its social and cultural boundaries tend to be.[26]

The Church

The most significant and influential institution of the early Hungarian-Canadian communities was the church. As Hungarian immigrants of the Roman Catholic faith outnumbered Protestants about two to one – reflecting fairly accurately the ratio between the two groups in Hungary – it is not surprising that the first Hungarian-Canadian religious organization was a Roman Catholic one, the parish at Esterhaz-Kaposvar. It was established in 1889 but did not have a resident priest for some time, and it would still be a number of years until a massive stone church would be built by the parishioners.

The Archdiocese of St. Boniface was on the very frontier of the Church of Rome and it took considerable time for innovations deriving from the modernization process at the centre to reach Winnipeg. This lag in cultural transmission was further increased by the desire of the prelate in charge to maintain strict control over local affairs in the Archdiocese. Thus, parish priests were kept under close watch and, until about 1911, were expected to govern their parishes almost in a patriarchal manner. Since no real efforts were made by the Archbishop of St. Boniface to obtain Hungarian priests, and since the few priests that were assigned to Esterhaz-Kaposvar and, later, elsewhere, achieved only a limited command of Magyar, Hungarian Roman Catholic settlers in all parts of Saskatchewan longed for religious services in their own language.[27] With the exception of Esterhaz-Kaposvar and Stockholm, however, Hungarian Roman Catholic communities rarely possessed enough determination and funds to maintain a priest of their own on a permanent basis.[28] As a result, most of the settlements remained "missions," with priests from other parishes visiting them once a month or once a quarter. Other colonies such as Plunkett, Howell, and Székelyföld maintained a priest for some time but later relapsed into mere missions.

Because of the centralized nature of the Roman Catholic Church, the ultramontane proclivity of some of its local leaders, and the cosmopolitan inclinations of certain priests assigned to serve Hungarian pioneers, the development of Hungarian ethnocultural institutions in Saskatchewan's Roman Catholic districts was very slow or nonexistent. A change in this respect began to take place only in 1910-1911, by which time there were several Hungarian priests residing in the Canadian West.[29]

In contrast to the Roman Catholic parishes, the Reformed Church of Bekevar would be a more typical institution produced by an ethnocultural island. Its success in this respect can be explained partly by the decentralized character of the Reformed Church and partly by the greater cultural and religious homogeneity that characterized this pioneer community. In fact, the Church of Bekevar was the colony's most significant social institution, surpassed in importance only by the family.

Particularly in its first five years of existence, Bekevar tended to be a wholly religious settlement, almost a community in the biblical sense. Families took turns hosting church services and thereby hosted the entire congregation. The minister boarded with one family after another. As the officers of the *presbyterium*, the governing body of the congregation, were elected annually at a general meeting of the members, there was ample opportunity for practising corporate leadership in the community. As time passed, the power of the *presbyterium* gradually grew, and so did its influence in matters not related to religion.[30]

The Family

The early Hungarian-Canadian family was the basic institution for the preservation of the native language, folkways, mores, and traditions; the handing down of these to the offspring formed the most important process of enculturation. The early Bekevar family, to take one example, resembled the old Hungarian extended family in that often the adult sons – even after their marriage – stayed for some time under the same parental roofs and co-operated in carrying out farming activities.[31] Families were almost inevitably large and virtually self-supporting even though they maintained, as a rule, close and frequent contacts with their kinfolk. Every member of the family would carry out some helpful function within the familial economy. Thus every child was useful and, therefore, welcome. As children were numerous, most of the time they entertained each other. The eldest daughter often looked after younger children and taught them various skills, including the speaking of the native language. In some families, elderly members regularly treated the young ones to stories and fairy tales, thus assisting in their enculturation. In certain cases, particularly when the elderly had been left behind in the old country, the more communicative of the parents undertook this task. Occasionally he or she would, at the end of the day, make one or another of the children read or recite passages from the Hungarian Bible or some other book, or would dictate a few lines for the child to take down. Although the rule was that when there was company youngsters were to be seen and not heard, they would follow with interest the adults' conversation in Hungarian, from which they would obtain much information regarding their culture.[32] Another source of family enculturation consisted of reading Hungarian books, usually borrowed from other families or from communal libraries. Even more common was the reading of Hungarian-language journals and newspapers published in the United States and, later, in Canada, or, in rare cases, sent from Hungary.[33]

The Rites of Passage

Associated with family and church life were certain rites such as baptismal, wedding, and funeral ceremonies. All these rites pertained to and marked major transitions in human life. Some incorporated elements derived from the past and reflected aspects of life no longer familiar or comprehensible. Rites of passage were important for Hungarian pioneers and for their communities, and for this reason they required attention marked with communal ceremonies.[34] Baptism not only signified incorporation into a religion, but also initiated a new human being into the community. Its solemnity was manifested by ceremonies which required witnessing by the whole or a part of the settlement. In a way, baptism also signalled the augmentation of the membership of the kin, the village, and so on. Consequently, celebrants at a baptism would include most members of the kinship and village networks. In the early days baptism was marked by *mulatás* (approximately, "merry-making"), in which the members of these networks participated. Among the most important celebrants were the *komas* (godparents).[35]

One of the early baptismal celebrations was reported in 1909 from Howell (Szent László): "A boy was delivered by a stork to . . . the farm of Mihály Andre. A big celebration was given. . . . All the relatives appeared and had a good *mulatság.*" Another baptism at the time in Cana is known to have attracted Hungarians "from far afield" and was celebrated with "heady wine and the Kossuth song until the next morning."[36] A similarly impressive celebration followed the baptism of István Varga's son in Otthon: "grandparents, relatives, and good friends came in great number and the celebration did not end until the wee hours of the morning."[37] At the baptism of András Bucsis's son at Saxon-Hill, near Otthon, many visitors from nearby communities were treated to midday dinner in the Hungarian style, which was followed by an *áldomás* (a special type of toast) with the help of a barrel of beer.[38]

Marriage and its ceremonial aspect, the wedding, are of central importance in human life. Consequently, they have been surrounded by more rites and ceremonies than the other two rites of passage, baptisms and funerals. Traditional wedding rites formed an essential portion of the culture of Hungarian-Canadian communities and thereby constituted, together with the baptismal and funeral, a segment of their socio-cultural "boundaries." One of the important components of wedding rites was the *leánykérés* (proposing) and the *eljegyzés* (betrothal).[39] For both the individuals involved and the community, the most important event was the *lakodalom* (wedding), and it was connected with the most numerous and intricate rites and rituals requiring the participation of many functionaries. For instance, the Elemér Herperger-Mariska Dancsok wedding at Benchonzie was attended by six *násznagy(s)* (best men), four *nászasszony(s)* (matrons of honour), six *nyoszolyolány(s)* (bridesmaids), and six *vöfély(s)*.[40] The leader of the last-named group, the *nagyvöfély* (the bridegroom's senior friend), was the most important person in the wedding party. His functions approximated those of master of ceremonies. The main qualifications for the role were a quick mind, a sense of humour, and a good knowledge of the *vöfély* rhymes.[41]

To act out all the traditional rites and rituals of the wedding and to have, in addition, a proper *mulatság*, unavoidably took a long time. The Benchonzie wedding, for example, went on until the evening of the second day.[42] As to the length of a wedding, the Lajos Göncy and Erzsi Szarka nuptials at Lethbridge probably set some kind of a record with a three-day celebration.[43] In terms of splendour, the József Mokay-Erzsébet Janoczko union stood out with twelve *násznagy(s)* and twelve *vöfély(s)* invited from various Hungarian-Canadian settlements of the West, and a *násznép* (wedding crowd) exceeding 400.[44]

It is of interest that some of the early inter-ethnic weddings took place in accordance with Hungarian traditions. Thus, for instance, Jim Smart and Mária Diósy were wed in 1911 surrounded by *násznagy(s), vöfély(s), nyoszolyó asszony(s)*, and the like.[45] There can be little doubt that wedding rites played an important part in the maintenance of Hungarian culture and traditions.

Funeral rites also played a significant role in the life of Hungarian-Canadian communities. In the early days, with practically no undertakers available, it fell to the individuals and the group to facilitate the passage of the dead, both in the physical and the spiritual aspects, out of this existence into the next. Thus, from the preparation of the casket to the interment itself, members of the kin and friendship networks assisted. Accounts of funerals reveal a definite structure. The rites included the *virrasztó* (approx.: the wake), the church service, and the graveside ceremony, consisting of the *bucsuztató* (farewell to the deceased) and the *temetés* (burial). Yet, for the living there remained one more rite, the funeral feast. Funeral rites provided still another mechanism for keeping the settlements culturally identifiable and socially cohesive.

The Community as an Agency of Continuity

In studying the early Hungarian-Canadian settlements on the Prairie, the fact emerges that they possessed, from the beginning, different levels of socio-cultural cohesion. Some of them became "culture centres" and displayed much cultural vitality. Others showed this type of creativity for a short time only, and still others, not at all.[46]

In addition to the church and the family, Hungarian community associations as well as institutionalized practices can be categorized as "instruments" for the maintenance and promotion of the communal ethnoculture. Hungarian-Canadian associations sprouted up in comparatively great variety and number, if we take all the Saskatchewan colonies into consideration. Nevertheless, they conformed to certain definite patterns. Most of them seem to have had a limited life span; and, as a rule, associations with manifold objectives proved to be the most enduring.[47] Today, even the memory of these early associations is often forgotten. This seems to have been the fate of the Wakaw and Area Hungarian Sickness and Death Benefit Society, one of the first of such associations in Saskatchewan.[48]

Denominational lay organizations first emerged at Bekevar, although, strictly speaking, the word "cultic" would be more fitting in the context. There is no doubt that the Christian Spiritists' Society was, for a while, the most controversial organization inside Bekevar or out. Its appearance suggests that the established churches could not or would not cater fully to the spiritual and socio-cultural needs of part of their membership. Yet the society contributed to the establishment of Bekevar as a leading culture centre.[49] Another significant association, the Self-Training Circle, was, judging by the membership, the socio-cultural side of the Spiritists' Society. This association was destined to become the predecessor to the subsequent Hungarian halls. The musical counterpart of the same complex was the Bekevar Brass Band. It contributed to the colony's self-sufficiency in communal entertainment and thereby to another "boundary" for the Bekevar ethnic enclave.[50]

Some organizations were established for a specific purpose. Among these were the committees in charge of holding "Hungarian picnics." Not only the larger colonies but also some of the smaller ones arranged these events. Their net receipts were usually assigned to some community project, such as a church fund. The picnics themselves brought together old and young, men and women, in merriment and friendly competition. But picnics were not strictly an "ethnic event," since everyone was invited, irrespective of religious and ethnic background.[51]

Somewhat similar to picnics, but usually more formal and often solemn, were community celebrations. The word "celebration" means the marking or observing of an event, place, object, or person, often with ceremonies. The solemn ingredients of a celebration include demonstrations of solidarity and socio-cultural cohesion, or a public reaffirmation of communal, religious, or national values. In early

73

Hungarian-Canadian folk communities an important element of such an event was the *mulatás*.[52] *Mulatás* basically resembled rejoicing on the individual or the group level, often accompanied by some singing or instrumental music; however, it could also be characterized by sadness and world-weariness. It was often an occasion for the release of pent-up emotions in a conspicuous manner. Sometimes it was an act of catharsis, but more frequently it was a convivial sharing of one another's hospitality and interaction. *Mulatás*, in a wider social context, complete with dancing and the taking of food and drinks, constituted a *mulatság*.

Celebrations on the *individual* level include, as seen above, the passage rites and the anniversaries connected with them, i.e., birthdays, wedding anniversaries, and the recalling of funerals.[53] In the same category could be listed the celebrations such as housewarming, grain milling, the slaughtering of a pig, and the *szüret* (vintage).[54] Celebrations of the *communal* type were events such as community foundation jubilees. The tenth-anniversary jubilee of Bekevar constituted a major event in 1910. The covert objective of these celebrations was to challenge the Kaposvarians to stage their forthcoming twenty-fifth anniversary in the same manner. The plan turned out to be successful. Despite the negative attitude of the Roman Catholic Church to demonstrations of ethnic awareness, the people of Kaposvar organized an even more conspicuous jubilee celebration than that which had been held at Bekevar.[55] Still another aim of these and other festivities was to create a more favourable image for Hungarians. In this the Magyars of Mátyásföld (Wakaw) excelled. At their 1910 festival they managed to draw a crowd of about 1,000 visitors of diverse ethnic backgrounds by staging horseraces and other popular diversions.[56]

Celebrations linked with the cultivation of a favourable image of Hungary and Hungarians included the annual March 15th and October 6th festivals commemorating the outbreak and suppression of the 1848-49 revolution respectively. These were complete with Hungarian costumes, displays of flags, and speeches about Hungarian history.[57] Celebrations of *religious* character included consecrations of churches, the most famous example of which was connected with the stately stone church of Kaposvar. This event was the occasion for the largest gathering of Hungarian Canadians up to 1908.[58]

Less solemn, and therefore probably more popular with the young, were the *mulatság(s)*. These informal events were undoubtedly effective instruments in the enculturation of the young. *Mulatság(s)* were held at carnival time at Cana. Easter *mulatság(s)* took place at the home of Mihály Viczkó at Howell.[59] The Corpus Christi holiday at Otthon proved to be a good opportunity for the Hungarian Canadians of Saxon Hill, Halmok, Cana, Otthon, and even Stockholm to get together and have a *mulatság*.[60]

Another activity important for the continuation of the ancestral culture was the writing of prose and poetry. Since most Hungarian immigrants to Canada had six years or less of formal education, writers and poets did not abound among them. Yet involvement in creative writing was not unusual for the early pioneers and, in a culture such as Bekevar, a veritable literary life existed under the guidance and inspiration of the Reverend Kálmán Kovácsi, himself a poet of some repute in Hungary.[61]

So far we have seen how former members of village communities in Hungary formed new settlements on the Canadian Prairies and what circumstances favoured the continued development of their native culture. In the following pages those influences will be discussed which, as agencies of modernization, were concurrently working for socio-cultural change.

AGENCIES OF CHANGE

Peculiarities of Land Distribution

The settlement of the West took place mainly on the basis of a land survey which had provided a very rational and accurate network of townships, each containing thirty-six square miles, or 23,040 acres. For the purpose of settling, one quarter-section (160 acres) constituted the basic unit.

Theoretically, 144 families could take up residence in every township, but in reality the system worked in a significantly different manner. First of all, only the even-numbered sections were thrown open originally as free homestead land, odd-numbered sections having been reserved for the railways. This way the railway companies could sell their lands at higher prices later when their properties appreciated in value as a result of the increase of population on the adjacent "free" lands. Secondly, only one or a few townships were opened up at a time in any one area.[62] This practice was designed to prevent land speculation; but one of its important consequences was that immigrants, unless they arrived in one big group, were likely to be dispersed in the various townships and ranges and would be mixed among immigrants of different national backgrounds.[63] And even in the case of a comparatively homogeneous *bloc* settlement an appreciable scattering of various ethnic elements was likely to occur. Thus, the peculiarities of land distribution formed a vigorous agency of ethnic intermingling and, as a result, of socio-cultural change.

Technological Change

Technological change was gradually bringing about a pervasive alteration in the early settlers' living standards and lifestyles. In the end, it affected most elements of Hungarian-Canadian culture.

The impact of farm mechanization can be gauged from production estimates that exist for the Otthon area in 1899 and 1909. According to these figures, in 1909 one big farmer, working with modern machinery, could produce more than what two or three townships could only ten years earlier.[64] Six years later, in 1914, still more advanced machinery appeared on the Prairies, at least according to advertisements published in the Hungarian-Canadian press. International Harvester's self-propelled diesels were supposed to be able to plough in twelve hours as much as a team of horses could in a month; and the diesel was able to plough, harrow, and seed, all in one operation.[65] Other types of new machinery, such as more efficient threshing machines and motor-saws, also became available about this time.[66]

Mechanization meant that farmers could increase the amount of land under cultivation. At the same time, the number of workers needed to produce the same crop declined. These developments caused sizable population shifts on the Saskatchewan plains. More enterprising and efficient farmers bought out the homesteads of others. Those who sold out – often at attractive prices – either moved north and started pioneering all over again or settled in the newly sprouting urban communities. A few, especially among the elderly, gathered their savings and returned to their native villages in the old country.[67] These changes brought an exodus from many of the Hungarian-Canadian ethnic islands, as well as a simultaneous scattering of Hungarians over the Prairies.

Technological change affected not only farm production but also the means and nature of transportation on the Prairies. The expansion of the West's railway network both provided easier and quicker travel for Hungarian Canadians and offered seasonal work for the less successful farmer in need of supplementing his income and for newcomers wishing to start saving money for a farm. In a different way, the building of branchlines and the establishment of more railway stations brought a dramatic change in the lives of many settlers. The difference that a new station made can be understood when it is realized that before the setting up of railway stations at Bender and Kipling, the farmers of Bekevar had to haul their crop – in the middle of winter – to Whitewood (about 64 km) and Broadview (about 30 km).[68]

When the railway did come to an area, it did more than decrease the distance that crops had to be transported. In the immediate vicinity of new stations, parcels of land were bought up by dealers, tradesmen, and speculators.[69] When the railway came to Bender and Kipling in 1908, both places began to show signs of early urbanization. In some cases, however, urbanization began before the coming of the railway, as was the case at Howell.

The motorcar began to appear in Hungarian-Canadian settlements in the early 1910's. Cars in those days often proved to be a nuisance both for their owners and the public; nevertheless, they were bought by people who wished to affect a higher social status or wanted to attract publicity for the sake of business. It is not surprising that the first Hungarian Canadian to own an automobile was a merchant, Kristóf Lukácsffy of Wakaw.[70] During World War I, the use of the motorcar began to spread in Hungarian-Canadian settlements. There is a report to the effect that a Hungarian wedding procession in Cana in 1915 included, besides fifty carriages, four cars; and that later on that year the fifth automobile was bought in Otthon.[71] By 1916 the number of cars in use around Matyásföld justified the setting up by E.L. Bakonyi, a Hungarian entrepreneur in Wakaw, of the "Grand Garage."[72]

Apart from other effects, the railway and the automobile gave the settlers of the West an increasing ease of mobility. Easier travel meant new and more contacts with the outside world. Out of these would come business opportunities, friendships with non-Hungarians, and even interethnic marriages. Spatial mobility, then, tended to interact with and reinforce social and economic mobility. Improved transportation helped to dissolve ethnic boundaries. It tended also to promote urbanization on the Prairies, which in turn further hindered culture maintenance by ethnic groups.

Urbanization on the Prairies

When planning railway branchlines and stations, the railway companies could not foresee the impending trend toward population decrease in the countryside. Consequently, the lines built and stations established proved far too close to one another. This meant that only a few railway centres could emerge as towns. For a community to become an urban centre, there had to be more going for it than a railway station. It had to have some attraction such as industrial or commercial activity or railway stockyards. With the passage of time some communities grew, while others stagnated or even declined. Esterhazy, the station established in 1903, prospered because it served as a distribution and supply point for Hungarian immigrants, as well as a market centre for Kaposvar and a few other farming settlements. In contrast, other Hungarian or partly Hungarian community centres lost out in the competition for urban growth. Otthon could not compete with Yorkton, nor St. László with Prud'homme, nor Plunkett with Saskatoon.[73] Bekevar, not a railway centre itself, lost its function as a marketplace to Kipling, a divisional point.[74]

As towns in Saskatchewan grew, more Hungarians were attracted to them. Many of these were transients such as domestic servants and railway maintenance workers. Others were entrepreneurs. János Terepoczky, for example, built an inn in the town of Mostyn. Lajos Gönzy, Sr., set up a billiard parlor and barbershop at Leross.[75] The already mentioned Lukácsffy was a general merchant, while Péter Németh, earlier an "ethnic newspaperman," became a dealer in farm machinery in Wakaw.[76]

The West's newly emerging towns were generally marketplaces for neighbouring colonies populated by a variety of ethnic groups; they used English as the *lingua franca* of trade and social life. Entrepreneurial success in these towns usually depended on the individual's degree of mastery of English and his connections among the English-speaking population. Here Hungarian Canadians were at a disadvantage in comparison with persons of British background. But despite the language barrier, many of them became prominent businessmen; however, only a few succeeded in the long run. Many of them were ruined or greatly weakened by the recessions of the post-World War I era. And even fewer among them would survive the Depression of the 1930's.[77]

The School as an Instrument of Change

The system of education that evolved on the Prairies was a decentralized one. A high degree of autonomy was vested in the local school districts, with a small board of trustees having responsibility for decisions. The school district was also responsible for the construction and maintenance of schools and for paying the teacher or teachers. While the system was effective in keeping expenses to reasonable levels, it caused difficulties in school districts inhabited by recent immigrants from non-English-speaking countries. The fact was that Hungarian peasant farmers, not knowing the language or the procedures of school administration, were at first too frightened to assume the role of school trustees.[78] Matters improved only in the case of the post-1900 immigrants. The people of Bekevar, for example, were apparently keen to assume the direction of formal education in their settlement; unfortunately, for some time they could not raise the necessary funds either among themselves or from the government.

The available evidence regarding early Hungarian-Canadian attitudes to schooling suggests that Hungarian parents wanted their offspring to acquire good command of English through attendance in schools with English as the language of instruction.[79] These parents were impressed by the egalitarian nature of Canadian society and by the prospects of socioeconomic advancement for their children. And, those Hungarian immigrants who were convinced of their eventual return to the old country thought that their "educated" children would easily acquire the ancestral culture once they arrived in Hungary. In any case, Hungarian or bilingual schools did not have a future in Saskatchewan. After the First World War, the provincial government abolished instruction in languages other than English.[80] Schools, then, were obviously important instruments in the acculturation of Hungarian children. Their effectiveness in some small country schools was limited only by the shortness of the school year, the frequent changing of teachers, and the presence among the pupils of a majority of Magyar-speaking children.[81]

Two Supracommunal Associations

The Hungarian settlements of Saskatchewan were scattered over a wide area. They were connected by an awareness of each other, reinforced by mutual visits by individuals, as well as by chance meetings of people at marketplaces. They were also linked through Winnipeg's role as the commercial, cultural, and religious metropolis for eastern Saskatchewan.

Winnipeg was the seat of the Archdiocese of St. Boniface. An equally important role in the lives of Hungarian-Canadian Calvinists was played by the Superintendent of the Presbyterian Missions for the West, also located in Winnipeg. It was through this office that the Kovácsi brothers – Kálmán, the poet, and Lajos – were brought to the Canadian West from Hungary. Their accomplishments were to include the founding of a Hungarian Reformed Congregation in Winnipeg, the launching of a new Hungarian newspaper, and the formation of the supracommunal organizations of 1908 and 1910.

The attempts to organize the scattered communities of Hungarian Canadians stemmed from concerns over culture maintenance.[82] At a meeting in February, 1908, a group of Winnipeg Hungarians established the Canadai Magyar Szövetség (Canadian Hungarian Association, henceforth CMSz) and set up an organizing committee with Lajos Kovácsi as its secretary. The CMSz's first branch came into being with fifty-three members in Bekevar under the leadership of Kálmán Kovácsi.[83] Apparently the Association expected to function through local branches, like the one established at Bekevar, and hoped to help member communities to obtain schools and clergymen. In the light of later developments, it can be assumed that the CMSz would have liked to get the local branches to opt for bilingual (Hungarian-English) separate schools, as well as for Hungarian priests or ministers. But the attempt of 1908 could not achieve its aims, as the CMSz proved abortive.[84] All it did was to point out the need for united action. Such action was demanded, for example, by a meeting of some 150 people in the Wakaw area where it was concluded that, in order to promote their interests, Hungarian Canadians had to "organize."[85]

Soon it became obvious to Hungarian-Canadian leaders that without adequate finances their organizational efforts were doomed. As good Kossuthist liberals, they had always been close to Canada's Liberal Party and turned to it for a subvention. Their plea fell on receptive ears, and money was channelled into their hands through the Hungarian-Canadian press.[86] As a result of this, Lajos Kovácsi and his associates could make a new attempt at creating a new supracommunal organization. After some preparations, they established the Canadai Magyar Testvéri Szövetség (Canadian Hungarian Fraternal Association, hereafter CMTSz) in 1910. In a rare instance of interdenominational co-operation, both the Reformed Congregation and the Roman Catholic Parish of Winnipeg joined the new organization.[87] They were followed by branch associations from such Saskatchewan communities as Bekevar, Benchonzi, Cupar, Viscount-Plunkett, Howell, and Wakaw.[88] But Kaposvar, Esterhazy, and Stockholm refused to join. Under pressure from their local priest, not one person from these places participated in the Association's work.[89] The reason for this was that by this time the Hungarian community of the Canadian West was deep in the throes of a dispute, the so-called Hungarian school question.

The School Question on the Prairies

The root of this dispute went deeper than the demands of the Hungarian-Canadian elite to obtain Magyar teachers and priests for a few settlements in Saskatchewan. The controversy seems to have been part of a Canada-wide disagreement within the Roman Catholic Church, as well as a conflict between the Archbishop of St. Boniface and his opponents both inside and outside the Catholic Church. The real issue was language and culture maintenance for the francophone population of the West. Central and East European immigrants of the Catholic faith became pawns in this controversy when the West's French-Canadian clergy, led by Archbishop Adelard Langevin, decided to achieve their objectives by applying political pressure through the threatened manipulation of the "Catholic vote." Accordingly, parishes of immigrant settlers were kept under the close control of the francophone priests assigned to them. In the parish of Kaposvar and its missions, Archbishop Langevin's agent-in-place was Father Jules Pirot. It became his task to "defend" the ultramontane Catholic position in the Hungarian school question controversy.

The controversy was triggered by three developments that appeared to threaten the position of the Archbishop. The first was the arrival, without the consent of the Winnipeg Church fathers, of a Hungarian priest, Father Menyhért Érdújhelyi, an advocate of Hungarian bilingual "separate schools." The second was the merger of the Canadian West's two Hungarian-language newspapers, *Canadian Hungarians* and *Magyar Farmer*, into the *Canadai Magyar Farmer* (hereafter *CMF*) early in 1910 under editors whose hostility to the ultramontane Catholic view was evident. The third and most important event was a public statement by the Austro-Hungarian consul in Winnipeg accusing the local church leaders of preventing Ukrainian and Hungarian Catholic settlers from obtaining priests of their own nationality. Although the consul's rather undiplomatic remarks had been occasioned by Ukrainian complaints, the Church authorities thought it wise to respond to the accusations without any reference to the Ukrainians, but to concentrate instead on a small and potentially weaker group, the Hungarians.[90]

The initial exchange between the consul and Father Pirot, the Church's unofficial spokesman in the matter, was followed by public recriminations between Pirot, on the one hand, and Érdújhelyi, Lajos Kovácsi, and some of their associates on the other. The debate became so bitter that Archbishop Langevin threatened to excommunicate any Hungarian Catholic who subscribed to the *CMF*, the chief mouthpiece of the CMTSz.[91] In the end both sides claimed victory, Pirot in a pamphlet he published on the dispute and the editors of *CMF* in the pages of their newspaper.[92] In reality, however, neither side was victorious. The Archbishop's victory consisted of excluding the *CMF* from most Hungarian Catholic homes. His opponents had equally little to show for their efforts. A very few Hungarians did go to teach in Hungarian-Canadian community schools as a result of the publicity caused by the dispute, but they did not stay long: they could not obtain permanent teacher's permits, and they found their salaries less than enticing.[93] True, the campaign for Magyar clergy appeared to have been more successful. During the next few years additional Hungarian priests arrived on the Prairies and they were put in charge of a number of Hungarian parishes and missions. However, this development was not so much the result of the schools question controversy but of administrative reform within the Roman Catholic Church.[94] As a postscript to this dispute it might be added that the actions of Kovácsi and his group, from the founding of the *CMF* to the frontal attack on the policies of Archbishop Langevin, seem to have been inspired and even "orchestrated" by the Liberals of the time who were not averse to seeing the ultramontane elements of the francophone clergy incriminated. Certainly, the CMTSz's organizational work and its propaganda campaigns could not have been carried out without considerable financial and moral support from the Liberals.

While the Kovácsi group's immediate aim was undoubtedly to obtain Hungarian teachers and priests for Hungarian-Canadian communities, it is perhaps safe to assume that their long-range objective was the reconciliation of the processes of continuity and change. Through the creation of Hungarian-Canadian co-operatives, which would have promoted technological and economic advancement without damaging the native culture, they wanted to take charge of modernization and make it an instrument of continuity. In addition, they hoped to obtain certain cultural and socio-economic favours for their compatriots through the creation of an effective pressure group.

The preconditions for achieving these objectives were the attainment of a consensus among Hungarian Canadians and the continued rule of the Liberals in Ottawa. In the end, neither of these conditions was realized. The denominational segmentation of Hungarian Canadians could not easily be overcome, nor was it possible to bridge the traditional social differences and mutual distrust between the peasant settlers and the members of the Hungarian elite. Furthermore, the resolute measure taken by the Archbishop against *CMF* greatly weakened the influence of Kovácsi and his associates in Roman Catholic communities. Success, in the form of replacement of francophone priests, proved too late – after the defeat of the Liberal Party in the elections of September, 1911 – to be politically helpful for Hungarian Canadians. The final blow to Hungarian-Canadian organizational and political hopes came with the outbreak of the war. By 1916 the CMTSz and many local associations had ceased to function, partly because of the war atmosphere[95] and partly as a result of the departure – for the same reason – of the Kovácsi brothers and other key persons to the still neutral United States. The *CMF* was taken over by Father L.J. Schaffer, who did not share the former editors' aspirations.

In the meantime, change continued to be an important aspect of the

Hungarian-Canadian settlers' lives. By the early 1910's many of them had become quite prosperous. From 1913 on, they were threatened by a major economic depression. The downturn in the West's economy was reversed by the war, which created a growing demand for food and brought unprecedented prosperity for Hungarian-Canadian farmers. It caused accelerated commercial, technological, and cultural change, and also turned many Hungarian Canadians' concerns away from politics. The sudden swerve of many of Hungary's leaders from the Kossuthist, anti-Habsburg attitude to support for Vienna's war effort proved too much to digest for many a Hungarian Canadian. Then there was the psychological problem created by the conflicting expectations that stemmed from the new citizenship and the old. Still another problem was the growth of nativistic antagonism to Central European immigrants in Canada and the resulting administrative measures taken against their organizations and institutions.[96] This was a good time to concentrate on wheat growing and to forget about ethnic loyalties and complex political questions. Nevertheless, many young Hungarian Canadians joined Canada's forces. Most of those who did saw action in Europe and some made the supreme sacrifice.

CONCLUSIONS

Between 1885 and 1914 thousands of peasants from Hungary's villages, driven by overpopulation and poverty and enticed by better economic prospects in Canada, immigrated to the Canadian West. There, they gradually reconstituted themselves into folk communities – complete with important socio-cultural institutions – on the pattern of their ancestral villages.

Within these "ethnic islands" certain social, cultural, and economic factors favoured the preservation of the immigrants' culture, while others worked for its modification. These "agencies" of continuity and change have been discussed in this chapter with the implied understanding that factors governing the evolution of ethnic communities cannot really be compartmentalized because they continually interact with each other as well as with society at large. Because of the nature of their traditions, lifestyles, and institutions, these folk communities were unable to resist the pervasive forces of modernization.

The fact that the Hungarian communities of Saskatchewan were waging a losing battle against the agencies of change was noticed and voiced, albeit in simple terms, by members of the Hungarian-Canadian elite. They proposed to counteract these trends by hiring native Hungarian teachers and priests, and in the long run, by obtaining certain socioeconomic benefits for Hungarians through the creation of an effective political lobby. While efforts in this direction had certain positive results, such as the establishment of a supracommunal association, the launching of a large newspaper, and the attack against the ultramontane franco-phone Church fathers, permanent success eluded the Hungarian-Canadian leaders. Consensus on a lasting and effective strategy of culture maintenance could not be achieved within an ethnic group divided by denominational and social differences.

The coming of World War I brought accelerated cultural and other change, especially in urban communities. In farming regions, the arrival of unprecedented prosperity helped to divert attention from cultural and political preoccupations. The war also brought the departure of influential Hungarian-Canadian leaders to the United States, the collapse of the Canadian Hungarian Fraternal Association, and the takeover of the Hungarian newspaper by an editor unsympathetic to his predecessor's aspirations.

By this time there were definite signs indicating that socio-cultural boundaries in Hungarian-Canadian islands were weakening. Even the speech used by the settlers was changing. In earlier years, when contacts with outsiders were few, and social interaction within the "ethnic island" consisted mostly of face-to-face communications, the language used was strictly Hungarian, with little difference between casual and non-casual speech. Later, with the growth of economic and social relations with out-siders, a certain degree of bilingualism evolved, and a form of English (depending on the speaker's efficiency) was used in contacts with non-Hungarians. By the 1910's, as a result of increasing urbanization and economic diversification on the Prairies, the incidence of bilingualism among Hungarian settlers grew, and so did speech stratification and stylistic variations. Individuals began to depart from traditional patterns not only in speech but also in social conventions and dress and even in eating habits. Yet within the ethnic island itself, English was still used only for communication with outsiders, for official transactions es-pecially with higher authorities, and for running the school system. It would be only decades later, after further inroads on the ancestral culture by modernization, urbanization, the schools, and the media, that the position of Hungarian as the language of the island's basic institu-tions would be undermined.

NOTES

1. Norman Macdonald, *Canada, Immigration and Colonization, 1841-1903* (Toronto, 1966), pp. 129, 147. See also D.J. Hall, "Clifford Sifton: Immigration and Settlement Policy 1896-1905," in Howard Palmer (ed.), *The Settlement of the West* (Calgary, 1977), pp. 76-7, 249.

2. A good study of a one-time village community in Hungary is Z.S. Papp, *The Life of the Beregdaróc People* (Budapest, 1975). Many significant points are given in István Rácz's "Peasant Migration from the Village," in István Szabó (ed.), *The Peasantry in Hungary during the Era of*

Capitalism 1848-1914 (Budapest, 1972), vol. II; and also, Leslie Konnyu, *Hungarians in the United States: An Immigration Study* (St. Louis, 1967), pp. 15-16.

3. M.L. Kovacs, "From Peasant Village to the Canadian Prairies," in Tom M.S. Priestly (ed.), *Proceedings of the First Banff Conference on Central and East European Studies* (Edmonton, 1977), pp. 364-72.

4. The fate of Hungarian transmigrants became known to Hungarian Americans mainly through the Hungarian-American press. See, for example, Péter Németh's report in *Új Hazánk* [Our New Country], New York, 2 December 1906. There was also persistent opposition in various American publications to the idea of transmigration to Canada. The first attack appeared in the *Austrian-American Journal* in 1885, quoted in *Fremden-Blatt*, Vienna, 24 July 1885. For a later attack, see *Szabadság* [Liberty], Cleveland, 26 September 1901.

5. Immigrants with money often preferred to buy land from railway companies at three to nine dollars an acre. Poorer newcomers usually applied to the government for free homesteads even if their soil appeared to be inferior. Chester Martin, *"Dominion Lands" Policy* (Toronto, 1973), pp. 16-19, 45-52.

6. For the names and activities of some of these agents, see the discussion below, as well as M.L. Kovacs, *Esterhazy and Early Hungarian Immigration to Canada* (Regina, 1974), pp. 1-15, 157-8. On Esterhazy's ambitions, see his letters to the Governor General of Canada, 9 and 21 May 1885, in Public Archives of Canada (PAC), Governor General's Records, RG 7 G 20, vol. 222, no. 395 and vol. 225, no. 456.

7. PAC, P.O. Esterhazy to John Carling, Minister of Agriculture, 1 October 1886, Department of Agriculture Records, RG 17, vol. 505, file 55, 534.

8. *The Regina Leader*, 16 June 1885; *Manitoba Daily Free Press*, 8 June 1886. Not all the newcomers in Esterhazy's party were Magyars. The first and last names on the list of settlers suggest Slovakian or Ruthenian (Ukrainian) descent. See Kovacs, *Esterhazy*, pp. 55, 160ff.

9. PAC, W.B. Scarth to H.H. Smith, 24 April 1893, Department of the Interior Records, RG 15 B 1a, vol. 104, file 90,895, part 2.

10. PAC, J. Lowe to P.O. Esterhazy, 23 July 1888, RG 17, vol. 1566, p. 102.

11. PAC, R.S. Park to H.H. Smith, 24 October 1890, RG 15 B 1a, vol. 104, file 90,895, part 2. Also, *Winnipeg Free Press,* 29 October 1890.

12. Mrs. L. Saxon, née Julia Brehoczky, Reminiscences (ms, 1948), pp. 1-6.

13. Interview with one of the original settlers, Péter Debreceni, aged ninety-six. Also, Gyula Izsák, "The History of Bekevar," *Kanadai Magyar Újság (KMU)*, 19 and 21 July 1925.

14. For one of Pinke's articles, see the *Amerikai Nemzetör (AN)*, 28 April 1897. Also, PAC, C.W. Speers to Frank Pedley, 22 December 1898, Records of the Immigration Branch, RG 76, vol. 178, file 60868, part 1.

15. Paul Sántha, writing in *KMU*, 27 April 1943. Cf. *Whitewood Herald*, 27 August 1903.

16. Paul Sántha, *Three Generations, 1901-1957* (Stockholm, 1959), pp. 15-17. Also, Sántha writing in *KMU*, 16 June 1953. Interview with Stephen Szmerekovszky.

17. Sántha, writing about the history of the region in *KMU*, November-December, 1942. Also, *Kanadai Magyarság (KM)*, December, 1905. A survey of the plan of Idavár is in the author's possession. Also, PAC, C.W. Speers to W.D. Scott, 28 January 1904, RG 76, vol. 132, file 60,868, part 2.

18. Sántha writing in *KMU*, 15 January 1943. Interview with Steve Miskolczi.

19. Sántha writing in *KMU*, 7 March to 18 April 1947. Sántha himself was of Bukovinan Székely background and had spent some time as a priest in Székelyföld.

20. P.O. Esterhazy, *The Hungarian Colony of Esterhaz, Assiniboia, North-West Territories, Canada* (Ottawa, 1902), pp. 8-9.

21. *Ibid.*, pp. 38ff. *Whitewood Herald*, 14 May 1903.

22. Several elderly male informants would address their wives in the familiar *second* person, while these used the courteous *third* person when speaking to their husbands in the course of the interviews.

23. Some settlers pretended to know English for the sake of improving their image and influence. Gyula Izsák, *A Szamaritánus* [The Samaritan] (Toronto, 1954), p. 50.

24. Acculturation is a complex and disparate process which affects individuals and groups in highly different ways and degrees. Cf. M. Clark *et al.*, "Explorations of Acculturation," *Human Organization*, 35 (1976), pp. 231-9.

25. F. Barth, "Introduction," in F. Barth (ed.), *Ethnic Groups and Boundaries* (Boston, 1969), pp. 9-13, 113.

26. Although the nature and effects of social, cultural, and ecological segregation have been known for a long time, their serious study in this country with reference to urban ethnic groups began with Raymond Breton's "Institutional Completeness of Ethnic Communities and Personal Relations to Immigrants," *American Journal of Sociology*, 70 (1964), pp. 193-205.

27. M.L. Kovacs, "The Hungarian School Question," in M.L. Kovacs (ed.), *Ethnic Canadians: Culture and Education* (Regina, 1978), pp. 333-5.

28. Wakaw (Mátyásföld) had the disadvantage of being divided both ethnically and denominationally; the initially united parish broke up into German-speaking and Hungarian-speaking entities, neither of which was strong enough to survive. Cana proved mostly too weak to progress beyond the stage of possessing its own church and having periodical visits from the priests of other parishes. See *Canadai Magyar Farmer (CMF)*, 31 March 1911, 5 July 1912; *KMU*, 1 January 1943.

29. The development of Hungarian ethnocultural institutions in Roman Catholic settlements after 1910 will be discussed in some detail below.

Hungarian Roman Catholic priests in Canada after 1908 were the Reverend Menyhért Érdujhelyi (1862-1925), Oszkár Sólymos (1872-1938), who arrived in 1911, and Istvan Soós (1864-1947), who came in 1914. Soós later became instrumental in bringing to Canada Pál (Paul) Sántha (1890-1962), who became one of the most influential Hungarian-Canadian priests in the interwar years. See the Files of the Clergy, no. 3393/1923, Archiepiscopal Archives, Esztergom, Hungary.

30.   The more democratic make-up of the Reformed Church was bound to show itself, as in the case of most Protestant denominations, in a higher proclivity for members to join other denominations, sects, or cults. In the early years the most successful in attracting members of the Reformed Church was the Baptist Church of Bekevar, founded in 1903 by immigrants recently converted in Hungary. The Bekevar church was one of four Hungarian Baptist congregations of Saskatchewan. Rev. John Monus, "History of Calvary Baptist Church, Kipling," in *Calvary Baptist Church, 1912-1972* (Kipling, 1972), pp. 1-2. The other three congregations: Leask, Prince Albert, and Wakaw. See *A Brief History of Wakaw Baptist Church, 1916-1976* (Wakaw, 1976), pp. 1-3. Other denominations appeared in the interwar years.

31.   John Kósa attempts to reduce – without much justification – the fairly complex social relationships of the peasant community into a "sib system" inherited from the nobility of old. Kósa, *Land of Choice: The Hungarians in Canada* (Toronto, 1957), pp. 13ff.

32.   Interviews. Portions of the present chapter referring to Bekevar are based on a more intensive study by this writer: *Peace and Strife: Some Facets of the History of an Early Prairie Community* (Kipling, Saskatchewan, 1980).

33.   Hungarian immigrants arriving via the United States often subscribed to Hungarian-American newspapers such as *Amerikai Nemzetör* (American National Guard) and *Szabadság* (Liberty). The first known Hungarian-language newspaper in Canada was *Kanadai Magyarság* (Canadian Hungarians); it appeared on March 15, 1905. In 1909 it was followed by *Magyar Farmer.*

34.   See Arnold van Gennep, *The Rites of Passage,* tr. Monika B. Vizedom and Gabrielle L. Caffee (Chicago, 1960), p. vii and *passim.*

35.   The *koma* network included the respective godparents of the parents, the *komas* acquired through the birth of earlier siblings, and the current ones. Interviews. Concerning "networks," see Jeremy Boissevain, *Friends of Friends* (Oxford, 1974), pp. 28ff.

36.   *CMF,* 10 May 1910.

37.   *CMF,* 15 June 1915.

38.   *CMF,* 15 October 1913.

39.   The *leánykérés* (formal proposing) was the result of a successful *udvarlás* (courting) of an *eladólany* ("girl for sale," that is, of marriageable age) by a *legény* (young single man) and it involved official suitors as well as the parents. The *eljegyzés* actually amounted to the conclusion

of a preliminary marriage contract, which fact was also shown by the technical terms applied in connection with it. Thus, the *kézfogó*, the solemn clasping of hands; the *jegyváltás*, the exchange of a *jegy*, that is, external evidence of contracting, a troth. The *jegypénz* (earnest money), a symbolic deposit, recalls the time of centuries ago when brides were purchased. The memory of the same era has been preserved in the designation *völegény* (shortened from *vevö legény*: "young man about to purchase"). Still, *jegypénz*, in the form of engagement coins, was given by Lajos Szabó to Etelka Izsák at their *eljegyés* at Bekevar in October, 1910. (Several interviews between 1972 and 1977.)

40. *CMF*, 9 June 1911.

41. The *vöfély* rhymes, written down by hand in booklets in practically every peasant community of the old country, showed a number of individual differences, due to changing times and circumstances, yet they contained certain surprising similarities, just like the wedding rites themselves. These common features, as found in the two *vöfély* books surviving at Bekevar, reveal the structure both of the wedding celebrations and of the *vöfély* lines. Thus the first major activity of the *vöfélys* was the delivery in person of wedding invitations with some rhymes. As to the wedding proper, the *nagyvöfély* assembled the *völegény's* wedding crowd and led them to the bridal house, where he effected "the delivery of the bride," despite the attempt to fob off a "limping bride" on him instead of the proper one. After the lunch at the bride's house the *nagyvöfély* had the opportunity to draw tears from his audience at the "farewell of the bride."

42. The account in *CMF* (9 June 1911), of course, does not go into a description of too many details, but clearly indicates the main stages of the Hungarian wedding, which also boasted a *bandérium* (mounted procession) of young men, followed by girls and boys in Hungarian folk costume.

43. *CMF*, 15 February 1910. Lajos Gönczy was one of the sons of Lajos Gönczy, Sr., one of the very early settlers of Esterhaz and Kaposvar. Kovacs, *Esterhazy*, pp. 95, 141, 142.

44. *KM*, 26 June 1908. The reason for the size of the celebration was the fact that János Janoczko, the bride's father, was one of the Esterhaz-Kaposvar pioneers who was already well-to-do in 1902. Kovacs, *Esterhazy*, pp. 114, 150-2.

45. The wedding vow was taken in the Kaposvar stone church on February 27, 1911, while the wedding meals took place and the ceremonies were performed at the home of István Diósy, the bride's father, at Grovepark, in the vicinity of Kaposvar. *CMF*, 10 March 1911.

46. There seems to have been a direct correlation between a community's artistic and literary creativity and the degree of homogeneity (both ethnic and religious) of its population.

47. Hungarians of Otthon, together with members of ethnocultural groups, readily responded to the establishment in 1910 of an association of the

"multicultural" type, a local branch of the Saskatchewan Grain Growers' Association. (*CMF,* 12 July 1910.)

48. The Hungarian Canadians of Wakaw area, counting 150, set up the above organization on May 28, 1908. The organization's founding and aims are described in *KM,* 12 June 1908. This newspaper report notwithstanding, one old-timer of Wakaw, Mrs. Mihály Nagy, née Rózsi Veixl, 84, thought she had never heard of the association (1 September 1977).

49. *CMF,* 15 March 1910. The members of the group were highly religious and they worked out a compromise solution for themselves to integrate the Calvinist teachings of their church in which they found motivation for intellectual creativity (in Hungarian, the same term expresses spirit and intellect alike) with the spiritist doctrines. For spiritism at Bekevar, see G. Izsák, *The Samaritan;* J. Pirot, *One Year's Fight for the True Faith in Saskatchewan; or, The Hungarian Question in Canada in 1910* (Toronto, 1911), pp. 6, 24, and *passim.*

50. The house of the self-training circle opened in the spring of 1910 (*CMF,* 3 May 1910). Other buildings in the Bekevar Centre were the Kossuth School, the "Great Church," the manse, the Baptist Church and manse, the cemeteries, and the Bekevar post office.

   By 1910 other communities also possessed musical groups, e.g., the Rákóczi Orchestra of Otthon (*CMF,* 30 August 1910), the János Barilla Band of Kaposvar and Cana (interviews), and the Stockholm Orchestra of József Kiss (*KM,* 26 February 1919).

51. *CMF,* 5 July 1912.

52. The derivation of the term *mulat* ("make something pass or fade away") seems to suggest an original meaning connected with "propitiatory sacrifice" by means of partaking of food, drinks, and merrymaking.

53. Birthday and wedding anniversary celebrations did not become prominent in the Hungarian-Canadian settlements until later years. A yearly minor, symbolic recollection of the funeral took place in the Roman Catholic parishes on All Saints' Days. On the other hand, the celebration of names' days were popular from the beginning: János Miskolczi's home at Howell became the scene of what amounted to a family reunion of thirty-three persons on his names' day (*KM,* 31 December 1919). At Wakaw, József Zsombor's names' day celebration was combined with that of March 15 "with the strains of the Kossuth song . . . under the full splendour of the Aurora Borealis." *CMF,* 15 March 1911.

54. József Zsombor's attractive new house at Mátyásföld-Wakaw was filled with good friends for its inauguration, two of whom provided music for "the inevitable dancing, which did not stop until 6 a.m." *CMF,* 1 November 1910. One instance of grain-milling *mulatás* is described by G. Izsák in his *The Samaritan,* p. 38. For a report on celebrations at the slaughtering of pigs at Otthon, see *KM,* March, 1905. The vintage *mulatság* was (and still is) a communal game in which some of the young participants (the "thieves") tried to snatch grapes suspended from net-

ting overhead. Those caught by the *csösz* (field guards) had to provide *zálog* (forfeit). *CMF*, 1 November 1910.

55. The tenth-anniversary jubilee involved the presence of the Austro-Hungarian consul of Winnipeg, a magnificent looking *banderium*, and the brass band, as well as the taking of numerous photographs. *CMF*, 26 July 1910. The Kaposvar jubilee included the participation of invited representatives from all of the major Hungarian colonies, with particular stress on Bekevar and Winnipeg. A commemorative medal was struck. Many speeches and poetry recitals were given. A large *banderium* re-enacted the "conquest" of Esterhaz-Kaposvar, headed by Lajos Gönczy, the second "Árpád." See Gönczy's "Conquest of the Land" in his diary (one copy of which is in the author's possession). Also *CMF*, 14 July 1911 and subsequent numbers; the jubilee itself took place in mid-August, 1911.

56. A gifted Hungarian-Canadian businessman, Kristóf Lukácsffy, had much to do with these developments. *CMF*, 19 July 1910 and 26 May 1911. In the latter issue there is a reference to the fact that Wakaw Lake was called "Balaton" by some individuals and that there were plans to make it into "the largest lakefront and holidaying resort in the West."

57. March 15 was also the day on which homage was paid to Lajos Kossuth and the Kossuth Song was invariably sung by the whole audience. As to the tone of speeches and recitations, the poem presented by Ida Gyore at Bekevar provides a sample:

> I am asking of you, grave, sacred for ever,
> Mournful reality, why have you swallowed up?
> Why . . . the sweet Messiah of this nation
> With the nightly pall of your silent solitude.
> We would yearn for the sage advice of his mind:
> We would follow him again into fire and flame;
> We would tolerate an hundred wounds and even death, smiling
> If only he were in charge; O, but this is out of reach!

KM, 27 March 1908. There were similar festivities in the other colonies, e.g., in Howell (*CMF*, 15 March 1910) and even earlier at Kaposvar, Otthon, and Yorktown (*KM*, March, 1905). The celebration of October 6, in recalling the sorrowful end to the War of Independence, 1848-49, was much less frequent; an instance of it was in Winnipeg (*CMF*, 15 October 1913).

58. This was the first public appearance of Father Menyhért Érdujhelyi, the first Hungarian priest in Canada. *KM*, 13 November 1908.

59. The repertoire of the Hungarian-Canadian country bands was usually restricted to Hungarian folk songs and popular music of the time. János Barilla (95) still recalled in 1975 about 150 tunes that he used to play with his band. For the above event, see *CMF*, 1 March 1912. On the Howell *mulatság(s)*, see *KM*, 30 April 1909.

60. *CMF*, 15 July 1914.

61. Kálmán Kovácsi (c. 1873-1931) is also listed in J. Szinnyei, *Magyar irók élete és munkái* [The Biographies and Works of Hungarian Writers], 16 vols. (Budapest, 1899), vol. 6, columns 1405-6. He recited one of his best poems, written at Bekevar, "The Song of the New Exiles" ["Új bujdosók éneke"], at the Kaposvar Jubilee celebrations on 15 August 1911. A copy is in the possession of the present writer. Kovácsi and Lajos Gönczy, Sr., excelled in writing accounts of events and personalities connected with the community. They also composed poetry, short stories, reminiscences, and notices and other items for the successive Hungarian papers. Gyula Izsák (1884-1960) became a successful and productive poet. He wrote, edited, and published the book, *Mezei Virágok* ("Prairie Flowers"), *Poems* (1905-1910). It was published at Kipling and printed by *CMF*, Plunkett (202 pages). In addition to numerous articles, he wrote and edited *A Samaritánus* (The Samaritan, a true history from the time of the first settlers.). It was published in Toronto in 1954. Gábor Szakács excelled as the author of accounts of contemporary events and happenings within the Bekevar community, which were published in Hungarian-language papers and occasionally in English ones. He tried his hand at poems as well and provided communal leadership in the staging of plays, the declamation of poems, and the presentation of musical items. Besides, he was a persistent promoter of the maintenance of the ancestral culture.

62. The two sections allotted to the Hudson's Bay Company and the other two set aside "as an endowment for purposes oᶠ education" were also released at different times. Martin, *"Dominions Lands" Policy*, pp. 16ff., 78-87, 98-9, 106-15.

63. There were exceptions in the early years of settlement; for instance, P.O. Esterhazy managed to exchange adjoining railways sections for homestead land for the purposes of the Esterhaz colony. Besides, "reserves" were set aside for future Hungarian settlement, which contained the even-numbered sections in Township 19, Ranges 1-5, and Township 19A, Ranges 1-5. (PAC, document dated 9 July 1886, RG 15, B-1a, vol. F90895/2, p. 392.)

64. *KM*, 22 October 1909.

65. *CMF*, 15 July 1914.

66. In the Wakaw and Leross areas, e.g., *KM*, 20 November 1908; *CMF*, 29 March 1910, 16 March 1912.

67. *CMF*, 7 April 1911.

68. *KM*, 15 February 1906.

69. Thus the Manitoba & North-West Railway Co. bought a lot adjacent to the Esterhazy station for one dollar; two acres were acquired by a James Sanders at the same station for $200. Contract Nos. 45 and 30, CPR Land Sales Records, vol. 16, p. 109 (Calgary).

70. *CMF*, 19 July 1912.

71. *CMF*, 15 June and 1 November 1915.

72. B.M. Frith, *A Short History of the Wakaw District* (Wakaw, 1932), p. 57.
73. *KM*, 12 November 1909, 28 August 1908.
74. Bender and Neelby developed from stations along the CNR in the vicinity of Kipling. See *The Citizen* (Kipling), 22 November 1978. The taking over of Bekevar's commercial functions by Kipling was a very gradual and slow process, which did not reach completion until the late 1960's.
75. *CMF*, 3 March 1911.
76. Frith, *A Short History*, p. 1; *CMF*, 1 November 1910, 26 January 1912.
77. Gyula Izsák, the farmer-poet of Bekevar, for instance, was to fall victim to the Great Depression.
78. Saskatchewan Provincial Archives, Regina (SPAR), Esterhaz Protestant Public School District No. 138, Records; SPAR, The East Otthon S.D. No. 462, Records.
79. According to a reliable contemporary observer some parents were concerned that their children would not learn "perfect English from Hungarian teachers" while other parents were indifferent to the question of schooling. *KM*, 19 February 1909.
80. See R. Huel, "The Public School as a Guardian of Anglo-Saxon Traditions," in Kovacs (ed.), *Ethnic Canadians,* pp. 300-1.
81. For instance, in the Mathyas S.D. No. 3141, "the school was in operation only 159 days due to difficulties in obtaining and keeping a teacher for a full year in a district which is entirely foreign and thus lacking a suitable place for a teacher to board. A teacherage was built, but very few teachers are willing to live alone in such a lonesome district. . . . The children are Hungarian Catholics and seven or eight school days were Church holidays. Furthermore, on many days the school was open, but, owing to bad weather, few children were able to come." (27 May 1918). SPAR, Mathyas S.D. No. 3141, Records. Teachers, usually females, could find neither "proper" company nor privacy in early prairie peasant communities.
82. We cannot discount the possibility of the impact of an American initiative upon some Hungarian Canadians, as 1907 witnessed the establishment of the American Hungarian Association. *Heti Szemle* (Weekly Review), 9 October 1907.
83. *KM*, 14 February 1908.
84. There cannot be any mistake that the notion of the Canadian Hungarian Association experienced, at that stage, rather a cool reception among Hungarian Canadians. *KM*, 6 March 1908. The meeting of the CMSz on April 11 could only attract "a very small portion" of the Hungarians (*KM*, 17 April 1908). In May there came the news that "in view of the paucity of interest and the fact that the Hungarians are led by a disruptive element . . . the CMSz is herewith declared dissolved." *KM*, 29 May 1908.
85. *KM*, 12 June 1908.

86. ". . . the Liberal Party agreed to support the new paper. They paid debts in the value of $400 and promissory notes falling due in connection with the printing shop equipment. Who it was that financed all the expenditures is unnecessary to state here, but he has invested on his own $2000 cash. The same person provided $3580 cash for the purchase of the *Kanadai Magyarság (Canadian Hungarians)* and the settling of all existing debts. So he alone supplied more than $5000." The extract from L.E. Kovacsi's confidential letter to G. Szakács and G. Izsák, Bekevar, dated Winnipeg, March 23, 1912, has been translated from the Hungarian original. A copy is in the author's possession.

87. *CMF*, 22 February 1910.

88. *CMF*, 12 April, 3 and 17 May, 14 and 28 June 1910, 13 January 1911.

89. *CMF*, 9 August 1910.

90. Kovacs, "Hungarian School Question," pp. 337-9, 345-51.

91. "The *Canadian Hungarian Farmer*, published in Winnipeg, has printed shameful slanders against the Hierarchy and the clergy and . . . the editor favours openly in his columns the union of the Hungarian people of this diocese with the reformed Calvinist Church. . . . We declare that no Catholic should receive the *Hungarian Farmer*. . . . The priests of our diocese are hereby authorized to refuse the sacraments of the Church to those who will receive a publication slandering the Church and striving against her. . . ." Extract from Archbishop Langevin's circular, addressed to "The Hungarian Catholic People" of the Diocese and dated September 22, 1910. For the full text see Pirot, *One Year's Fight,* p. 16. Part of the circular was published in *Manitoba Free Press,* 31 October 1910.

92. Pirot, *One Year's Fight*, p. 24. *CMF*, 31 December 1910.

93. The small country school boards had very tight budgets, which often had to be contributed to by a dozen or so families; therefore, its members were out to economize as much as humanly possible. (Interviews.)

94. *Acta Apostolicae Sedis*, 31 August 1910, vol. II, no. 16, p. 637. The unpopularity of the priest within his parish was now judged a cause sufficient for his removal from office. *CMF* quickly (27 September 1910) noticed this new arrangement and in the next few years petitions of parishioners did result in the transfer of unpopular priests to other assignments from Kaposvar, Stockholm, and other Hungarian-Canadian settlements.

95. The war atmosphere was echoed in *CMF*, 1 November 1915. "On the declaration of war, the non-naturalized Hungarians in urban areas were instructed to report to the police, or were placed in internment camps. . . . The appreciation accorded to Magyar farmers thus far began to turn to coldness. They who had been labouring with unflagging tenacity for their adopted country for over a quarter-century, were now regarded as enemies. They themselves sadly contemplated the

vanishing of their old renown and reputation, as if *they* could have been blamed for the war.''

96. According to a recent study, the wartime prosperity of ''minority-group'' farmers contributed to the growth of nativism, which in turn led to the introduction of compulsory ''unilingual education'' and to the War-time Elections Act of 1917, which took away the right to vote from *citizens* ''of enemy origin.'' John Herd Thompson, *The Harvests of War: The Prairie West, 1914-1918* (Toronto, 1978), pp. 80-95.

FOUR

The Years of Growth and Change, 1918-1929

N.F. Dreisziger

THE GREAT TRANSFORMATION

One of the most remarkable aspects of Hungarian-Canadian history between World War I and the Great Depression is massive demographic
change. Within a little more than a decade, Hungarians had evolved
from a small, rural, and largely Saskatchewan-based ethnic group into a
fair-sized and quite highly urbanized minority spread across much of
Canada. This extensive transformation was brought about by a number
of factors, the most important being the arrival of thousands of
Hungarian immigrants whose values and attitudes were often different
from those of the pre-1914 settlers. These newcomers were more prone to
seeking jobs in the cities and settling in parts of Canada that previously
had been avoided by their countrymen. They often assumed lifestyles
that differed from those of the early pioneers. The result was the
emergence of a Hungarian-Canadian community quite unlike the one
which had existed before the war.

Hungarians in Canada's Mines and Cities to 1914
Simultaneously with the establishment of the first Hungarian agricultural settlements on the Prairies, Hungarian miners started arriving in
the Lethbridge area. They were brought there from Pennsylvania to provide cheap labour for Sir Alexander T. Galt's newly opened coal mines.[1]
In the beginning this first non-agrarian "Hungarian colony" in Canada
seems to have been made up mainly of Slovaks,[2] but around the turn of
the century its Magyar element was reinforced by new arrivals, many of
whom came directly from Hungary. By 1901 there were enough Magyars
in the town to establish the First Hungarian Sick-Benefit Society of
Lethbridge, the first known association of Hungarian workers in
Canada.[3] Four years later, a Hungarian church dignitary, the Reverend
Peter A. Vay, visited Lethbridge and reported meeting "hundreds" of

his countrymen there.[4] Vay also found Hungarians living in the mining communities of the Crowsnest Pass region of the Canadian Rockies. At the other end of the country, Vay found a colony of Hungarian miners in North Sydney, Nova Scotia.[5] Another contemporary source mentions a group of Magyar miners in Michel, British Columbia.[6]

The appearance of Hungarian transients in Canada's cities had actually predated the establishment of their first colonies on the agricultural and mining frontiers. In the 1850's and 1860's several of the post-1849 Hungarian emigrés to the United States had apparently crossed the international boundary to seek employment in cities like Toronto and Montreal. The most famous of them was Márk Szalatnay, a workingman's advocate and trade union organizer.[7] Neither he nor any of his revolutionary compatriots seem to have chosen Canada as their place of permanent residence. It was only at the turn of the century that Hungarians began to settle in Canadian cities. When the Reverend Vay toured the country in 1905, for example, he encountered Hungarian workers in Niagara Falls, Ontario, and in Sydney, Nova Scotia.[8] According to other sources, by this time there were Hungarian immigrants living in such Ontario cities as Windsor, Galt, Welland, Brantford, and Hamilton.[9]

While small Hungarian communities were being created in a few central and eastern Canadian centres, a larger one was being formed in Winnipeg. It had its beginnings around 1900. Within five years, it numbered several hundred. 1904 saw the establishment of the First Hungarian Sick-Benefit Association of Winnipeg. Two years later, a Presbyterian congregation was established; and the following year another sick-benefit society, serving Hungarian Roman Catholics, came into being. There were also a club for German-speaking immigrants from Hungary and the beginnings of an ethnic press.[10] As has been mentioned in the previous chapter, by 1908 Winnipeg had become one of the foremost centres of Hungarian activity in Canada.

Little is known about the life of Hungarians in Canada's mining and manufacturing centres during the early years of our century. The historian examining the meagre evidence is impressed by the hardships that confronted most of these people. Whether working in mines, at blast furnaces, or on construction sites, they were constantly under the threat of industrial accidents. Many of them lost their lives, others were permanently disabled. Still others succumbed to various industrial diseases in the unsafe work environment. Nevertheless, most of them persevered in order to save enough money for a farm in Canada or in Hungary. In times of prosperity, saving was possible; but during recessions unemployment often eroded all savings.[11] The religious, social, and cultural needs of these people were not fulfilled. For example, Vay was the first Hungarian priest ever to visit many of their communities. Plagued by economic insecurity, inhuman working conditions, and social and cultural isolation, these Hungarian miners and workers often found solace in alcohol. The Lethbridge police records offer a glimpse of the wretched lives many of that town's immigrant miners must have led. The drunken brawls and fracases with the police over the making of home-brew earned these unfortunate beings the contempt and hostility of local authorities and residents alike. The *Lethbridge News*, for example, used to denounce the town's "uncivilized," "despicable," and "brutal" Hungarians in the most vehement manner. We may presume that the for-mation of the sick-benefit societies, which doubled as social clubs, had a salutory effect on immigrant life. Through them, the worst effects of economic uncertainty were often eliminated, and the social life of most newcomers was improved.[12] But only in Winnipeg was there potential for richer cultural life, made possible by the presence of a small circle of bet-ter educated individuals.

World War I

The First World War accelerated the processes of the Hungarian group's dispersal and urbanization. While the interruption of immigration from Hungary stopped the growth of some colonies, and the dislocations caused by the war even led to the decline of others,[13] the war witnessed the emergence and growth of new foci of Hungarian ethnic life. Espe-cially impressive was the growth in the industrial belt of southern On-tario. The rapid expansion of manufacturing in this region attracted im-migrants from many parts of Canada. Scores of Hungarians migrated there from the West, and still others seem to have joined them from the United States. Besides jobs, the area had other attractions: nuclei of Hungarian communities in several cities, active Hungarian life across the international boundary in cities such as Detroit and Buffalo, and a milder climate. Particularly impressive is the wartime and post-war growth of the Hungarian "colony" of Welland, where in 1921 a self-improvement society was established with sixty-six members. Brant-ford's and Hamilton's Magyar communities continued to grow, and several other cities in the area, which do not seem to have had Hungarian residents before, acquired a few in this period. A handful of Hungarians are known to have settled even in Toronto, a city which until then had been avoided by them.[14]

The 1921 census records are probably not very good indicators of the true growth of the Hungarian community in southern Ontario during the war and its immediate aftermath. The depression of that year probably drove some Magyars out of manufacturing centres, and there may have been quite a bit of confusion about just who was Hungarian as a result of the dismemberment of historic Hungary. But the census figures are still interesting: Toronto, a mere 59; Port Colbourne, 73; Windsor, 86; Hamilton, 200; Brantford, 247; and Welland, 234, with hundreds of others living in adjacent townships. In fact, with 719 residents, Welland riding had the largest Hungarian element of any electoral district in Canada outside of Saskatchewan.[15]

Despite the growth of the Hungarian communities of southern Ontario during the war, on the eve of the 1920's Saskatchewan continued to be the main centre of Hungarian immigrants in Canada. With a few exceptions, such as Winnipeg and Welland, all the important foci of Hungarian activity were still in that province. So were two-thirds of the country's Hungarian residents.[16] The 1920's were to change this state of affairs in a dramatic fashion. Within the course of a single decade changes were to be wrought in the group's distribution pattern which make this decade into a watershed between the predominantly rural, "Saskatchewan" past and a mainly urban, "Canada-wide" future.

The Post-war Era

The 1920's, particularly the second half of the decade, witnessed the first really large-scale immigration of Hungarians to the Dominion. The Canada of this period was a very different country from the one that had received the first Hungarian settlers a generation earlier. From the late 1890's to the end of the Great War, the Dominion had undergone a rapid and thorough transformation. During this quarter-century, vast districts of the previously near-empty Prairies had been settled. Many hitherto inaccessible regions, such as the northern zones of Quebec, Ontario, and British Columbia, had been opened up to mining and lumbering. In central Canada, manufacturing had expanded by leaps and bounds. The country's population had increased by more than three million. The influx of a great number of new immigrants from Central and Eastern Europe had marked the beginning of a truly multi-ethnic Canada, while the migration of thousands of people from the farms to the cities pointed toward an urbanized future for the country. The 1921 census marked a symbolic milestone in this respect: it recorded a near-balance in the nation's urban-rural distribution.[17]

While the years of prosperity and expansion brought increased complexity and sophistication in the country's economic, social, and cultural life, their effects were not purely beneficial. A price had to be paid for progress. Rapid urbanization resulted in city slums; industrialization, in labour strife. The emergence of new centres of population and new social groupings exacerbated existing regional and social conflicts and made the country's political life more unsettled. The farmers' protest movements, the growth of labour radicalism, and the weakening of old party alignments were but a few of the manifestations of these developments.

The type of transformation the country had undergone since the turn of the century continued during the 1920's. Population growth proceeded unabated, and so did urbanization. After a post-war depression, the growth of manufacturing resumed. The frontier of agricultural settlement, as well as the mining and lumber frontiers, kept expanding throughout much of the decade. Social and regional conflicts, aggravated by dislocations caused by the Great War and its turbulent aftermath, continued to plague the country. Large-scale immigration from Central and Eastern Europe resumed, causing a further shift in the ethnic composition of many parts of Canada, particularly the Prairies.

While Canada was to progress along the path of national development during the 1920's, her Hungarian community continued its evolution into an increasingly diverse and geographically dispersed group. Within a decade, its numbers were to more than triple, its geographic distribution was to change radically, and its social make-up would become more complex. Its cultural and organizational life would betray new vitality, culminating, almost symbolically, in the establishment of a Canada-wide organization of Hungarians. But, just as in the case of the rapid expansion of Canada's economy, this growth had many adverse effects. Expansion fostered intra-ethnic strife and, in the end, some of the expectations stemming from it proved unwarranted. Not surprisingly, when hard times arrived in the 1930's, serious setbacks occurred in Hungarian ethnic life.

The New Immigration

The mass migration of Hungarians to Canada during the mid- and late twenties had its origins in developments elsewhere in the world: in Central Europe and the United States. In the former region, the post-war dismemberment of historic Hungary by the peacemakers caused many hardships for her peoples, and enhanced many Hungarians' desire to try their fortunes overseas. Equally important from the point of view of post-war Hungarian emigration was the introduction in 1924 of the American quota system. This measure reduced to a trickle the flow of Central and East European immigrants to the United States.

Just about the time the U.S. virtually closed its doors to Hungarians, Canada lifted its wartime ban on the immigration of "enemy aliens."[18] Furthermore, two years later the Dominion's gates were flung wide open as a result of the notorious "Railways Agreement," which empowered the country's two railway companies to recruit thousands of agricultural immigrants from Central and Eastern Europe. The fact that Canada's admission regulations were relaxed just as those of the United States became more and more restrictive assured that there would be no shortage of Hungarian applicants for admission.[19]

Canada's post-1923 regulations limited entry to two groups of Hungarians: farmers with money to buy land, and agricultural labourers with guarantees of farm work. All immigrants had to be in good physical and mental health and had to be able to read. They had to have valid passports and railway tickets to their destinations in Canada. The latter requirement was designed to prevent the new arrivals from drifting to the cities before undertaking farm work on prairie homesteads. Wives and minor children of farmers legally landed in Canada were exempted from many of the above requirements. After 1925, the recruitment and initial screening of prospective immigrants were entrusted to agents of the railway companies, who issued so-called "occupational certificates" to agriculturalists, authorizing their entry into Canada.[20]

The post-war Hungarian immigration to Canada began in March of 1924 when a group of 160 peasants boarded a Cunard liner in Antwerp. They were to be accompanied by a Cunard Line employee all the way to Winnipeg. From there they were to be distributed to Hungarian farms on the Prairies. Only those for whom placement with Magyar settlers was not found were to be directed to farms of non-Hungarians. A contemporary newspaper report speculated that some 1,000 more farmhands were about to leave Hungary for Canada within the same month.[21] Indeed, the news of the re-opening of Canada's gates spread like wildfire in the Hungarian countryside. In the absence of accurate immigration information, many people got the mistaken impression that free homesteads awaited them in Canada, and that the Canadian government assisted in paying passage. From some villages as many as 500 persons applied to emigrate to Canada. Many sold all their belongings in order to enable at least one member of the family to emigrate. The other members were to follow as soon as he earned enough money to pay for their transportation.[22]

The issue of Hungarian immigration was one of concern not only to the Canadian government but also to authorities in Hungary. Statesmen in Budapest were unhappy about the spreading of the "Canadian fever" in Hungary's villages. Accordingly, they forbade the distribution of immigration propaganda. But their attitude to North American immigration was by no means wholly negative. They maintained an interest in North America's Hungarian communities and in the welfare of the individual immigrant. Their concern for the latter manifested itself in the establishment, in 1922, of the Immigrant Protection Bureau (IPB) in Budapest. Originally the Bureau was to provide help to both people leaving Hungary and those returning there from abroad, but in time its work increasingly involved aiding people in the former category. In Hungary, the IPB assisted people in obtaining passports, travel documents, and foreign currency. It tried also to protect people from unscrupulous agents who, for ample compensation, falsely promised to deliver people to their desired destinations in circumvention of immigration regulations.[23] In time, the Bureau's activities were extended beyond Hungary.

The beginning of the IPB's work in Canada coincided with the visit to this country in 1923 of Iván Hordossy, a special agent from Hungary. Hordossy toured the major Magyar settlements of the Canadian West and found them to be quite prosperous. Conditions awaiting new settlers, however, were difficult. These people needed loans, preferably from Canadian sources, and protection from unscrupulous agents.[24] To achieve the latter aim, the IPB established a branch office in Winnipeg – the Canadian Hungarian Immigrant Protection Bureau (CHIPB) – and effected the launching of a viable Hungarian-language newspaper, the *Kanadai Magyar Újság* (Canadian Hungarian News). The Winnipeg bureau and the paper strove to protect newcomers from irresponsible agents, to provide them with useful information, and to establish contact between them and native-born Canadians.[25] By doing so, they served to allay some of the Hungarian government's concerns regarding the fate of immigrants to Canada. As a result, limited emigration from the impoverished and often overpopulated Hungarian countryside to the Canadian West was allowed to continue and, in fact, to increase.

As has been mentioned in an earlier chapter, the governments of Romania, Yugoslavia, and Czechoslovakia were not at all unhappy about the emigration of their Magyar minorities. In Yugoslavia, for example, immigration propaganda was permitted among non-Slavic groups, such as Magyars and Germans, but was expressly forbidden among Serbs and Slovenes.[26] Given the prevailing social, economic, and political circumstances in the Magyar-populated regions of East Central Europe, it is not surprising that, once Canada's gates were opened, a steady stream of Hungarians kept coming until the gates were again closed with the onset of the Depression.

Immigration Statistics

Several factors make it difficult to give accurate statistics on this movement. As has been said, Hungarians were coming from four East Central European states; and there was always a trickle of them arriving from the United States. To complicate matters, not all immigrants from Hungary were Magyars: every year a few hundred Germans came, and a handful were listed by Canadian authorities as "being of the Hebrew nationality" (*sic*). No accurate statistics were kept in Ottawa on the number of people who returned to Hungary, nor on those who, after staying for some time in Canada, migrated to the United States.

Statistics maintained by the Department of Immigration and Colonization, the ministry in charge of these matters since October of 1917, record the number of immigrants from Hungary in the 1923-24 fiscal year (April 1, 1923, to March 31, 1924) as being 364. In 1924-25, the first year of renewed immigration from Hungary, the figure climbed to 1,052; and in 1925-26, to over 4,100. In the following fiscal year 4,863 came, and in 1927-28 their number reached 5,318. In 1928-29 a record 6,242 Magyars entered Canada. In the fiscal year ending March 31, 1930, the last year of large-scale immigration, 5,688 came, bringing the total of arrivals since 1923 to over 27,600.[27] It is not possible to establish how many of these came from countries other than Hungary, but there are statistics which give a good indication. In the 1926-27 fiscal year, for example, some 530 came from Czechoslovakia, 100 from Yugoslavia, and over 400 from Romania. For 1928-29, the corresponding figures, given in round numbers, are 600, 200, and 700.[28] Monthly returns kept by the department disclose that most Hungarian immigrants arrived in the spring and that their usual port of entry was Quebec City, although many landed in Halifax.

100

According to official statistics, the overwhelming majority of the new-comers were agriculturalists, reflecting regulations barring the entry of other occupations except in the case of persons coming to join members of their families living in Canada. The records also reveal that each year the majority of arrivals were young adult males. Their ratio to adult females improved as the decade drew to a close. In the 1927-28 fiscal year, for example, out of over 5,300 arrivals, there were 3,673 males and only some 850 females and 800 children. For 1929-30 the corresponding approximate figures are: 6,240 (total), 2,600 (males), 1,550 (females) and 1,500 (children).[29]

The social composition of this large group of Hungarian immigrants is difficult to establish. The fact that the vast majority of them were classi-fied as "agriculturalist" may suggest that the group was entirely of lower-class origin. But it was not so. All social classes seem to have been present among the new arrivals.[30] Even a handful of aristocrats came under the 1923 scheme allowing Hungarians with money to purchase farms in Canada. Other members of Hungary's middle and upper classes, deprived of their estates or government jobs as a result of the post-war peace settlements, managed to enter the country disguised as agricultural labourers. As former estate owners or managers, they had no trouble answering the Canadian immigration inspectors' questions on agriculture, and they could also make their hands appear similar to those of real peasants. One of them, in preparation for his interview with Canadian authorities, repeatedly immersed his hands in mud and al-lowed it to dry on his skin. In a few weeks his hands became indis-tinguishable from those of a poor peasant.[31]

In reality, most of these middle- and upper-class people were political refugees, the victims of a radical reordering of much of East Central Europe in the wake of the war. Taken together, their number amounted to a couple of thousand at the most,[32] but by the end of the decade they were to play a role out of proportion to their numbers in the cultural, religious, and political life of Hungarian-Canadian society. But the most visible result of the arrival of many people for whom life on the prairie farm was evidently not attractive was to reinforce the shift of Hungarian-Canadian life to the more urbanized regions of Canada.

Geographic Dispersal and Urbanization

The influx of the mid- and late-1920's helped the Hungarian community of Canada to more than triple its size. In addition to this dramatic in-crease, the group underwent or, more precisely, continued to undergo two other important demographic changes. One of these was the accele-rated dispersal across much of Canada; the other, rapid urbanization. A brief look at census data will illustrate the magnitude of these changes. Between 1921 and 1931 Saskatchewan's Hungarian population increased only by 48 per cent. In the same period Manitoba's more than doubled, British Columbia's increased close to four times, Alberta's five, and Ontario's underwent an eight-fold increase. Quebec's Hungarian population grew from less than 100 to over 4,000. In 1921 slightly more than two-thirds of Hungarian Canadians lived in Saskatchewan. A decade later less than a third did.[33]

The increase in the group's urban concentration is equally remarkable. In 1921 some 9,748 of Canada's 13,181 Hungarians were rural residents; only 3,433 lived in towns and cities. A decade later more than 20,000 lived in urban areas, nearly half of the group. In 1921 only 11 per cent, i.e., close to 1,500 Magyars, lived in cities of 30,000 and over. By 1931 this figure grew to over 30 per cent, representing about 12,600 individuals. From being the twenty-fifth most urbanized ethnic group in 1921, Hungarians became the twelfth in the course of a decade.[34] In 1921 five Canadian cities had a Hungarian population of over 200 people; by 1931 there were at least a dozen such cities, with half of these boasting a Magyar population of at least 1,000.[35]

As has been seen, the trend toward dispersal and urbanization was not new in the history of the Magyars in Canada: the 1920's only brought an acceleration of this dual process. Particularly impressive was the trend toward concentration in urban areas. The fact that this happened in the period of large-scale immigration from Hungary was not a coincidence. The available evidence suggests that it was the newly arrived who flocked to the cities. The reasons were manifold. There was a general trend toward urbanization throughout much of Canada; manufacturing continued to expand; city life was becoming more and more attractive. On the negative side, cheap, good agricultural land was a declining commodity. Particular reasons also explain the urbanization of Hungarians in many regions. The opening of Hungarian consulates in Montreal and later in Winnipeg gave a definite impetus to those cities' Hungarian life. Large public works, such as the construction of the new Welland Canal in the 1920's, attracted many Magyars to the urban centres of the Niagara Peninsula.

The first signs of the new urban expansion came in the same region that had experienced the greatest expansion during the second half of the previous decade: southern Ontario. In 1926 a Hungarian journalist by the name of Ödön Paizs toured this region and, in addition to encountering his countrymen in the older, pre-war centres of the area, found some in Oshawa, St. Catharines, Port Colbourne, Thorold, and St. Thomas. The largest colony by this time was in Hamilton. In fact, Paizs described this city as the "Hungarian capital of Eastern Canada."

Hamilton's Magyar community had been growing until the post-war economic slump of the early 1920's. In 1921 it declined to a couple of hundred people only, but with the return of better economic conditions in 1924 and the start of the new wave of immigration, the colony rapidly resumed its growth. By the time of Paizs's visit there, it numbered over 1,000 residents. The vast majority were casual labourers, but there were about 100 people – mechanics, tradesmen, and railway employees – who had steady jobs. These formed a more or less permanent core for Hamilton's Hungarian community. In winter months the colony was augmented through an influx of hundreds of unemployed seasonal farm workers from nearby areas. Most of the temporary residents, as well as many of the permanent ones, lived in the city's east side, where housing was the cheapest. By the mid-twenties, the colony had a couple of clubs, a Reformed congregation, and even a newspaper. The continued influx of Hungarians during the next four years caused still further growth in the city's Magyar population. By the time of the 1931 census, Hamilton's Hungarians numbered well over 2,000.[36] Despite this continued increase, Hamilton failed to remain the undisputed "Hungarian capital of eastern Canada" for long. By the last quarter of the decade, two new large Hungarian urban communities had grown up in central Canada, one in Montreal and the other in Toronto.

Hungarians in Montreal and Toronto

The largest centres of Hungarian life in Canada today are Toronto and Montreal. Neither of these cities possessed a Magyar community worthy of note during the formative stages of the Hungarians' history in the Dominion. It was only during the mass immigration of the 1920's that viable Hungarian groupings developed in them. From about 1926 on, however, the Magyar communities of Montreal and Toronto grew by leaps and bounds and surpassed, first in size and then in importance, all of central Canada's older centres.

Of the two cities, Montreal had the rudiments of a Hungarian community first. During the pre-war years several families and single people took up residence in the city. This tiny group seems to have been mainly Jewish. It even had its own "Austro-Hungarian synagogue."[37] The size of the city's Hungarian community changed little during the war. The 1921 census found only sixty-seven Magyars in Montreal and about ninety in the entire Province of Quebec. The situation remained the same for several years, but after 1925 the group began to grow. It is not known for certain what attracted Magyars to a city so distant from existing centres of Hungarian life in North America. Most important, probably, were jobs. Business opportunities attracted Jews, while the city's cultural life must have been a magnet for a few individuals. Indeed, by the end of the decade, several Hungarian artists and musicians took up residence in the city. Montreal's cosmopolitan atmosphere must have appealed to middle-class people, and the existence of a Hungarian consulate from 1922 on made the city better known among Magyar immigrants, educated and less educated alike.

The organized life of Montreal's Hungarian community began mainly along religious lines. In the spring of 1926, a young minister came to the city at the invitation of the United Church of Canada and established a congregation. At first it had some forty members, many of them Székelys from Transylvania. The city's Roman Catholics obtained a priest about two years later. In the meantime, the colony's first lay organization, the Hungarian Social Club, also began its activities. It was followed by the establishment of the Székely Cultural Society, the German-Hungarian Club, the St. Emerick Sick-Benefit Society, and the Kata Bethlen Women's Club. The latter two were affiliated with the Roman Catholic and Protestant congregations respectively. By the end of the decade, Montreal's Magyar population was approaching the 3,600 mark and may have even exceeded that figure during the winter months as a result of the usual influx of unemployed seasonal workers.[38] The colony's size, and its high degree of concentration in the St. Laurent Boulevard and Pine Street area, made a rich social and cultural life possible.

Toronto's Hungarian community had a rather late start. A few immigrants from Hungary, mainly Jews, did settle in the city prior to the war, but were not joined by an appreciable number of others until the 1920's. By then the city's main attraction had become the availability of industrial jobs. Toronto seems also to have been the way station for those who came to Canada with the often vain hope of gaining admission to the United States. Under the circumstances, it was to be expected that Toronto's Magyar community fluctuated in size and was slow to develop the institutions of a stable ethnic grouping.[39] Nevertheless, in 1926, organized life did start in the city. In the spring of that year the Presbyterian Church established a mission among Hungarian Calvinists. Two years later both the Lutheran Church and the United Church of Canada decided to follow suit. In the meantime, the city's growing Hungarian Roman Catholic community was also being served by visiting priests. Late in 1929 the Hungarian Catholic Club was formed and soon began working toward the establishment of a Roman Catholic parish.[40]

The Catholic Club seems to have been Toronto's first important Hungarian lay organization. In time it was to be followed by others, representing different political and recreational interests. It is noteworthy that no influential economic association was formed in the city for many years. Toronto's proximity to other, older Hungarian-Canadian centres acted as a hindrance to the growth of its Magyar colony's influence. The closeness of Hamilton and Brantford, for example, made it unnecessary to set up sick-benefit associations in Toronto. Just as clergymen had served the city's Hungarian community for years from outside centres, the sick-benefit associations of Hamilton and Brantford attended to the health insurance needs of Toronto's Hungarian immigrants.

Despite its size, numbering close to 2,000 people by the end of the decade, Toronto's Magyar colony remained a sort of a satellite of older communities in smaller urban centres. At the end of the 1920's, Hamilton was still the "Hungarian capital" of Ontario. Further east, Montreal had a Magyar colony that was larger than Toronto's, and there was still much influence wielded by urban Hungarian groupings of the West, particularly that of Winnipeg.[41]

Urban Groupings in Western Canada

The early history of Winnipeg's Magyar community has been traced. That colony, which had a promising start in the decade before the war, declined after 1914. By 1918 nearly all of Winnipeg's Hungarian clubs and associations had ceased to function. A resurgence in this respect did not come until 1924 when a new Presbyterian congregation and a Roman Catholic parish were founded, and the First Hungarian Sick-Benefit Society of Winnipeg, inactive since 1918, resumed its activities. As has been mentioned, 1924 was also the year of the founding of the Immigrant Protection Bureau in the city and the birth of the *Canadian Hungarian News*, Hungarian Canada's most influential newspaper through four decades. During the next few years several other lay organizations came into being. Also important was the opening, in 1927, of the Hungarian consulate in the city. The consulate's staff was to play an active though advisory role in Winnipeg's Hungarian-Canadian affairs.

Although Winnipeg's Hungarian community never rivalled in numbers the larger conglomerations that had grown up in eastern Canada by the end of the decade, it retained a great deal of influence. Several factors account for this. The presence of the consulate and the *News* was one important reason. Another was the city's location nearly halfway between the Hungarian groupings of the Lower Great Lakes-St. Lawrence region and those of the West. Not surprisingly, when an attempt was made during the late 1920's to form a nation-wide organization of Hungarian Canadians, Winnipeg was the site of the founding convention. It would be only after even further demographic shifts to the east that Winnipeg's Hungarian community would relinquish its powerful influence on Hungarian-Canadian affairs.

Aside from Winnipeg, five prairie cities possessed Hungarian groupings by the end of the decade. In Saskatchewan, Regina had had the nucleus of a Hungarian community since the early 1900's. It grew slowly until, during the mid-1920's, it reached a size that made organized life feasible. Many of Regina's Hungarian residents came from farming districts north of the city; others directly from Hungary; still others from the Hungarian villages of Bukovina, one-time province of Austria-Hungary which became part of Romania after World War I.[42] For many years, the city's Hungarians were served by priests and ministers stationed elsewhere in the province. But the proximity of more influential centres of Hungarian-Canadian life did not deter the community's members from forming their own social clubs. The most notable of these was the Canadian Hungarian Cultural Club, which came into being in 1922. In 1927 the club's Roman Catholic members established the First Catholic Funeral Society of Regina to enable the organization's members to have proper funerals. Unlike most other urban Hungarian communities, Regina's was relatively stable in membership, even though most local Magyars were casual labourers who were buffeted from job to job with the fluctuations of the labour market.[43] The problem of economic instability was more acute among the Hungarian population of Saskatoon, where a nucleus of a Hungarian ethnic community was established only after 1924.[44]

Neither Regina's nor Saskatoon's grouping wielded much influence in Hungarian-Canadian affairs on the national or even the provincial level. The large majority of Saskatchewan's Hungarians continued to live in rural areas.[45] Consequently, small, rural Hungarian centres played a more important part in the province's Hungarian-Canadian affairs. For instance, Regina's Magyar Roman Catholics were served from Stockholm, the foremost centre of Hungarian Roman Catholic influence in the province. The Regina-Stockholm relationship is a good example of an urban ethnic community being the satellite of a rural one. Saskatoon's Hungarians, being further removed from the traditional centres of Hungarian influence in the province, do not appear to have been similarly affected. In fact, when Hungarian newcomers began to settle on homesteads in northern Saskatchewan during the late twenties, the city's Magyar community began to act as an ethnic resource centre to the new settlements. It provided the services of a travelling minister and a doctor as well as those of a few craftsmen and shopkeepers. Nevertheless, Saskatoon functioned mainly as a temporary haven, where Hungarians stayed as long as they had casual employment and moved on when they were laid off or found better jobs elsewhere. Saskatoon's Magyar population waxed and waned with economic conditions; during the Depression, it would shrink to a third of its pre-1930 size.[46]

In Alberta, the Lethbridge area had a sizable Hungarian community throughout the 1920's. Its members worked on sugar beet farms and in coal mines and sugar factories. The region attracted few educated Hungarians, and those who did come did not stay long. Partly as a result, the community lacked the type of leadership that would have enabled it to play an important role in community affairs. Somewhat different was the case of the grouping that was emerging in Calgary. Only a handful in membership at the beginning of the decade, it grew into a several-hundred-strong community by 1929. Its members had been attracted to the city by jobs in manufacturing and in the service industry. In the winters the colony was augmented by the influx of unemployed miners and sugar beet workers. The founding of a Roman Catholic parish in 1926 marked the beginning of organized life among Calgary's Hungarians. It was followed a few years later by the start of a Presbyterian congregation and still later by the establishment of a non-sectarian social club. Alberta's third urban colony of Hungarians, started in about 1926 in Edmonton, would not challenge the other two for a long time. Even more than the Hungarian groupings of the other prairie cities, Edmonton's seems to have been plagued by unstable employment conditions.[47]

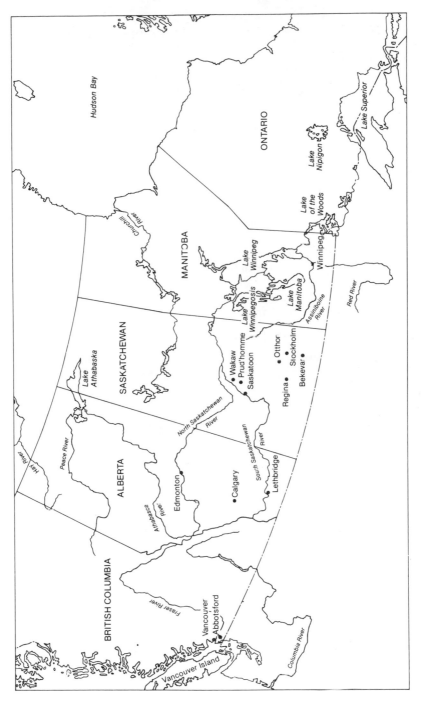

Toward an Urbanized Future

By the end of the 1920's, then, more than a dozen Canadian cities had Hungarian communities ranging in membership from a few hundred to several thousand. Six were located in the Prairie Provinces, one in Quebec, the rest in southern Ontario. Of the six prairie urban groupings, only three, Lethbridge, Regina, and Winnipeg, had existed as such before 1920. In the East, the story was similar. Rudimentary Hungarian communities had been present prior to 1920 in a few cities, but the real growth came after 1923. It is noteworthy that the largest Hungarian urban groupings grew up where practically no Magyars had resided before 1920.

The Hungarian community's increasing urbanization and geographic dispersal was in tune with demographic developments in Canada. Improved transportation and communications created more opportunities for travel and personal contact, as well as a greater familiarity with conditions and opportunities in other parts of the country. These factors, along with the continued expansion of manufacturing and service industries in the cities, affected the native-born and immigrant alike. It was the latter who was more easily disposed to move. For example, to a Hungarian who had exchanged the familiar ways of the Hungarian village for prairie wilderness, moving from the farm to the city was not an unthinkable undertaking. The switch to urban life became easier as more Hungarians had settled in cities. After Canada's manufacturing had been "explored" by Hungarian "urban pioneers," the mass migration could begin with the newcomers knowing what to expect and where to turn for aid and comfort.

In a sense, the rapid urbanization of the Hungarian-Canadian population was an unexpected development. The vast majority of Magyar immigrants to Canada had been admitted as agriculturalists and, indeed, they were mostly people whose roots had been in the countryside. Census data reveal that the trend toward urbanization was weakest among the "most Canadianized" of Hungarian Canadians, the second-generation population. Among the first-generation category, the immigrants themselves, there was an inverse relation between the length of residence in the country and the degree of urbanization. That is, it was the most recent arrivals who showed the highest urbanization ratios at the time of the 1931 census. How accurately the 1931 figures reflect the general trends of the late 1920's is difficult to determine since we have only a limited knowledge of the impact of the first year and a half of the Depression on Canada's immigrant population. Indeed, it has been pointed out that the onset of bad times may have accelerated the migration of agricultural workers and disappointed homesteaders to the cities.[48] But because no figures exist to illustrate the state of urbanization at the end of 1929, we have to rely on data for 1931.

The theory that urbanization took place at a slower pace among second-generation Hungarian Canadians than among immigrant Magyars is borne out by the fact that, while only 37.9 per cent of the former were urbanized in 1931, some 56 per cent of the latter were found to be urban residents.[49] Within the immigrant population itself, the process of urbanization was least advanced among the older groups and had gone the farthest among recent arrivals. About 29 per cent of those who came to Canada before 1910 had become city dwellers by 1931. The figure for the 1911-20 group was 39 per cent, for the 1921-25 group, 54 per cent, and for the very numerous 1926-30 group, 62.4 per cent. To put it simply, less than a third of the "old" immigrants had ended up in the cities by 1931, while almost two-thirds of those who arrived in the late 1920's had become urban residents. What is even more interesting is that this relatively high urbanization ratio for the 1926-30 group was true of every province with a mixed urban-rural population, even Saskatchewan. Of course, the ratios were higher in the more urbanized regions of the country. In Ontario, for example, 76 per cent of the post-1926 arrivals had become city dwellers by 1931.[50]

At the end of the 1920's, Hungarian-Canadian urban settlements were very young entities in more than one sense of the word. They were the result of recent growth and were populated predominantly by recent arrivals.[51] Being very new, they displayed all the characteristics of young ethnic communities. They were unstable in size and membership and were very much at the mercy of fluctuating economic conditions. Yet, they possessed much vitality, often a characteristic of young immigrant communities. Above all, they pointed toward a new way of life for the Hungarian-Canadian group: a predominantly urban future.

SOCIAL CONDITIONS AND LIFESTYLES

The conditions governing the lives of Hungarian Canadians were the same as those which determined the nature of Canadian society and the lifestyles of its members. These were geography, climate, economic conditions, political traditions, and social realities. The factors of great distances, bitterly cold winters, and an economy based mainly on the production of staple foods and raw materials had a great impact on the host society and the Hungarian ethnic group alike. Almost equally important was the existence of a political and social system based on a mixture of *laissez-faire* capitalism and a brand of statism that provided welfare for the rich. Another set of determining factors stemmed directly from the immigrant heritage. These included a high degree of linguistic isolation, a lack of familiarity with British (and French) manners and traditions, and a lack of effective leadership. The last of these factors was not an inherent trait of Hungarians but was mainly the result of Canada's "agriculturalist only" admission policy, which restricted (though did not completely prevent) the entry of educated middle-class elements. Thus, Canadian conditions and the "immigrant heritage" combined to shape a Hungarian-Canadian community which differed not only from Canadian society but from other Canadian ethnic groups and Hungarian society in Hungary as well.

Demographic Characteristics

One source that helps us to understand the nature of Hungarian-Canadian society is the Canadian census. From the mass of statistics we can derive glimpses of the group's demographic characteristics. The census reveals, for example, that Canada's Hungarian communities suffered from a skewed population structure. The population curve bulged at the twenty-five to thirty-nine age bracket. Over 52 per cent of the Hungarian immigrants were in this age group. The equivalent figure for Canada's British population was about 19 per cent. This unevenness was not striking among immigrant Hungarians in Saskatchewan (42 per cent) and Manitoba (46 per cent). In Ontario it was marked (56 per cent) and tended to be most pronounced among the male population: three out of every five Hungarian males in that province were twenty-five to thirty-nine years old.[52]

The second major irregularity in the Hungarian ethnic group's population structure was the uneven ratio between men and women. In 1931, out of Canada's 40,582 Hungarian residents, about 25,000 were males. The ratio was most prominent for adults (twenty-one years of age and over). Slightly over 17,000 of these were males and less than 8,000 were females. Since a much larger fraction of Hungarian men were single than women (a third of all males of fifteen years and over, as opposed to only about a fifth of women), these figures meant that the ratio of eligible males to eligible females was very high. The census results place this figure at 3.27. This ratio exceeds by a wide margin the corresponding figures for all other ethnic groups of European origin except that given for the "Czechs and Slovaks."[53] The census data also indicate that this imbalance between males and females was most pronounced among immigrant Hungarians and urban residents. One set of figures should suffice in the way of illustration. In Ontario's cities, there were 2,419 Hungarian immigrant males in the thirty to thirty-nine age group and only 846 women.[54]

The abundance of young adult males, combined with the scarcity of women, had unusual effects on marriage practices and fertility rates. First of all, a higher proportion of Hungarian women were married than were the females of any other ethnic group, with the exception of Canada's East Asian residents. Furthermore, Hungarian-Canadian girls married younger. Close to 13 per cent of girls in the fifteen-nineteen age bracket were married according to the 1931 census. This compared with the national average of slightly over 5 per cent and exceeded by a wide margin the figures for all immigrant groups.[55] The high marriage rates for women, combined with a greater than average tendency for early marriage and the youthfulness of the male population, resulted in very high fertility rates for the Hungarian group. The 1931 census established the group's fertility index at 151, which was double the figure given for the country's British population and was exceeded only by the Chinese, Japanese, and Yugoslavs. Magyar-Canadian society's 6,186 married women in the fifteen to forty-four age bracket bore an estimated 1,271 children a year, a remarkable figure topped only by mothers of Yugoslav and Chinese background, and by French-Canadians.[56] It seems, then, that while many Hungarian-Canadian men, especially recent arrivals, were denied the blessings of family life, others were busy establishing families almost as if they had to assume responsibility for their ethnic group's numerical growth.

While the census offers a fair insight into Hungarian-Canadian society's marriage statistics, it presents a much less complete picture about its degree of integration. Yet, some helpful statistics can be found in this regard, also. The acquisition of the host country's language or languages is a useful indicator of an ethnic group's potential for adjustment. 1931 census data indicate that of the 31,000 Hungarians ten years of age and over who were not English-speaking from childhood, some 25,500 had acquired English at some stage of their lives. This is an 82.2 per cent rate, which lags behind the figures for all other European groups except the Finnish.[57] Magyars and Finns had a less impressive record than other groups because the majority of both were recent arrivals. They were also hindered by their "ethnic heritage": mother tongues that were very different from English. The extent of an immigrant group's naturalization, the acquisition of citizenship status, often can be another indicator of its degree of integration into the host society. Much useful information exists in this connection as well. Slightly more than 22 per cent of Hungarian immigrants had acquired citizenship status by 1931. The ratio for adult males was lower, 19.7 per cent.[58] Furthermore, the naturalization process was less complete in the provinces with the bulk of the new immigration: Ontario (17.8 per cent), Alberta (10.4 per cent), and Quebec (5.6 per cent). But it was among city dwellers that the record was the poorest. Less than 5 per cent of urban Hungarian immigrants had attained citizenship status by 1931.[59]

These data reinforce the impression that, outside of the old Saskatchewan centres, Canada's Hungarian community was a young ethnic group, hardly touched by the process of integration. It was a group characterized by a highly unnatural population structure, as well as by uneven rates of development among the various urban and rural settlements scattered throughout much of the country. Problems stemming from such conditions were numerous. The absence of certain sections of a normal population, in particular homemakers, greatly reduced the quality of life for many Hungarian immigrants. The lack of knowledge of English by some, often coupled with the failure or inability to attain citizenship status, reduced economic opportunities and reinforced feelings of helplessness and isolation. The differing rates of ethnic development in general and adjustment in particular among the various regional, rural, and urban groupings of Hungarian Canadians were conducive to the growth of distrust and jealousies among them.

Living Conditions and Lifestyles

The everyday lives of Hungarian immigrants to Canada were partly controlled by the same factor that greatly influenced the lives of most ordinary Canadians: climate. Canada of the 1920's was still very much an "eight-months country,"[60] in which virtually all economic activity was determined by the weather. It was still a country where the frontier loomed large in national life. Undeniably, there had been improvements in such fields as transportation, communications, public health, and education; but many of the "new technology's" blessings, such as the telephone, the radio, the motor car, and indoor plumbing, had only marginal impact on the life of the lower class, to which the vast majority of Hungarians belonged. Whether on the farms, on construction sites, or in logging camps, their work was governed by the seasons. On the prairie farm there was work in the spring, from the middle of April on. This was followed by a period of relative inactivity lasting until August, when all hands were needed to bring in the harvest. After September the demand for farm help rapidly declined and did not resume until next spring. This pattern was imposed by the West's wheat economy. Wheat was supreme, and there was little diversification to provide a somewhat different work cycle. Most homesteads offered year-round work for the farmer and his family, but farm workers could put in only a few weeks' or, at best, a few months' work in any one year. At other times they had to find work elsewhere. Thus, the farm worker became a migrant labourer. Even those who managed to acquire a homestead often had to supplement their income through outside employment. Only after most debts had been paid did the farmer stand a chance of making it on his own.

Not many Hungarian immigrants to Canada in the 1920's escaped the fate of being migrant labourers at least for a few years. The life stories of those who did not reveal a great variety of patterns. As has been mentioned, the immigrant's "career" usually began on the prairie farm to which he had been directed by the agency responsible for his placement. Some newcomers stayed at their designated destination; others, who found the wages or working conditions unsatisfactory, looked for farm work elsewhere. Problems rarely arose until September, when most farming operations came to an end and the immigrant became unemployed. The placement agency was no longer concerned with him – now he was on his own. Some people waited and contented themselves with seeking a few days of work here and there in the region to which they had been directed originally. Often they could supplement their summer savings by odd jobs such as clearing land and cutting firewood for farmers or townspeople. Unfortunately, these jobs paid very little.

Other newcomers found unsettling the prospect of having no full-time work until the spring, and thus they set out to find work in other parts of the country. A few found employment in mines, in particular the coal mines of southwestern Alberta. As temporary helper and most recent arrival, the newcomer received the least desirable job and was laid off at the first sign of slackening demand for coal. But if his job lasted through the winter, he escaped having to work in the bitterly cold open air and could supply himself and his family with coal picked from heaps of rock scattered around the mine's entrances. For those who failed to find work in the mines, or who didn't try to, there was often casual work for the railways, either in track maintenance or on the construction of branch-lines. Still others headed for logging camps, logging being generally the only type of work available in the winter on Canada's vast frontiers. Neither railway construction work nor logging appealed to family men unless they were willing to part with their wives and children for many months at a time. A part of the workers' earnings were consumed by payments they had to make for meals and lodging in the camps.

Still others headed for the cities. They were often followed by those who had first tried the country's mines, railways, or logging camps and had failed either to find jobs or to keep them. In the cities there was a variety of possibilities: woodsplitting or snow removal around people's homes and shops, construction work when it was not monopolized by members of another ethnic group, and, for a fortunate few, even work in factories. Those who couldn't find work spent their time looking for it and lived on their meagre savings or on money borrowed from relatives or acquaintances. Expenses were cut by living frugally, with several people sharing a room in a crowded boarding house maintained usually by one of their countrymen. The proprietor of such an establishment, known as the *burdosgazda* ("landlord"), was often a fairly recent arrival who supplemented his family's income by subletting part of his home to permanent lodgers and transients. The city often seemed to promise much, but it gave little in the way of employment. However, it offered a life less harsh than that on the frontier, and it also saved the newcomer from the isolation of the labour camps.

In the spring the cycle would start anew as people returned to the land for farm work, and this yearly pattern would go on until broken through the immigrant finding a farm he could start cultivating or some kind of urban employment he could count on. If anything was certain in this world of uncertainty, it was the fact that nothing was fixed, settled, or permanent. Very few could ever feel ensured against having to lead the life of a migrant labourer. The farmer could fail and go bankrupt; in the city, even the surest jobs could disappear; illness, fire, or some other calamity could strike, throwing men and families back into a most uncertain type of existence. For many there appeared only one escape: a return to Hungary and the familiar people and ways of the native village. Hundreds of disappointed newcomers chose this course of action.[61]

The basic feature of new Hungarian-Canadian life in the 1920's seems to have been mobility sustained by economic instability and personal restlessness. Repeated migration became part of the lifestyle for many. Often, the travelling was senseless and counterproductive. In the early spring of 1928 a public building burned down in Saskatoon. A decision was made to replace it. As soon as this was announced, Hungarian transients converged on the city in the hope of finding well-paying construction jobs.[62] Such usually useless travel helped to consume many a newcomer's savings or put him deeper into debt. Later, during the Depression, Hungarian transients learned to save the cost of transport by travelling on the roofs of freight cars, a practice which cost many lives as cold, numbed bodies fell beneath the wheels. Those who were less enterprising resorted to an ancient method of travel: walking. According to a popular myth, one Hungarian in search of a job walked from Winnipeg to Toronto barefoot, carrying his only pair of boots in his hand. When he found a job, he went back to fetch his family in the same manner.[63]

Special Handicaps

While climate and general economic conditions affected the lives not only of Hungarians but those of other immigrants and most of Canada's poor, Hungarian newcomers had to contend with several handicaps which were more or less peculiar to their kind. One of these was the fact that a large number of Magyar newcomers to Canada came with money borrowed often at usurious lending rates. Consequently, their first concern was to rid themselves and their families of this debt. In doing so, they often missed opportunities to invest in a farm or to start a small business of some sort. In fact, these debts tended to condemn many a newcomer to years of existence as a migrant labourer. Indebtedness could not be simply forgotten, as usually it had been contracted against family assets in Hungary.[64] Closely connected to this state of affairs was the fact that many Magyar immigrants were young heads of families who felt obliged to save for the transportation of their wives and children to Canada. Such hopes were often dashed by economic setbacks. Many Hungarian-Canadian men did not reunite with their families until after the Depression or the Second World War.[65]

Perhaps the most severe handicap new Hungarian arrivals had to contend with was their near-total lack of occupational and language skills. As peasants they had no training in anything but subsistence farming, Hungarian style, and most of them had no knowledge of English. Given the absence of opportunities for learning the language and trades, the acquisition of these skills was a slow and painful process. Furthermore, the lack of knowledge of English and Canadian conditions made the newcomers prey to unscrupulous persons, often of their own nationality, who took advantage of the newly arrived's ignorance. Older residents of the country would take money from newcomers in return for promises of suitable employment, but the jobs were rarely delivered. Also common was the practice by foremen in mines and factories and on construction sites to take bribes when new help was being hired and to go on exacting a tribute from workers whose continued employment lay within their discretion. Another type of fraud perpetrated on new arrivals was to promise them passage to the United States, where conditions allegedly were better. The victims were made to pay handsomely and were taken near the border but not across it, or worse, were allowed to fall into the hands of American authorities. A less nefarious, though often equally effective way of helping newcomers to part with their savings was for their *burdosgazda* to provide illegal alcohol for them along with their meals and lodging. In 1929 it was estimated that such a practice could cost a boarder an extra $15 to $20 a week. It must be stated that such an arrangement was not entirely the fault of the landlord. Some boarders preferred "wet" boarding houses to "dry" ones, and the pressure to provide drinks was there.[66]

The Fate of Female Domestics

The difficulties of new Canadian life were not confined to the male members of the group, just as immigration was not restricted to them. During the height of the post-1924 influx of newcomers, several thousand women came to Canada from Hungary. Most of them arrived to join husbands or other close relatives. Others came as single persons under Canada's scheme of admitting female domestics. These people were recruited to work as household servants in the Canadian West. After their arrival, they were placed on farmsteads where they were expected to help with housekeeping and other chores, such as milking. The scheme did not work without difficulties and disappointments. Some Hungarian arrivals did not know, or refused to accept, what awaited them. A few were not familiar with most aspects of domestic work on the farm. Many seem to have come with the conviction that they could avoid becoming servants and could find employment as sales clerks or factory workers in the cities. In 1930, the Hungarian consul in Winnipeg complained to authorities in Budapest that in 1929 there had been an unusually large number of difficulties in regard to Hungarian female domestics. Many of them had abandoned their assigned jobs. Others did not even show up in their places of destination but insisted on staying in Winnipeg, which offered few if any employment opportunities.[67]

It appears, then, that the importation of female domestics from Hungary was no more successful a scheme from the immigrants' point of view than the admission of agricultural workers. Perhaps it was an unreasonable expectation on the part of Canadian policy-makers to suppose that young, unmarried women, usually without any language skills and often without other appropriate skills as well, would take to the demanding life and isolation of prairie homesteads. The whole program, it seems, added much to human misery and contributed to the influx of unemployed and in some respects unemployable people into the cities.

Community Life

The lifestyle of a large section of the new Hungarian-Canadian society was not conducive to the development of any meaningful community life. Hungarian groupings in most cities were made up of transients. There were some rural enclaves in which, for a few years until the Depression struck, Hungarian homesteaders could sustain some form of social life. Most of these were in Saskatchewan (Leask, Aldina, Norbury, Spiritwood, Rabbit Lake, Rothmere, etc.) but there were some in Alberta and Manitoba, also.[68] Little is known about these mostly temporary Hungarian settlements and the community life in them. Much better known is the social activity developed by the new urban groupings of Hungarian Canadians.

The style of Hungarian-Canadian social life in cities like Montreal and Toronto was greatly influenced by economic realities. No statistics exist regarding the disposable incomes of Magyars in the big cities, but there is every reason to believe that they earned much less than the estimated $1,500 a year needed to keep a family out of poverty.[69] But the lack of adequate financial resources did not mean that social life could not be at times rich and satisfying for the participants.

The new Hungarian-Canadian society's community life centred on existing or newly established religious or lay organizations. Not many of these have left a record of their activities; but the ones that have illustrated the social life of Hungarian Canadians during the closing years of the 1920's. One grouping whose activities are well-known is the Protestants of Montreal. Along with the start of their religious work in 1926, cultural and educational efforts were undertaken almost as if they were more important than fun and entertainment. English classes were organized and a library was established with books donated by the government of Hungary. From 1928 on, however, an active social life developed, supplementing the religious and cultural work started earlier. Social functions included dinners, dances, plays, picnics, bazaars, and exhibitions of embroidery.[70] Similar activities were carried on by the city's Roman Catholic Magyars and the members of two lay organizations, the Hungarian Social Club and the Székely Club. Occasionally, larger projects, such as concerts or musical productions, were undertaken jointly with most if not all of these groups and clubs participating. Besides the social activities, two other closely related ethnic enterprises were initiated: Hungarian school for children and soccer matches for sports-minded youths. The highlight of the group's annual community routine came with the celebration of March 15, Hungary's national day. The focal points of most of these activities were the churches and a clubroom right on St. Laurent Boulevard. Another place of gathering was the Hungarian consulate on St. Catherines Street. Here, immigrants exchanged stories of their fortunes or misfortunes as they arranged for the transportation of family members to Canada or, in the case of the disappointed, their own return to Hungary. In Montreal, Hungarian presence was noticeable even to the casual passerby. In the St. Laurent Boulevard-Pine Street area there were Hungarian shops with Magyar signs and billboards on them.[71]

In Toronto active social life developed somewhat later. There, one typically new Canadian organization was the Hungarian Roman Catholic Circle. Established in the fall of 1929, it soon embarked on regular meetings, dances, and English classes in a large room rented in a house on Beverley Street. For some time, the club prospered in every way except financially. Its membership quickly grew from eighteen to nearly one hundred. Public lectures were arranged. In the summer there were ice cream parties and picnics. A small library was started. Next, a house was rented with enough room for larger English classes and dances and even for amateur theatrical productions. The home became the hub of Hungarian social and cultural activity in Toronto. Some functions were held jointly with the city's Magyar Reformed congregation. Other times the dancehall was rented to another recently established institution, the Hungarian Club, or to a visiting theatrical troupe from Hamilton. For more casual entertainment, magazines, chess sets, and the like were acquired and a billiard table was rented.[72]

At the time, most of Toronto's Hungarians lived within walking distance of Beverley Street. The area, bounded by Queen and College Streets on the south and north sides respectively, and extending a couple of blocks both east and west, was inhabited by several East European immigrant groupings. It never became a "little Hungary" the way other sections of the city became "Chinatowns" or "little Italies." Nevertheless, it served as the "home" area of a relatively compact Magyar group, perhaps geographically the most concentrated ever to be had by Hungarians in Toronto. The district had seen better days, but with the original owners gone to more fashionable sections of the city the Beverley Street district became a residential area with large, deteriorating rooming houses. In time, the adjoining business districts, located along Queen Street, Spadina Avenue, and College Street, also became ethnicized through the establishment of ethnic businesses and institutions. In the case of the Hungarians this process took place partly after the migration of Hungarian residents out of the Beverley Street area had started.[73]

Social Stratification and Leadership

The new Hungarian-Canadian society was more heterogeneous than the old one had been. In the first place, the social composition of the immigration stream of the 1920's was more complex. Secondly, most of the new arrivals were better educated, public education having made some advances in Hungary since the turn of the century. The new arrivals often had a richer life experience: most of them had served in the war, had travelled, and had been exposed to new ideas and ideologies. Some of them even used "big words" unintelligible to the old-timers.[74] Not surprisingly, the differences in outlook led to a sociocultural chasm be-

117

tween the new and earlier immigrants. The newcomers, in a typical fashion, resented the material success of the previous arrivals, especially when contrasted with their own apparent lack of progress. At the same time, the older residents disliked what they considered to be "lack of perseverance" on the part of the newcomers. Recounting the great difficulties they had to overcome in their own time, they often reproached their newly arrived countrymen for their desire to "get rich quickly" and their reluctance to do backbreaking physical labour. But the old immigrants' greatest distrust seems to have been directed against the new immigration's gentry and middle-class elements, some members of which tended to treat their lower-class countrymen with condescension yet tried to act as their leaders and to make a living from them as ticket agents and insurance salesmen. This situation often gave rise to misunderstandings and caused ill-feelings toward the "men in trousers" [nadrágos emberek] and "gentlemen rogues" [úri csirkefogók].[75]

Closely related to this issue of intra-ethnic social disharmony was the problem of leadership within the ethnic grouping. People with good education were rare among the old immigrants. Among the new arrivals they were more common, but before these could rise to positions of leadership they had to earn the trust of their countrymen and acquire a familiarity with Canadian conditions. The absence of capable and tactful individuals who had a good command of English and who could have acted as effective spokesmen for their ethnic group in influential Canadian circles was a definite disadvantage for Hungarian-Canadian society. Indicative of the dearth of qualified Hungarian-Canadian professionals is the fact that a search by the Hungarian consultate of Montreal in 1930 produced only one practising Magyar-Canadian physician in all of central Canada (Miklós Sole [Zóla?] of Hamilton). Three years later a well-informed Hungarian-Canadian newspaperman had reason to complain about the utter lack of Canadian-trained Hungarian lawyers in the country.[76]

Although some students of Hungarian affairs have made various generalizations about the "inability" of Hungarians to provide effective political leadership for their own kind, no convincing evidence has been produced that this is really the case. Hungarian-Canadian society's failure to produce good leadership appears to have been the result of certain specific causes. Canada's "agriculturalist only" admission policy restricted the entry of educated, potential leaders into the country; and the lifestyle of most old immigrants was not conducive to preparing children for positions of influence and leadership. General conditions existing within most newly established Hungarian-Canadian groupings – especially the lack of residential stability – also hindered the emergence of effective leadership. With the passage of years, leaders did emerge. The fact that they failed to produce the calibre of leadership their fellow Hungarian Canadians expected of them (or they of themselves) was, as shall be seen below, not so much the result of their group's inherent social or psychological weaknesses but of the brutal conditions which

Hungarian Canadians had to face at the time, and especially, during the Great Depression.

Problems plaguing the emerging Hungarian-Canadian society during the 1920's were numerous. The most serious were a distorted demographic structure, geographic dispersal, economic insecurity, social disharmony, and a dearth of effective leaders. Given these factors, it is not surprising that all was not well with the ethnic group's institutional network and political strategy. Nevertheless, the Hungarian-Canadian community's organizational efforts and political initiatives in these years were not without results, and they betrayed a great deal of determination and dynamism.

INSTITUTIONS AND POLITICS

Ever since Hungarians began arriving in greater numbers in Canada, they had striven to establish their own associations. The growth and increased complexity of their communities in Canada in the 1920's brought about a corresponding increase in the number, size, variety, and sophistication of Hungarian-Canadian associations and institutions. At the same time, within certain sections of the Hungarian ethnic group, interest in politics seems to have become more common than ever before.

The nature of Hungarian-Canadian organized life in the 1920's was determined partly by the patterns and traditions established in the group's older centres in the West and southern Ontario, and partly by Hungarian-Canadian society's social and economic circumstances. The group's religious traditions, combined with its members' thirst for spiritual comfort, resulted in efforts to expand the group's network of religious associations. The economic insecurity of Hungarian Canadians gave rise to new mutual benefit and self-help organizations, while their isolation and alienation from the host society drove them into their own social clubs. Their desire to preserve the ethnic identity of their children induced them to establish "ethnic" schools for them, and their need to be better informed prompted them to launch and maintain their own press organs. To improve their position of influence in Canadian society and to achieve many of their collective aims, they embarked on the ambitious project of establishing their own unified, Canada-wide organization. The origins, nature, and consequences of these efforts are the main themes of the following paragraphs.

Religious Associations

It has been said that the organization of Canada's Hungarian immigrants was possible first only along religious lines.[77] While there are exceptions to this generalization, many examples bear it out. Moreover, whenever worldly associations preceded the spiritual ones, the reason was probably a simple lack of priests or ministers who could start religious work.[78]

There can be little doubt that the vast majority of Hungarian immigrants to Canada, both before and after World War I, were devout Christians. Nevertheless, Canada's Hungarian community, much like society in Hungary, was divided along religious lines. According to the 1931 census, 72.5 per cent of its members were Roman Catholics, 10.3 per cent Calvinists, and 5.3 per cent Lutherans. The remaining were divided among followers of the United Church, the various smaller Protestant churches, and the Greek Catholic and Jewish faiths.[79] It is noteworthy that the equivalent figures for post-1920 Hungary (65 per cent Roman Catholic, 21 per cent Calvinist, 6 per cent Lutheran and 5 per cent Jewish) were slightly different,[80] indicating that Calvinists and Jews were under-represented in Hungarian immigration to Canada. Another difference between the religious divisions of Hungarians and Hungarian Canadians was the fact that, while the proportions of the various religious groups differed from region to region in Hungary, all Canadian provinces with large Hungarian populations had a religious distribution basically similar to the Canada-wide average.[81]

The organization of this religiously divided ethnic group into parishes and congregations had been well under way by 1920. The 1920's brought two important developments in this connection: Church Union, and increased geographic dispersal of Hungarian Canadians. For the Protestants of English Canada in general, Church Union was mainly an event of unification; for Hungarian-Canadian Calvinists, it resulted in division. While most of their existing congregations remained with the Presbyterian Church, in some areas Hungarian Calvinists joined the United Church. The other development, the spreading of Hungarians to newer and newer regions in Canada, necessitated constant organizational work on the part of all religious-minded Hungarians, Protestant and Catholic alike. In trying to overcome this challenge, the latter had some advantages. In most areas they were more numerous than any other denomination, were not affected directly by the problems stemming from Church Union, and had a few centres of their own established even before the immigration of the late 1920's. Nevertheless, the establishment of parishes in Hungarian-Canadian society's newer centres proved to be a slow and painful process. There were not always enough Hungarian-speaking priests to handle this work, and some elements of Canada's Roman Catholic hierarchy doubted the value of "ethnic" parishes and opposed their establishment. Partly as a result of these factors, only a few Magyar-Canadian centres managed to set up their own Roman Catholic parishes in the 1920's.[82]

Hungarian Calvinists were less favourably situated. Even though they had had a long record of organizational work within and even outside of Saskatchewan (in particular, in Winnipeg and Hamilton), in the early 1920's they had no active congregations outside of the "mother Province." Moreover, when the new centres of Hungarian Canada came into being as a result of the new immigration, the Presbyterians failed to establish their own congregations in many of them. They lost Winnipeg,

Young pioneer couple from the Kaposvar district of Saskatchewan, ca. 1905.
(Courtesy M.L. Kovacs)

Early Hungarian pioneers and their sod house on the Saskatchewan prairies.
(Courtesy M.L. Kovacs)

The "Great Church" of Bekevar, Saskatchewan. (Courtesy M.L. Kovacs)

The stone church of Kaposvar with historical monument to the early pioneers. (Courtesy M. Simko, Toronto)

Members and meeting-hall of the First Hungarian Sick-Benefit Society of Lethbridge. (Public Archives of Canada)

Members and home of the Self-Improvement Circle of Welland, 1931.
(Public Archives of Canada)

Homesteader and his family in central Saskatchewan, ca. 1925.
Photo by Paul Koteles. (Courtesy M.L. Kovacs)

The "Justice for Hungary" flight welcomed in Budapest, August, 1931.
(Hungarian Air Force Museum, Oshawa)

Hungarian-Canadian family during World War II.
(Courtesy the Rev. Charles Steinmetz, Toronto)

"First Hungarian Day," Welland, Sept. 2, 1935. (Multicultural History Society of Ontar.

Hungarian workingmen's picnic, 1940's. (Multicultural History Society of Ontario)

*Demonstration in Toronto demanding freedom for Hungary and other enslaved nations Nov. 4, 1956. Photo by Harold Robinson. (*The Globe and Mail, *Toronto)*

Refugees wearing identification tags about to embark on the long journey to Canada. Photo by L. Denes. (Courtesy Edmond de Fay, Toronto)

Hymn singing at a refugee reception centre. Photo by L. Denes. (Courtesy Edmond de Fay, Toronto)

Refugees being processed before departure for Canada. Photo by L. Denes. (Courtesy Edmond de Fay, Toronto)

*The soccer team of refugee students at the University of British Columbia.
(Courtesy F. Kurucz, Vancouver)*

Graduating class of the Sopron School, 1959.
(Courtesy Prof. O. Sziklay, Vancouver)

Students and faculty of the
Sopron School of Forestry of the
University of British Columbia.
(Courtesy Prof. O. Sziklay,
Vancouver)

The post-1956 period saw a flowering of Hungarian-Canadian cultural organizations such as the Kodály Ensemble of Toronto. These photographs show the Ensemble's choir (top), its dancers (middle), and its members on a visit to Winnipeg during Canada's Centennial celebrations in 1967 (bottom). Photos by S. Selmeczi and L. Soltay. (Courtesy K.I. Dreisziger)

Sculptor Victor Tolgesy's memorial to the freedom fighters of the 1956 Revolution. Photo by S. Selmeczi. (Courtesy Dr. G. Nagy, Toronto)

Dedication ceremonies for the memorial, Budapest Park, Toronto, Oct. 1966. Photo by N.F. Dreisziger.

Saskatoon, Montreal, and Regina to the United Church, but managed to set up congregations in Hamilton (1926), Welland (1926), Windsor (1927), Toronto (1928), and Calgary (1930). In some centres, such as Toronto and Welland, they had to accept "co-existence" with congregations belonging to the United Church.[83]

Among Canada's churches, the United Church seems to have showed the most interest in the country's immigrant ethnics. As a part of these efforts the church established various "all nations' churches," "friendship houses," and "all peoples' missions." Ministers and volunteer workers were recruited from the ranks of immigrants or were invited from their mother countries. Several capable Hungarians joined the United Church's efforts. Perhaps the two most colourful were Ferenc Hoffmann and Ambró Czakó. The former was an ex-professor of agriculture who, after escaping Russian captivity in the First World War, was "smuggled" into Canada by friendly British officers. He later entered divinity school and became a United Church minister. His command of several languages enabled him to carry out effective missionary work among various ethnic congregations on Saskatchewan's expanding agricultural frontier. A man of a great deal of energy and charisma, Hoffmann was to serve his church and Hungarian Canadians of all denominations in this area for many years.[84] Czakó, though a man of different temperament, was also a very able and colourful person. In Hungary he had taught philosophy in a Roman Catholic collegiate but had to leave the country because of his association with the revolutionary regime of Mihály Károlyi. After staying in England for some time, Czakó came to Toronto and became a minister of the United Church. Unlike Hoffmann, Czakó preferred to live the life of a scholar and avoided contacts with Hungarians, except for those who shared his political views.[85] Both of them edited a Magyar-language periodical for their church. Hoffmann's journal, *Az Otthon* [The Home] (1923-1937), offered spiritual guidance for its readers along with down-to-earth advice on farming and husbandry. Czakó turned his *Tárogató** (1937-1950) into a highbrow review of the arts, humanities, and politics whose covert message was socialism.[86] Through these publications, and through the work of men like Hoffmann, Czakó, and others, the United Church was able to reach a great many Hungarian Canadians. By the end of the 1920's it had a network of Hungarian congregations extending from the West (Otthon, Saskatoon, Regina, and Winnipeg) to central Canada (Montreal, Toronto, and Welland).

Among the other Protestant denominations, the Lutherans were most numerous. Faced by geographic atomization and the lack of ministers and outside support, their organization into Lutheran congregations proceeded slowly and did not succeed in some places. Their work was begun in 1926 by János Papp of Toronto. Two years later he moved to Windsor

---

* Hungarian wind instrument.

to serve the newly formed Hungarian congregation there but continued to conduct missionary work in the large urban centres of central Canada. Before the end of the decade Jenö Ruzsa, a young man just out of divinity school, relieved Papp of some of his work by assuming the leadership of the congregations of Kitchener, Hamilton, and Toronto.[87] Among the smaller Protestant groups, the Baptists had established a congregation of their own long before 1914 in the Bekevar area of Saskatchewan. In 1929 they succeeded in establishing two congregations in Ontario as well, in Toronto and Welland. From these centres they tried to serve their co-religionists scattered from Windsor to Montreal. In their organizational work, the Magyar Baptists were helped by the American Hungarian Baptist Federation.[88]

The efforts of the various Hungarian-Canadian denominations to establish parishes or congregations were usually followed by attempts to acquire church buildings. In many cases these aspirations were frustrated by economic problems. In rural areas or in small towns, where land was cheap, the problem could often be overcome through extensive use of volunteer labour. But in cities building lots were expensive, and money had to be collected if the congregation wished to build or buy its own church. Since the vast majority of Hungarian-Canadian newcomers lived in poverty, the task of collecting sufficient funds was difficult. An additional problem was the fact that in Hungary people had grown accustomed to parishes and congregations with little need for new organizational work. As well, churches in the old country had an ample supply of ministers and priests and had their expenses defrayed with income from estates and state-collected taxes. People coming from such circumstances often did not appreciate the need to pay for their clergymen's upkeep, let alone for capital expenditures.[89] Yet, many Hungarians gave freely to their churches, and those who did not or could not, often volunteered their free labour. Two fine examples of such generosity are the Roman Catholic and Baptist churches of Welland, both built toward the end of the 1920's.[90]

Schools

Closely associated with Hungarian-Canadian churches were the Magyar "ethnic schools." Their purpose was twofold: the religious education of children and the passing of the Hungarian heritage on to the second generation. There have been five types of such schools in Hungarian-Canadian history: full-time bilingual, summer, weekend, Sunday, and late afternoon. The latter four were designed to supplement the education children were receiving in the regular Canadian school system.

No full-time bilingual (Magyar and English) schools seem to have come into existence outside Saskatchewan.[91] Summer schools, lasting up to eight weeks, were maintained by several denominations in many locations. The most active Roman Catholic promoters of the summer school movement were the Sisters of Social Service. From the arrival of their first members in Canada in 1923, these Roman Catholic nuns expanded their teaching (and other social work) activities from their base in Stockholm to many areas of the Prairies and eventually to central Canada.[92] Weekend schools were even more common. They provided training in the Hungarian language and taught reading, composition, and history at the elementary level. At the Montreal United Church school, for example, instruction was provided for each child three times a week, twice on the weekend and once on a weekday after school.[93]

Like the organization of congregations, the establishment and maintenance of schools were plagued by problems. Hungarian Canadians' geographic and religious atomization made stable, good quality schools feasible only in the largest centres. One problem was the attitude of parents, some of whom did not believe in sending their children to ethnic schools. Others were reluctant to walk their children to classes, especially if these were held in another part of town. Then there was the shortage of qualified teachers, arising from the fact that members of the teaching profession were virtually excluded from Canada. As a result, the task of teaching often devolved on an already overburdened priest or minister, a minister's wife, or volunteers whose qualifications may not have been the best. As virtually all congregations experienced financial difficulty, the paying of more than a token salary was out of the question. The schools had to make the best with the volunteer work offered to them. Unlike the churches, which occasionally received help and helpers from the mother country, the schools were lucky if they could receive textbooks from Hungary through one of the consulates.[94]

Lay Associations

Hungarian-Canadian churches and denominational schools were supplemented by a variety of lay organizations. Some of these were social clubs established mainly for the purpose of good fellowship and entertainment. The activities of one such organization have been described above. Other lay organizations were primarily economic in nature. They were mutual sick- and death-benefit associations aimed at reducing the economic insecurity that faced Hungarian Canadians. The earliest of such organizations, already mentioned, was formed in Lethbridge in 1901. By the end of the 1920's, this society had 240 members and a tested scheme for providing payments to the ill and relatives of the dead.[95] The West's second and third sick-benefit associations were established in Winnipeg. The First Hungarian Sick-Benefit Association of Winnipeg came into being in 1904. It functioned until 1918 and again between 1924 and 1929. The King St. Stephen Roman Catholic Sick-Benefit Association was established in 1907 and flourished for several decades. This organization was a good example of a multi-purpose ethnic club. Ostensibly, its main function was the payment of modest illness and death benefits to its members. It served also as a social club and a cultural centre, which maintained a library and a summer school for children. It worked in close collaboration with Winnipeg's Hungarian Roman Catholic parish, although from 1926 on it was officially independent from it.[96]

In central Canada the first sick-benefit organization was established in 1907. It was the First Hungarian Workers' Sick-Benefit Association of Hamilton. Like its western counterparts, this institution served a variety of economic, social, and cultural aims. Unlike the associations in Lethbridge and Winnipeg, the Hamilton group had wider than local aspirations and significance. From the start, it worked toward the establishment of branch organizations in other cities. Its first successful subsidiary was established in 1913 in Brantford. In 1926 this particular branch split from the main body and established the Hungarian Sick-Benefit Association of Brantford. Within two years both the original and the new association were reorganized and became the focal points of two rival mutual benefit insurance movements. The Hamilton group, with its ranks and leadership swelled by people who had arrived to Canada in recent years, formed the Canadian Hungarian Sick-Benefit Federation. The Brantford club became the Eastern Canadian Hungarian Sick-Benefit Association. The two were incorporated in 1927 and 1928 respectively. Both embarked on the establishment of branch units in many parts of the country. By the end of the decade there were distinct ideological differences between the two groups, differences which were to become more pronounced later. The Hamilton group became a centre for people with leftist tendencies, while the Brantford federation appealed to the non-radical, "patriotic-Christian" elements of Hungarian-Canadian society.[97]

These two federations of mutual-benefit associations never gained a monopoly over the Hungarian-Canadian insurance business. A few large lay organizations retained independence from them. The Self-Improvement Society of Welland, for example, maintained an independent mutual-benefit scheme for its members from the very start. Moreover, other Hungarian centres continued to establish their own independent mutual-benefit or funeral societies. In fact, by the end of the 1920's, apparently every large Hungarian-Canadian centre had some kind of an insurance association as well as a local branch of one or both insurance federations based in Hamilton and Brantford.[98]

Just as the establishment of religious associations was often followed by the acquisition of church buildings, the creation of social clubs and mutual-benefit societies was followed by attempts to build or purchase "Hungarian halls" or "Hungarian houses." These efforts were frustrated by the kind of problems that confronted the religious associations wishing to acquire their own houses of worship: meagre finances and social atomization. With each larger Hungarian-Canadian concentration establishing several, often rival clubs and mutual-benefit societies, much money was spent on the rental of meeting places, dancehalls, and auditoriums. In smaller towns Hungarian clubs could acquire their own buildings through buying an inexpensive lot and erecting a structure on it, piecemeal, with the help of volunteer labour. In larger centres the same couldn't be done. There, money was needed, but it was difficult to obtain. Under these circumstances it is understandable why in none of their new, large centres did Hungarian Canadians acquire any "Hungarian halls" during the 1920's. Indeed, at the end of the decade, only three of their lay organizations (the sick-benefit associations of Lethbridge and Winnipeg, and the Self-Improvement Society of Welland) had buildings of their own. A few more might have been close to getting one but had their plans dashed by the arrival of the Depression. It was not until the 1940's that the movement for Hungarian-owned places of culture and entertainment could resume with some prospect for success.[99]

The Press

The Hungarian Canadians' religious, educational, social, and economic institutions were supplemented by still another manifestation of their organized life: the ethnic press. On the whole, the maintenance of Hungarian-language newspapers and periodicals was prompted by the same needs and desires that drove Hungarians to establish their own religious and other organizations, and it was plagued by similar problems.

In the period under discussion, Canada's Hungarian-language press had a great potential for playing an influential role within Hungarian-Canadian society. Theoretically, it was in a powerful position because it provided the much needed link between the isolated immigrant or immigrant grouping and the outside world. As few Hungarian Canadians knew enough English (or French) to read Canadian newspapers, and their lives were not yet affected by that other powerful medium of mass communication, the radio, the Hungarian press had a near-complete monopoly on the dual role of dispensing information and trying to formulate public opinion among Hungarian Canadians. Nevertheless, the Hungarian-Canadian press failed to become a powerful and effective tool of ethnic communications and co-operation. While there was no lack of effort to make it such an instrument, a host of problems, such as sparse financial resources, the dearth of experienced leaders, and serious social disunity, prevented it from becoming influential and successful.

The years 1905-1924 constituted the formative period of Canada's Hungarian-language press. These two decades saw the rise and demise of several newspapers, including the *Kanadai Magyarság* (Canadian Hungarians), the *Canadai Magyar Farmer* (Canadian Hungarian Farmer), and the *Canadai Magyar Néplap* (Canadian Hungarian People's Paper). Then, in the winter of 1924-25, a group of people, including two Hungarian-Canadian newspaper editors and two emissaries from Hungary, joined forces and established the *Kanadai Magyar Újság* (Canadian Hungarian News). The editor was Iván Hordossy, the man who had been put in charge of the Immigrant Protection Bureau of Winnipeg. With the help of a small subsidy from Hungary, the paper became Canada's largest and most prosperous Hungarian newspaper during the interwar years.[100]

The *Canadian Hungarian News* had started as a small weekly paper in Kipling, Saskatchewan, but soon moved to Winnipeg. Its size and coverage expanded. By 1927 it was produced in ten pages and had a network of agents and volunteer reporters in many parts of Canada. In 1928 Hordossy returned to Hungary and was replaced as editor by a bright and dynamic young man, Béla Bácskai-Peyerle. The following year the paper was bought by the Hungarian magnate Zsigmond Perényi, bringing the paper even more under the control of Hungary's establishment.[101]

Attempts to start Hungarian newspapers in central Canada date from the mid-1920's, a period which saw the launching of three small papers in the Niagara Peninsula. These were the *Kis Újság* (Little Newspaper), the *Kanadai Magyar Népszava* (Canadian Hungarian People's Voice), and the *Kanadai Magyar Hirlap* (Canadian Hungarian Journal), which later moved to Toronto. Except for the *Little Newspaper*, which published for seventeen years, none of these ventures lasted long. They either collapsed or were absorbed by the *Canadian Hungarian News*. A more lasting central Canadian undertaking was the *Kanadai Magyar Munkás* (Canadian Hungarian Worker). Launched in 1929 as an unpretentious little paper, its fortunes improved when it became the chief Hungarian-language organ of the Communist Party of Canada.[102]

Besides the newspapers, there were the religious periodicals. Hoffmann's *The Home* has been mentioned. Its Roman Catholic counterpart was Father Jeromos Hédly's *Örszem* (Sentinel). In Hamilton, Ferenc Kovács published the *Figyelő* (observer) for his Calvinist followers. In Toronto, the Reverend Charles Steinmetz launched the *Gyertyafény* (Candlelight). At one time or another, Jenő Ruzsa edited the journals *Evangélikus Élet* (Lutheran Life) and *Evangélikus Otthon* (Lutheran Home). The Reverend Mihály Fehér of Montreal for many years put out the *Református Hiradó* (Reformed Herald). The Baptists also had a journal, the *Világosság* (Light). Aside from the heavily subsidized *The Home*, only a very few of these periodicals survived for more than a few years. Yet, while journals appeared and folded and editors came and went, the religious press remained, with a fluctuating number of embattled periodicals trying to reach rather small audiences.[103]

It is probably not unfair to say that, aside from the publications which managed to attain a subsidy, the Hungarian-Canadian press was in a sorry state. Part of the problem was atomization, which was particularly evident in the case of the religious press. Still another problem was the lack of experience and skill on the part of editors and publishers. Putting out an ethnic newspaper was a small-scale yet complex undertaking that required the publisher to be a journalist, printer, editor, and businessman rolled into one. Few if any Hungarian Canadians combined all the necessary talents and skills.[104] Contrary to what might be expected, the geographic dispersal of Hungarian Canadians was not always a negative factor; in fact, a few of the newspapers benefited by it to some extent. It is noteworthy that while the *Canadian Hungarian News* and the *Little Newspaper*, serving the Canadian West and the Niagara Peninsula respectively, tended to prosper, no viable ethnic newspapers could come into existence in large, rather compact ethnic communities such as those in Montreal and Toronto. The fact was that a Hungarian Canadian residing in one of these cities needed an ethnic paper less than one living in the isolation of the prairie homestead or a southern Ontario small town. But when it came to having a paper that could serve the whole of Hungarian-Canadian society, Canada's huge size proved a disadvantage. It was simply not possible for a small team of men to be familiar with Hungarian-Canadian affairs both in the West and in the East. The editors of the *News* tried to do so, but with thousands of miles separating them from the new centre of Hungarian Canada, they could do no more than to rely on volunteer "eastern" reporters and send a member of their staff on an "eastern tour" every now and then. It was not a satisfactory arrangement.[105] In fact, a paper published in Winnipeg could hardly command more interest in central Canada than one produced in New York or Cleveland. And there were many of these, as the United States' Magyar community boasted over forty Hungarian-language newspapers, including two dailies. The circulation of these papers in Canada is not known, but we know that some of them had promotion agents in Hamilton and Toronto.[106]

Relations with Hungary

The establishment and maintenance of congregations, insurance companies, Hungarian houses, and Hungarian-language publications constituted Hungarian Canada's everyday organizational life. The history of these has never been told adequately, and may indeed never be written in view of the paucity of available information. More important and interesting but equally little known are the relations of the Hungarian-Canadian ethnic community with Hungary and the attempts to establish a Canada-wide organization.

The Hungarian government's interest in Canada's Hungarian immigrants has been mentioned. The establishment of the IPB in Winnipeg, the launching of the *News*, and the re-opening of the consulates in Montreal and Winnipeg had been manifestations of this interest. The consulates played an imporant role in local and national Hungarian-Canadian affairs, as the consulates' staffs often advised Hungarian-Canadian leaders, helped to mediate in their disputes, and occasionally intervened with Canadian government and railway officials on behalf of Hungarian immigrants.[107] This type of work was supplemented by visits from Hungary by public figures and government officials. These were usually parts of North American fact-finding missions, and were designed to help to reinforce the stature of those elements of Hungarian-Canadian society which stood for close co-operation with the government in Budapest.[108]

Hungarian Canadians seem to have reacted to these efforts with a mixture of awe and appreciation. Visitors from Hungary were always welcome and were treated with respect by all but the political left. Some visits were returned with a Hungarian-Canadian leader or group visiting Hungary. Only in the 1930's did relations become strained at times, when the novelty of the visits wore off and each side began expecting more and more of the other.[109]

A Hungarian-Canadian Federation

One of the Hungarian government's aspirations was the promotion of unity among the various Magyar ethnic communities scattered from Western Europe to South America. Budapest's prime concern was the populous and influential Hungarian group in the United States. The reason was obvious and not entirely unselfish. Through the leadership of this group, the Hungarian government could strengthen its influence in Washington. In the spring of 1928 these hopes came a step closer to realization when almost a thousand Hungarian delegates from all over the United States gathered in Buffalo and established the National Federation of American Hungarians.

In Canada, the campaign for the creation of a Hungarian-Canadian umbrella organization roughly coincided with the gestation period of the Hungarian-American federation, and it does not seem to have been inspired from Hungary. Early in 1927, at the invitation of the Reverend János Kovács of Bekevar, representatives of many western Canadian organizations met in Regina and called for the creation of a Canada-wide federation to look after the interests of Hungarian Canadians. The work of the Regina meeting was to be continued by a larger gathering in Saskatoon. Meanwhile, the idea of a national federation found another advocate in the person of György Szabó, a Cunard Line agent in Winnipeg. On his initiative, preparations for a national convention were started. An eastern Canadian preparatory conference was held in Welland, under the leadership of Ferenc Kovács of Hamilton.[110]

The founding convention took place in February, 1928, in Winnipeg. It was an impressive affair with a great many leading Hungarian-Canadian personalities in attendance. Since one group of organizers had connections with the Canadian National Railways, the company provided free passage to some of the conference-goers. Not to be outdone, the Canadian Pacific Railway Company gave free tickets to many others and threw a gala reception for all those in attendance at the convention. The railway companies' keen interest in immigration matters and their competition for influence in ethnic affairs greatly enhanced the budding rivalries among the various factions of Hungarian-Canadian leadership.

All was not well behind the facade of pomp and rejoicing that characterized the gathering.[111]

To the uninitiated, the convention certainly seemed a success. A national organization, the Canadian Hungarian Federation (CHF), was proclaimed. Its aims were outlined: the advancement of Hungarian Canadians' interests, their education for good citizenship, the improvement of
their reputation in Canada, and so on. A constitution was adopted and
voting procedures were worked out for the election of an executive.
Then, the eighty-five accredited delegates proceeded to elect the federation's leaders. Interestingly, the people who received the most votes were
not those who had inspired the CHF's creation in the first place. The
presidency went to János Újváry, a Regina ticket agent. The Reverend
István Csutoros of Welland was elected vice-president. Miklós Istvánffy,
a delegate from Hamilton, became national secretary.[112] The results of
the election caused keen disappointment in some circles. It was claimed
that the old homesteaders were not properly represented in the executive:
that Újváry lacked the necessary stature and dedication required by his
post and that he was a newcomer, a CPR man, whose public role conflicted with his business interests. The *News*, for a long time an advocate
of the planned federation, condemned the convention's outcome. Next,
a group of disappointed leaders founded a rival organization, the
Hungarian Relief of West-Canada, at a convention in Saskatoon. To add
insult to injury, they established their headquarters also in Winnipeg, in
György Szabó's ticket office.[113]

The defection of the *News* and the establishment of a rival federation
were only two of the many problems facing the federation. The most
serious was financial. The CHF had no reliable source of income. It
hardly had a membership; therefore, it could not count on membership
dues.[114] Closely associated with the above was the question of staff. The
convention voted a handsome salary to Istvánffy and persuaded him to
relocate in Winnipeg, but there was no way of paying him. Istvánffy,
keen and optimistic about the federation's future, accepted; for two
years he spared no effort to save the organization. Indeed, during the
spring and summer of 1928 some problems were solved. As a result of
negotiations with the rival federation, and the intervention of the visiting
Hungarian statesman Perényi, the two federations resolved their differences. Istvánffy went on a cross-Canada tour and managed to drum
up some support for the CHF. Plans were made for the selling of health
insurance. Next, Újváry resigned, making way for the election of a president more acceptable to the various factions within the membership. The
CHF's 1929 convention produced more satisfactory results than the
previous one. The president-elect was József Csávossy, a wealthy Alberta
farmer of upper-class background whose ranch had just been voted
Canada's "best managed farm" by a Canadian organization. János
Kovács, the greatly respected Presbyterian minister of Bekevar, became

associate president, while Istvánffy remained as national secretary. The rest of the executive was made up of a combination of "new" and "old" and "western" and "eastern" Hungarian-Canadian leaders. The meeting's atmosphere was warm, which augured well for the federation's future.[115]

The first half of 1929 was spent in feverish activity. More tours were undertaken by the members of the new executive. Negotiations were started in order to acquire a press outlet. The health insurance scheme was pushed with renewed vigour. Yet, a host of problems remained. The geographic dispersal of Hungarian Canadians was something that no amount of organizing could overcome. The worsening economic situation frustrated the success of the health insurance scheme. No press organ was acquired, although an agreement was reached with the *News* giving the CHF space for news and announcements. But the greatest problem was funds. The federation never had a large membership and found it difficult to collect fees from the members it had. Without adequate income, it tried to survive with the aid of loans and to pay one loan with the help of another. Its bank accounts tell a sad story. They never showed a balance of over $400. By February of 1931, a mere three years after its founding, the balance of the federation's last remaining bank account dwindled to $14.75. By that time the organization had disintegrated into small, hardly viable "provincial chapters."[116] The Canadian Hungarian Federation fell victim to quixotic planning, general apathy, and the Depression.

The experiment in establishing a national federation brought to an end a distinct period of Hungarian-Canadian history lasting from the post-World War I years to the onset of the Great Depression. It was an age characterized above all by change. During this brief time span Canada's Hungarian population more than tripled in size, its social composition became more complex, and its urban-rural ratio and geographic distribution underwent dramatic changes. Largely as a result of these developments, new centres of Hungarian ethnic life emerged and organizational activity became much more diverse. Especially during the late 1920's, much creativity was displayed in the realm of social, cultural, and political undertakings.

Much of this new vitality was generated by the new arrivals who were anxious to establish their own associations and institutions in order to better cope with the innumerable social, economic, cultural, and psychological problems facing newcomers. But there can be no doubt that the widespread optimism prevalent in Hungarian-Canadian circles was also a reflection of the general economic prosperity enjoyed by the whole of Canada at the time. It is not surprising, then, that when the euphoria of the twenties yielded to the despair of the thirties, much of the ardour vanished from Hungarian-Canadian community life. In fact, the Depression years were to bring untold hardships for most Hungarian immigrants and crushing problems for their organizations.

NOTES

1. A.A. den Otter, "Sir Alexander T. Galt and the Northwest: A Case Study in Entrepreneurialism on the Frontier" (Ph.D. thesis, University of Alberta, 1975), p. 230, especially note 35.
2. *Ibid.*, pp. 230-3. For police views on Lethbridge's contemporary "Hungarian problem," see Superintendent R.B. Deane's reports to his superiors in "North-west Mounted Police, Annual Reports," printed each year in Canada, Parliament, *Sessional Papers.*
3. *Kanadai Magyar Újság (KMU),* 12 October 1929.
4. Péter A. Vay, *Amerikai naplókivonatok: utijegyzetek, levéltöredékek* [American Diary Excerpts: Travel Notes, Letters] (Budapest, 1910), pp. 100ff.
5. *Ibid.*, p. 114.
6. *Amerikai Magyar Népszava Képes Naptára* (1907), pp. 180ff.
7. Charles Lipton, *The Trade Union Movement of Canada, 1827-1959* (Montreal, 1966), p. 55. On Szalatnay, see the *Dictionary of Canadian Biography,* X, pp. 670ff. A few of the post-1849 emigrés might have participated in the Fraser Valley gold rush. See W.E. Ireland (ed.), "First Impressions," *British Columbia Historical Quarterly,* 15 (1951), p. 97.
8. Vay, *Amerikai naplókivonatok,* pp. 98, 114, 118.
9. Ödön Paizs, *Magyarok Kanádaban* [Hungarians in Canada] (Budapest, [1928]), pp. 197-215. Jenö Ruzsa, *A kanadai magyarság története* [The History of the Hungarians of Canada] (Toronto, 1940), especially the chapter on Ontario. Also, information from Géza Kertész and László Jakus of Welland, Ontario, August, 1973.
10. *KMU,* 14 July 1928, 12 October 1929, and 12 February 1931. Péter Németh, "A Prérik Fövárosa" [The Capital of the Prairies], *A Bevándorló,* II, no. 64 (20 December 1906), pp. 11ff. Vay, *Amerikai naplókivonatok,* p. 94. István Nagy, *A winnipegi Magyar Református Egyház félévszázados története, 1906-1956* [The Winnipeg Hungarian Reformed Church's Half Century of History, 1906-1956] (Winnipeg, 1956), pp. 5ff. Ruzsa, *A kanadai magyarság,* pp. 54, 61. Interviews with Mr. Julius Köteles, 26 October 1975, and the late Reverend Kálmán László, 27 October 1975.
11. Vay, *Amerikai naplókivonatok,* pp. 100, 114, 118. Németh, "A Prérik," pp. 11ff. John Kósa, "Immigration and Adjustment of Hungarians in Canada," p. 59. For a general treatment of life in Canadian railway construction camps, see Edmund Bradwin, *The Bunkhouse Man,* with an introduction by Jean Burnet (Toronto, 1972).
12. Den Otter, "Galt," pp. 230-3; the reports of Superintendent Deane, especially the report for 1888 (printed in Sessional Paper no. 17 for that year, *Sessional Papers,* vol. 8, Ottawa, 1889) and the report for 1892 (printed in Sessional Paper no. 15 for that year, *Sessional Papers,* vol. 9, Ottawa, 1893). For a bitter attack on Hungarians in the *Lethbridge News,* see the issue for 28 June 1888.

13. In particular, Winnipeg's Hungarian colony. Nagy, *A winnipegi Magyar*, p. 1; Ruzsa, *A kanadai magyarság*, pp. 54, 60ff.

14. Paizs, *Magyarok*, pp. 197-215 *passim*; Ruzsa, *A kanadai magyarság*, pp. 156-261 *passim*. On the origins of the Welland community, interviews with Kertész and the late Mrs. L. Jakus (Anna Kovács), August, 1973; also, *KMU*, 11 June 1931.

15. *Census of Canada*, 1921, I (Ottawa, 1924), Tables 28, 26. Statistics for a few other cities are: Winnipeg, 344; Regina, 277; Sydney, 120; and Edmonton, 65.

16. More precisely, 67.8 per cent (8,946 out of the 13,181 living in the country). Of those living outside of Saskatchewan, 41 per cent resided in Ontario, 24.7 per cent in Alberta, 19.6 per cent in Manitoba, 8.1 per cent in British Columbia, 2.1 per cent in Quebec, and 4.6 per cent elsewhere, mainly in Nova Scotia. *Ibid.*, Table 24.

17. R.C. Brown and Ramsay Cook, *Canada, 1896-1921: A Nation Transformed* (Toronto, 1974), Chapter I.

18. An attempt at rescindment failed in November, 1920. PAC, Memorandum by S.D. Scott, Assistant Deputy Minister of Immigration and Colonization, 23 November 1920, RG 76, vol. 145. Also, *ibid.*, copy of letter, J.A. Calder, Minister of Immigration and Colonization, to F.H. Auld, Deputy Minister of Agriculture, 20 November 1920.

19. The lifting of the ban was preceded by lobbying by the Hungarian-Canadian community. *Ibid.*, Departmental memoranda, 7 November 1922, 19 May 1923.

20. Provincial Archives of Saskatchewan (PAS), Testimony of Ferenc Hoffmann before the Saskatchewan Royal Commission on Immigration and Settlement (1930), Hearings of the Commission, vol. 2, p. 123.

21. Translation of an article by Ödön Paizs in the *Az Est* (Budapest), 9 March 1924, in PAC, RG 76, vol. 145.

22. *Ibid.*; also, interview with Sister Mary (Schwartz) of the Sisters of Social Service, August, 1972.

23. PAC, memorandum by I. Hordossy and S.E. Janossy, 31 December 1924, in the Arthur Meighen Papers, vol. 95. A translation of the Royal Hungarian Ministry of the Interior circular, no. 44,700/1921, in PAC, RG 76, vol. 145. *Cf.* Miklós Szántó, *Magyarok a nagyvilágban* [Hungarians in the Wide World] (Budapest, 1970), pp. 101-10 *passim*.

24. Memorandum by Hordossy and Jánossy, 31 December 1924.

25. Hordossy writing in *Külföldi Magyarság*, 2 May 1925. Also, interview with Gusztáv Nemes, 24 October 1975.

26. Testimony of Ferenc Hoffmann before the Royal Commission on Immigration and Settlement, pp. 124ff. Kósa, "Immigration and Adjustment," p. 66.

27. Report of the Department of Immigration and Colonization for the Fiscal Year Ended March 31, 1928, Table 5 (p. 12), in *Annual Departmental Reports, 1927-28,* vol. II (Ottawa, 1929). Report for the Year

ended 31 March 1930, Table 5 (p. 12), in *Annual Departmental Reports, 1929-30*, vol. II (Ottawa, 1931).

28. Report for 1926-27, pp. 22ff., in *Annual Departmental Reports, 1926-27*, vol. II (Ottawa, 1928). Report for 1928-29, pp. 20ff. Officials in Ottawa estimated that by 1928 between 500 and 1,000 Hungarians had been shipped back to Hungary on account of being destitute. It was suspected that some of these "destitutes" had some money but wanted a free return voyage. PAC, Walker to Egan, 11 May 1928, RG 76, vol. 145.

29. Report of the Department of Immigration and Colonization for 1927-28, p. 14; Report for 1929-30.

30. Kósa, "Immigration and Adjustment," p. 70.

31. Francis Grob, "Recollections," incomplete ms in the author's possession. I am indebted to Mr. Grob for portions of this manuscript.

32. Kósa, "Immigration and Adjustment," p. 70.

33. Estimates based on figures provided by *Census of Canada, 1921*, Table 24; W. Burton Hurd, *Racial Origins and Nativity of the Canadian People*, Census Monograph based on the 1941 census, Table 6.

34. *Census of Canada, 1931*, I Table 35. W. Burton Hurd, *Racial Origins and Nativity of the Canadian People*, Census Monograph no. 4 (Ottawa, 1937), p. 97 and Table 40. Also, Hurd (1941), p. 61.

35. Kósa, "Immigration and Adjustment," p. 340, Table 24.

36. Paizs, *Magyarok*, pp. 198-206. Ruzsa, *A Kanadai Magyarság*, pp. 210f. *Census of Canada, 1931*, vol. II, Table 33.

37. Ruzsa, *A Kanadai Magyarság*, pp. 285, 287.

38. Mihály Fehér, *A Montreáli Magyar Református Egyház Jubileumi Emlékkönyve, 1926-1966* [The Jubilee Album of the Hungarian Reformed Church of Montreal, 1926-1966] (Montreal, 1966), p. 17. Aladar Komjathy (ed.), *Magyar Református Egyház: Hungarian United Church* (Montreal, 1976), p. 37. Ruzsa, *A Kanadai Magyarság*, pp. 287-312.

39. Ruzsa, pp. 156f. Letter, Ferenc Grob to the author, 20 October 1975, in my possession.

40. Ruzsa, pp. 162, 167, 176ff.; Fehér, *Montreáli*, p. 17; *KMU*, 14 July 1928; interview with the Reverend Charles Steinmetz, 28 November 1976.

41. Ruzsa, pp. 56-68 *passim*.

42. Speculations on the origins of Regina's Magyar population derive from the three main secondary sources of early Hungarian-Canadian History, Paizs, Ruzsa, and Sántha. See Paizs, pp. 134ff.; Ruzsa, p. 100; Sántha, writing in *KMU*, 7 December 1937.

43. Ruzsa, pp. 101-104; Paizs, *Magyarok*, pp. 134f; *KMU*, 12 October 1929 and 3 September 1931.

44. Ruzsa, pp. 106ff.

45. Hurd (1941), Tables 11 and 15.

46. Ruzsa, p. 104.

47. Paizs, p. 125; Ruzsa, pp. 18-19, 29.
48. Ruzsa, p. 337; Fehér, *Montreáli,* p. 52.
49. Calculations based on figures provided in *Census of Canada,* 1931, I, Tables 30, 35.
50. Calculations of urban-rural ratios are based on figures provided in *ibid.,* Table 30. The urban ratio of the 1926-30 group in Manitoba was 59 per cent, in Saskatchewan 29 per cent, in Alberta 34 per cent. In Quebec and Nova Scotia these ratios were very high for all groups, not just for the post-1926 arrivals.
51. Recent arrrivals (1921-30) made up 66 per cent of the immigrant Hungarian population of Saskatchewan's towns and cities, 80 per cent of Manitoba's, 92 per cent of Ontario's, and 97 per cent of Quebec's. Percentages calculated on the basis of figures provided in *ibid.*
52. Percentages based on figures provided in *Census of Canada,* 1931, I, Table 38.
53. Hurd (1931), Tables 16, 18, 24, 26.
54. *Ibid.,* Tables 73, 74. The statistics for Ontario are taken from *Census of Canada,* 1931, I, Table 38.
55. *Ibid.,* Table 25.
56. *Ibid.,* Tables 73, 74.
57. *Ibid.,* Tables 55, 58, 59.
58. *Ibid.,* Tables 45, 47. Indicative of the drastic change in the general status of the group in the decade after 1921 was the fact that the equivalent figure for the previous census was 72 per cent.
59. *Ibid.,* Tables 50, 52.
60. Leonard Marsh quoted by Terry Copp, *The Anatomy of Poverty: The Condition of the Working Class in Montreal, 1897-1929* (Toronto, 1974), p. 141.
61. For several biographical sketches of Hungarians who came to Canada in the second half of the twenties, see Ruzsa, *A Kanadai Magyarság,* pp. 441-6. Three autobiographical pieces are presented in Linda Dégh's *People in the Tobacco Belt: Four Lives* (Ottawa, 1975), Chapters I, II, IV.
62. Consular memorandum, 28 April 1928, Winnipegi Konzulátus (K 139), Külügyminisztériumi Levéltár, Polgári kori központi kormányhatóságok levéltárai, Magyar országos levéltár [Winnipeg Consulate, Ministry of External Affairs Archives, Archives of the Central Authorities of the Bourgeois Era, Hungarian National Archives], Budapest (cited hereafter as Consular Records).
63. Béla Bácskai-Payerle, "A Kanadai Magyarság" [Canadian Hungarians], *Magyar Szemle,* 18 (1933), p. 221. Interviews with Sisters Mary and Columba of the Sisters of Social Service, and taped conversations with old-timers in Lethbridge, kindly placed at my disposal by Father S. Molnár of the St. Elizabeth of Hungary Parish in Calgary.
64. Paizs, *Magyarok,* p. 75.
65. Interview with Sister Mary.

66. *KMU*, 8 June 1929. Also, Paizs, *Magyarok*, p. 51; and Bácskai-Payerle, "A Kanadai," p. 220.

67. Consular Records, Memorandum, 28 May 1930.

68. Frank Hoffmann, "People of Hungarian Origin," *Encyclopedia Canadiana*, v, p. 199. Hoffmann had been responsible for the processing and immigration of many of these settlers to Canada; later he served some of them as an itinerant missionary of the United Church. PAS, Records of the Saskatchewan Royal Commission on Immigration and Settlement (1930), vol. 2, pp. 109-30.

69. Copp, *Anatomy of Poverty*, pp. 40ff. The average yearly income for an unskilled labourer in Montreal during the 1930-31 period was $836. It is safe to suppose that immigrants earned less. In Toronto incomes were slightly higher. *Ibid.*, p. 140.

70. Fehér, *Montreáli*, pp. 23f.

71. Ruzsa, *A Kanadai Magyarság*, pp. 308-10. Paizs, *Magyarok*, p. 47. *KMU*, 26 May 1928, 27 March and 4 December 1930.

72. A Torontoi Magyar Katolikus Kör Jegyzőkönyve [Minutes of Meetings of the Toronto Hungarian Catholic Circle], ms, 24 November 1929 and after, St. Elizabeth of Hungary Parish Office, Toronto.

73. John Kósa, "Hungarian Immigrants in North America: Their Residential Mobility and Ecology," *Canadian Journal of Economics and Political Science*, XXII, 3 (August, 1956), pp. 369ff.

74. Paizs, pp. 102, 169.

75. *Ibid.*; Bácskai-Payerle, "A Kanadai," p. 220.

76. Consular Records, Consular memorandum, 8 September 1930. Bácskai-Payerle, p. 221. The lack of Canadian-trained Magyar lawyers was to be remedied somewhat a few years later when Elemér Izsák, a second-generation Hungarian Canadian, became a lawyer in Toronto.

77. Paizs, p. 172; *cf.* Ruzsa, p. 333.

78. Geraldine Vörös, a Ph.D. candidate in sociology, has argued in a study of Welland's Hungarian community that the pattern of religious organizations preceding political ones does not fit a highly politicized ethnic group such as the Hungarian group was during the interwar years. The suggestion is interesting but there is not enough evidence to warrant the drawing of any historical conclusions from it. G. Vörös, "Formal Institutions: Community Independence and Community Factionalism," paper presented at annual meeting of Canadian Sociology and Anthropology Association, Laval University, Quebec, May, 1976.

79. *Census of Canada*, 1931, XIII, Table 86. The figures for Hungarian Canadians born in the territories of Trianon Hungary were slightly different: 72 per cent Roman Catholic, 9 per cent Calvinist, 6.5 per cent Lutheran, 3.6 per cent United Church, and 9.2 per cent "other." *Ibid.*, Table 87.

80. György Ránki *et al.* (eds.), *Magyarország Története, 1918-1919, 1919-1945* [Hungary's History, 1918-1919, 1919-1945] (Budapest, 1976), p. 786.

81. *Census of Canada*, 1931, I, Table 45. In contrast, in Hungary, the western part of the country was predominantly Roman Catholic, while the easternmost counties had large Calvinist majorities.

82. Notably, Calgary (1926), Welland (1928), and Montreal (1928). Among older Hungarian-Canadian urban centres, Winnipeg had had a Roman Catholic parish since 1924. Ruzsa, pp. 19, 60, 301. Bácskai-Payerle, p. 222.

83. Ruzsa, pp. 211, 252, 264, 163, 19; Bácskai-Payerle, pp. 222ff.

84. John Murray Gibbon, *Canadian Mosaic: The Making of a Northern Nation* (Toronto, [1938]), pp. 360ff. PAS, Saskatchewan Royal Commission on Immigration and Settlement, vol. 2, pp. 110ff. Report of the Commission on City Missions and non-Anglo-Saxon Work, 4 February 1944, Board of Home Missions, vol. 16, United Church Archives, Toronto.

85. Letter, Béla Bácskai-Payerle to the author, 30 December 1975, in my possession; interview with the Reverend Károly Steinmetz, 28 November 1976.

86. PAS, Saskatchewan Royal Commission on Immigration and Settlement, vol. 2, p. 109; Report of the Commission on City Missions; Ruzsa, *A Kanadai Magyarság*, pp. 363, 368.

87. Ruzsa, pp. 375ff.

88. *Ibid.*, pp. 342-50.

89. *Ibid.*, pp. 333ff.

90. *Ibid.*, pp. 249, 347, illustrations on pp. 250, 351.

91. Ruzsa mentions the existence of such a school within the Calvinist (United Church) congregation of Montreal (Ruzsa, p. 357), but elsewhere (p. 300) describes this school as being part-time. In Saskatchewan the most noteworthy day school was maintained in Stockholm. Paul Sántha, *Three Generations, 1901-1957: The Hungarian Colony at Stockholm, Saskatchewan* (published by the author, n.d.), pp. 83-5.

92. Interviews with Sisters Mary and Columba; Ruzsa, pp. 111ff. Sántha, *Three Generations*, pp. 51, 80ff.

93. Fehér, *Montreáli*, pp. 32ff. József Tamás, *Magyar iskolák Kanadában* [Hungarian Schools in Canada] (Montreal, 1966), pp. 21ff.

94. Many of the above observations are based on facts and opinions presented by Ruzsa, pp. 356ff., and Bácskai-Payerle, p. 223.

95. Any healthy person under the age of fifty could join the society on the recommendation of the group's general meeting and the payment of an entry fee, ranging from $1 to $7 depending on age. The monthly membership fee was 75¢. Sick benefits were paid at the rate of $1 a day up to three months, and 50¢ thereafter. Payments could be discontinued after six months. Death benefit was $50 plus a dollar for each member of the society. *KMU*, 14 July 1928.

96. *KMU*, 12 October 1929; Ruzsa, pp. 61ff.

97. Ruzsa, pp. 199-204, 211, 372-4; *Az Uttörö*, 10 April 1958; *KMU*, 9 April 1935; PAC, Records of the Canadian Hungarian Federation, file 2

in the Records of the *Canadian Hungarian News*, Box 47, cited hereafter as *CHN* Records.

98. *KMU*, 12 and 19 October 1929, and June, 1931.
99. Most of the above observations are based on Ruzsa, pp. 359ff.
100. *KMU*, 29 November 1974. Ruzsa, pp. 364ff.; interview with G. Nemes. For a study of this newspaper's early history, see Carmela Patrias, "The *Kanadai Magyar Újság* and the politics of the Hungarian Canadian Elite," Occasional papers in ethnic and immigration studies, Multicultural History Society of Ontario, no. 3, 1978.
101. *KMU*, 13 July 1929 and 29 November 1974.
102. *CHN* Records, copy of memorandum, [Istvánffy] to Csávossy, May, 1928. *KMU*, 13 July 1939 and 30 January 1930. Ruzsa, pp. 386-71.
103. Ruzsa, p. 363; Fehér, p. 25; Hoffmann, pp. 199ff.
104. Ruzsa, p. 362.
105. On the subject of the *Ujság's* relations with eastern Canada, see *KMU*, 30 January 1930; and the Istvánffy memorandum of May, 1928. Also, Ruzsa, p. 367.
106. Szántó, *Magyarok a nagyvilágban*, pp. 120, 127; Ruzsa, pp. 191ff.; *KMU*, 19 January 1929. The two largest dailies, *Szabadság* [Liberty] and *Amerikai Magyar Népszava* [American Hungarian People's Voice], had subscription agencies in Toronto. The left-wing *Új Előre* [New Forwards] was promoted by the sick-benefit federation based in Hamilton.
107. Ruzsa, pp. 327ff. *KMU*, 12 October 1929.
108. On one of these tours, see *KMU*, 21 April 1928. For a Marxist analysis of the Hungarian government's aspirations in regard to the Hungarian communities of North America, see Szántó, pp. 89-132 *passim*.
109. For Hungarian-Canadian complaints about the unfulfilled aspects of the relations with Hungary, see Bácskai-Payerle, pp. 222ff.; Ruzsa, pp. 357, 383ff.
110. Ruzsa, pp. 71ff. Grob, "Recollections," pp. 6ff. Letters, Ferenc Grob to Joseph Kohári, 21 May and 29 June 1974, kindly loaned to me by Dr. Kohári.
111. *CHN* Records, vol. 47, Report of György Szabó to the 1929 Convention. Gyula Izsák, "A Kanadai Magyar Nemzeti Szövetségekről" [About the Canadian-Hungarian National Federations], ms, n.d., in *ibid.*, vol. 30a. Letters, Grob to Kohári, 21 May and 29 June 1974. Ruzsa, p. 72. *KMU*, 28 January 1928.
112. *CHN* Records, vol. 47, Minutes of the founding convention. Grob's letters to Kohári. Ruzsa, p. 74.
113. *CHN* Records, Box 47, Draft memorandum submitted by the Saskatchewan delegation to the founding convention; *KMU*, 14 February and 10 March 1928.
114. *CHN* Records, CHF file 30, Istvánffy to Újváry, 7 March 1928. Individual membership in the CHF was set at $1 a year. Often the fee was only paid when someone approached the federation for legal advice or some other favour.

115. *CHN* Records, Box 47, Minutes of the CHF's Central Executive Meeting, 22 June 1928; *KMU*, 28 April 1928; Istvánffy's correspondence for this period, in *CHN* Records.
116. PAC, *CHN* Records, unorganized parts, CHF bank accounts.

FIVE

A Decade of Setbacks: The 1930's

N.F. Dreisziger

LIFE AND SOCIETY DURING THE DEPRESSION

Perhaps no event had a more profound and more lasting impact on the history of Hungarian-Canadian society during the first half of the present century than the Great Depression. The crisis wrought havoc on the economic and social development of all of Canada. It ruined the country's staple economy, drove farm prices to record lows, forced thousands of farmers and businessmen into bankruptcy, and produced an unemployment rate in excess of 25 per cent of the labour force. The brunt of the adversity was borne by the poorer classes and minorities, and few groups suffered more than the Hungarians.

The Human Toll

It is not possible to recapture here in detail the misery inflicted by the Depression on individual Hungarian Canadians. Attempts have been made to convey it in fiction and in autobiographical accounts.[1] All that can be done in a survey of this type is to illustrate, through a few generalizations, the fate of the various elements of Hungarian-Canadian society during the 1930's.

First to feel the severe effects of the economic crisis were the migrant farm workers of the West. These people had had their share of difficulties even before 1930, but the Depression made their lot even more miserable. Evidence indicates that their situation became appreciably worse right at the outset of the crisis, during the winter of 1929-30. In his May, 1930, report to Budapest on unemployment among Hungarians in the West, Winnipeg consul István Schefbeck talked of people who had been unemployed for five to six months, and even of some who had not worked for eight months. He explained that the difficulties of the West's wheat economy during 1929 had led to decreased railway traffic and the end of railway construction work in the northern prairie regions. Manufacturers also curtailed their operations and some of them closed down for months during the winter. The result was wide-scale unemployment. Some of the unemployed found work through municipal relief projects or in bush-clearing, but none of these jobs lasted longer than three or four weeks. In the spring the situation became worse. With the end of the winter's forest-clearing operations, thousands of unemployed flocked to the cities. They were soon joined by the usual spring wave of fresh arrivals from Europe. Unlike in previous years, when the crowds of migrant workers dispersed to work on farms and railway construction sites, in the spring of 1930 most of them remained unemployed.[2]

What happened in the spring of 1930 was to repeat itself for almost a whole decade, the only substantial difference being that, after 1931, the ranks of the unemployed were no longer swelled each spring by masses of fresh arrivals from overseas because Ottawa had closed Canada's gates to most types of immigrants. Nevertheless, the number of unemployed continued to grow for some years as idle farm workers were joined by others whom the economic crisis deprived of their jobs or livelihood. Many of these were Hungarians who had taken up farming during the 1920's or even earlier. The fact was that the Depression dealt a particularly severe blow to the West's farm economy. The prices of agricultural produce became so low that it did not pay to raise crops. In 1932 wheat sold for as low as thirty-four cents a bushel. The price of firewood, a staple product of new homesteads in some northern regions, was so low that it was not worth transporting it to nearby towns and cities. In addition to the low prices, many areas of the Prairies were afflicted by natural calamities such as prolonged drought, plagues of grasshoppers, and soil erosion caused by wind and drought. In some regions farmers suffered nine successive years of total or near-total crop failures.[3] The results were disastrous. Farmers in debt were unable to meet their obligations. Mortgages were foreclosed and settlers had to abandon their homesteads. Thousands of Hungarians drifted away from prairie farms and sought a better life in other regions of the country, often in the big cities.

Misery in the Cities

Conditions were not better in most urban centres either. In those days there were no federally financed welfare programs. In most cases, relief was provided by municipalities. These faced the problem of having to care for more and more unemployed at a time when fewer and fewer people were able to pay municipal taxes. To prevent the influx of unemployed from places where no relief could be provided, municipalities tried to keep out newcomers and to restrict relief to long-term residents. As early as June of 1930, Winnipeg's city council began insisting that unemployed with less than a year's residence should be expelled from the city and that non-citizens on welfare should be deported from Canada.[4] Such attitudes made the lot of the recently arrived migrant worker very difficult. But even those who qualified for relief had a tough time. They received nothing more than handouts of food from public food depots or food and rent vouchers. Still other city residents managed to find a few weeks of work each year, which provided a meagre living for their families. A very few, mainly blue-collar workers whose firms did not go bankrupt succeeded in hanging on to a job. They were truly lucky. Even with low incomes – wages were often cut during the Depression – they could provide for their loved ones and even save for a piece of real estate or a farm, which in those days could often be had for a song.[5]

Whether unemployed or not, on relief or not, everyone lived frugally. Although at first it was believed that things would soon get better, after years of increasing unemployment people began to believe that economic depression was here to stay. Accordingly, they tried to get by with spending as little money as possible. They lived in crowded, unheated houses and bought only the most basic necessities. They walked to and from work or church, even if it took them hours to do so, rather than spend five cents on streetcars. They even denied themselves the chance to get warmed up by going to a movie in a heated movie theatre, because it cost ten to fifteen cents to do so.[6]

While many of the economic hardships affected immigrant and native-born alike, Hungarians often faced problems not shared by Canadians. As recent arrivals they were first to be fired and last to be rehired when it came to employment. As has been mentioned, many of them had come to Canada on borrowed money and had left their families in Hungary. Those among them who had not paid their debts and had not brought out their wives (and children in some cases) before the onset of bad times faced the prospects of losing their collateral (often a piece of family real estate in Hungary) and of no reunion with their loved ones.[7]

Deportations and Relief Camps

Still another threat that confronted the recent arrival was deportation from Canada if he was found to be a public charge. Not being able to find work and forbidden to apply for relief, many recent Hungarian Canadians found themselves in a desperate situation. Some solved it by deliberately going on municipal relief and thereby effecting their own deportation to Hungary. Conditions during the Depression were miserable there also, but in the Hungarian countryside people could at least expect to avoid actual starvation. Official statistics give an indication of the size of this more or less involuntary movement back to Hungary. Before the economic crisis, about two dozen Hungarian immigrants were deported from Canada each year (at the expense of the shipping companies), for various reasons ranging from ill-health to criminality. This was not a large figure considering that in 1929 some 1,500 people were returned to the United Kingdom. But in 1930 the figures for Hungarians began to climb. In that year thirty-one of them were deported; in the next year, 121, and in 1932 the number of Magyar deportees reached an all-time high of 170. Eighty-six of these were convicted of having accepted relief. In the following year the number of people returned to Hungary declined to 101, and by 1934 the number of deportees had returned to the pre-1929 levels.[8]

There were definite reasons why deportations declined after 1932. By then, those who were least able or least willing to cope with the adversities had been sent back to Hungary or left Canada of their own volition. The federal government was anxious also to find some solution to unemployment. Its principal measure was the establishment in 1932 of camps for the unemployed under the control of the Department of National Defence. In these camps, young men could get board and lodging plus twenty cents a day in return for working on government construction projects often in some remote part of Canada. The scheme did not solve anyone's economic problems, but it kept many desperate men off the streets where they could resort to crime and violence. We don't know how many Hungarians lived in these camps, but indications are that there were many. We know also that some were happy with their lot while others had complaints. Many did not like the living conditions and were dissatisfied with the twenty cents a day pay. Others charged that "English" camp-dwellers got preferential treatment when it came to getting leave from the camps.[9]

Migrations and New Settlements

Those among the Hungarian unemployed who were neither deported nor confined in labour camps roamed the country in search of jobs. One prominent Hungarian newspaper editor wrote in 1933 that it was not uncommon for him to receive a letter from the same unemployed Hungarian one day from Montreal and two weeks later from Vancouver. Nor was it unusual to find twenty or thirty Hungarians perched on top of a freight car in spite of the watch maintained by the Mounted Police and the bitter cold of the winter. There were days, the editor claimed, when as many as three Hungarian migrants were reported dead, having fallen off speeding freight trains.[10]

Not all the migrants kept travelling aimlessly year after year. Sooner or later many of them found something to do, or gave up trying. Others probably made one or two trips and settled in a part of the country where economic prospects looked better. Only massive research could provide a comprehensive picture of these migrations or their consequences. Census data offer only limited information on their final outcome. But before the statistics are analysed, it should be stated that these Depression-time migrations led to the birth of still more new Hungarian settlements in Canada. The most important of these grew up in the lower Fraser and Okanagan Valleys of British Columbia and in the "tobacco belt" of southern Ontario.

Hungarians were not new to British Columbia in the 1930's. There had been many of them in the province before. In 1921 they numbered over 300, and by the next census their number reached 1,300. Most of them lived scattered in many regions of British Columbia. Only in the lower Fraser Valley was there a noticeable concentration. The influx of the Depression years changed this situation by increasing considerably the trend toward geographic concentration in a couple of regions. While many Hungarians remained in scattered districts, by the time of the 1941 census the majority of them lived in a few areas along the lower Fraser River and in the Okanagan Valley. This development had been made possible by an influx of some 1,600 Hungarian Canadians, which brought their numbers almost to 2,900 by 1941. The growth was experienced almost exclusively by two census divisions (numbers 3 and 4) incorporating the above mentioned districts. These accounted for 78 per cent of the increase in British Columbia's Hungarian population.[11]

In the lower Fraser Valley the most notable Hungarian colony developed in the Abbotsford-Huntington area. The first Magyar settlers arrived in this prime agricultural district during the mid-1920's. Many of them were from the Prairies, particularly from Stockholm, Saskatchewan; most of them seem to have been Roman Catholic.[12] They came for a variety of reasons. Perhaps the most important was the desire to escape the long, harsh winters of the Prairies. Later, during the 1930's, many sought refuge here mainly for economic reasons. All commentators agree that the colony was successful. A few of its members tried tobacco growing; they were the first to do so in the area. Others went into dairy farming, fruit growing, sugar beet production, or various types of mixed farming. A few made a living from non-agricultural pursuits. By the end of the decade the colony had about four hundred members and a thriving social and organizational life.[13]

In the Okanagan Valley, the largest concentration of Hungarian settlers developed in the Osoyoos-Oliver area, not far from the American border. Most of the colony's members came during the Depression and became involved in mixed dry farming and gardening. In numbers this settlement has apparently never exceeded 200. According to the census, somewhat smaller Hungarian colonies existed in the 1930's further north in the valley, in Summerland and Kelowna.[14]

In addition to the largely rural Hungarian settlements of the Fraser and Okanagan Valleys, by 1941 many urban Magyar colonies had also grown up in British Columbia. By far the most important of these was in Vancouver. Hungarians had started settling there in the second half of the 1920's. By 1931 their number exceeded 200. In 1941 they numbered about 550. Life was not easy for them – during the Depression many were often out of work and had to compete with the city's numerous Oriental and other immigrants for jobs at very low wages. Yet, many found periodic employment in lumberyards and industrial shops. Moreover, by the end of the 1930's, a handful of Vancouver's Hungarians managed to establish themselves in business. By this time the colony as a whole had an active organizational and social life.[15]

Any discussion of significant new Hungarian settlements in Canada during the 1930's must include the so-called "tobacco belt" of southern Ontario. As in the case of the new British Columbia settlements, Hungarians were not entirely new to this region. The 1931 census found 153 of them in Norfolk County, a region of sandy soil to which tobacco had been introduced probably by Belgian (Flemish) farmers. But it was only in the early Depression period that Magyars began to show up here in substantial numbers. They worked as hired hands during the summer months and, especially, at harvest time. For hundreds of them this work must have been the major source of income in those years of adversity. In 1933 so many of them came to seek work that their presence (they camped in overcrowded, makeshift shacks) gave rise to public concern in the town of Delhi.[16]

Gradually, some fieldhands became sharecroppers, while others bought unprofitable farms in the area and converted them to tobacco growing. Despite the heavy investment required and the many risks involved, some of them succeeded and became prosperous tobacco farmers. Others, not so experienced or just less lucky, failed. These were often replaced by still other Hungarians willing to give this demanding occupation a chance. They had no alternatives. In a world where wheat and mixed farming had become unprofitable and where jobs were non-existent, an immigrant trained only in the cultivation of the soil had to turn to some cash-crop growing, no matter how risky, if he were to break out from the vicious cycle of unemployment and poverty. Under these circumstances it is not surprising that, by 1941, Norfolk County's Hungarian population had grown to just over 1,300, exceeding an 850 per cent growth rate over the decade. Most seem to have been directly involved in tobacco growing, either as sharecroppers or as outright owners of farms. The Hungarian ethnic group had become firmly entrenched in the economic life of the region.[17]

Demographic Changes

The birth of new Hungarian settlements in British Columbia and southern Ontario was only one manifestation of the great transformation the "dirty thirties" wrought in Hungarian-Canadian society. Despite a definite slowdown in immigration by 1931, the group continued to increase in size during this decade. From 40,582 in 1931 it grew to 54,598 a decade later, that is, it underwent a 34.5 per cent expansion. Although nowhere near the over 200 per cent growth rate of the previous decade, this was a substantial increase considering that Canada's total population grew only by 11 per cent in the same period. Immigration accounted for only a third of this growth. Less than 4,700 people came to Canada from Hungary between 1931 and 1941. Probably most of them were sponsored family members, virtually the only type of immigrants permitted to enter the country from Eastern Europe after 1931.[18] Hungarian-Canadian society's growth, then, was due mainly to natural increase. As has been pointed out, the Hungarian birthrate at the outset of the decade had been very high because of the youthfulness of the population, early marriage of girls, and high marriage rates for women. But there may have been still other reasons for the large statistical increase from 1931 to 1941. It is probable that in 1931 some Magyars from Hungarian-populated districts of Romania had been enumerated as Romanians, but ten years later they insisted on being listed as Hungarians or were deemed such by enumerators because their birthplaces had been returned to Hungary by the Second Vienna Award of August, 1940. It is also possible that in 1941 some ethnic Germans from Hungary, who had previously identified themselves Germans, declared themselves Hungarians, members of a nation still at peace with the Allies on the date of the 1941 census (June 2).[19]

The increase in the Hungarian group's size was not distributed evenly among the provinces. The largest growth was experienced by Ontario, whose Hungarian population grew by more than 8,000 and topped 22,000 in 1941. Next came Alberta, with a Magyar community increased from about 5,500 to almost 7,900. British Columbia's grew by nearly 1,600 and Saskatchewan's by 1,200. Manitoba's increased only by 463 people and Quebec's by 116. The Maritime Provinces' Hungarian population continued to remain small. In terms of rates of change, the picture was somewhat different. Here, British Columbia took the lead with a 120 per cent growth. Ontario followed with 60 per cent, and Alberta took third place with 43 per cent. Manitoba's growth rate was 24 per cent, while Saskatchewan and Quebec experienced rather low growth rates, 9 and 3 per cent respectively.[20]

A few words should be said about the regional distribution of this growth. British Columbia has been discussed already. In Ontario, Norfolk County probably had the fastest growth, but there were three other census districts that saw the addition of more than 1,000 Hungarians to their population. Welland County's Magyar colony grew by over 1,300 new members. More than half of these had settled in the industrial region of Welland and Crowland Township. The Windsor region of Essex County experienced a similar growth. Toronto's Magyar community also increased significantly, but Hamilton's Hungarian population remained Ontario's largest with 2,628 residents.[21] Elsewhere in the country growth had been less spectacular. In fact, the Magyar colony in Montreal had declined slightly in size. Nevertheless, with close to 3,800 residents, metropolitan Montreal remained by far the largest settlement of Hungarians in the country. Winnipeg's Magyar colony did not change in size, but Regina's increased considerably. Elsewhere in Saskatchewan, the Touchwood area's Hungarian population underwent a significant expansion. Most other census districts showed small changes only, some declined, others increased slightly.[22] In Alberta, almost all districts show at least some increase, but most of the growth seems to have taken place in the southern regions of the province, where irrigated agriculture, particularly the cultivation of sugar beets, remained a viable activity even during the Depression. In Calgary the number of Hungarians declined, while Edmonton's very small colony doubled in size.[23]

The changes in the regional distribution of Hungarian Canadians during the Depression were parallelled by an equally interesting although not so marked transformation of the urban-rural division. As has been seen, the 1921-31 period had been one of rapid urbanization for the group. The 1930's brought a halt to this trend and even witnessed a return-to-the-land movement in some regions of the country. In 1931, 49.5 per cent of Hungarians were classified as urban residents; ten years later, the figure was 47 per cent. At the outset of the decade some 31 per cent of them lived in cities of 30,000 or more inhabitants; in 1941 only about 29 per cent did.[24] The provincial breakdowns of urban-rural ratios are also revealing. Quebec's Hungarian community remained very highly urbanized. In Ontario, where the ratio had been 73 per cent in 1931, the trend toward urbanization had been reversed. The new rate was only 63 per cent. In Manitoba and Alberta similar trends prevailed. In the former the urbanization ratio was 46 per cent, down from 54 per cent ten years earlier. In Alberta, the rate had declined from 31.4 per cent to 24.7 per cent. Only in Saskatchewan was there a slight increase in urbanization, from 18.6 to 20.7 per cent.[25]

Several conclusions can be drawn from a survey of changes in the Hungarian group's geographic distribution during the 1931-41 period. The most obvious is that the trend toward dispersal continued in this decade. The appearance of Hungarian colonies in the Fraser and Okanagan Valleys of British Columbia and in Ontario's tobacco belt are only a few important illustrations of this trend. A comparison of the detailed statistics of the 1931 and 1941 censuses gives a much better picture of this geographic dispersal. The record is full of census divisions that report an increase of Hungarian residents from a handful to a few dozen, or from a few score to a couple of hundred. It is very characteristic of this scattered group that neither in 1931 nor in 1941 was there a single census division west of the Manitoba-Ontario border that did not report at least one Hungarian resident. In Ontario there had been nine such districts in 1931. By 1941 their number had declined to four (Lennox and Addington, Haliburton, Prescott, and Russell Counties).

The trend toward increased geographic dispersal coexisted with an apparently contrary trend pointing toward consolidation in certain regions of the country. The fact is that while some Hungarians were dispersing to the four corners of Canada, others were resettling in parts of the country more heavily populated by their fellow ethnics. Some of these areas of new consolidation had served as the group's centres for many decades (e.g., Windsor and Welland), others (such as Toronto and Vancouver) were of fairly recent origin. Viewed from a wider perspective, it can be said that the growth of the group in Ontario was part of this process of "new consolidation." That province alone accounted for 59 per cent of the total increase in Hungarian-Canadian population between 1931 and 1941. Its position as the most populous "Hungarian" province had barely been established in 1931. During the next ten years Ontario's lead had widened. In 1941 the province was the home of 40.4 per cent of all Hungarian Canadians. The equivalent figure for its closest rival, Saskatchewan, was by then down to 26.7 per cent.

It is evident beyond doubt that the most important facts of life for Hungarian-Canadian society were repeated and large-scale internal migrations. It can be safely presumed, too, that these migrations had been prompted by economic rather than political, social, or other factors. There is no evidence, for example, that prejudices against Hungarians sufficiently differed in intensity in the various parts of Canada to induce them to change their residence. With the exception of the few who were deported to Hungary, no Hungarian Canadian was compelled to abandon his home for political reasons. In theory at least, the migrations of the 1930's were undertaken voluntarily. In reality, they were prompted by dire economic necessity. During the Depression many of the traditional Hungarian-Canadian occupations became unproductive or simply disappeared. As a result, people who previously had made a living from these pursuits had to find alternative sources of subsistence. Certain economic opportunities existed for people even during the Depression but usually in another corner of the country. The migrations to the fertile fields of the lower Fraser Valley, to the orchards of the Okanagan, to the sugar-beet lands in the Lethbridge area, or to Ontario's tobacco belt were all undertaken in search of these alternate opportunities. That these areas were in milder climates was probably an incidental though welcome secondary factor. It should be kept in mind that the census shows that while thousands of Hungarians had migrated to these warmer regions, hundreds of them had gone to the northern districts of Ontario, British Columbia, and the Prairies. No doubt more would have gone north had there been more and better economic opportunities for them there. The fact that the Depression had caused such extensive dislocations in Hungarian-Canadian society's geographic distribution suggests that the group was still very weak and vulnerable. Consequently, residential mobility remained an important, if not the most important, feature of its life.

The 1930's had their impact not only on the Hungarian group's geographic distribution but also on many aspects of its demographic makeup. Many of these were simply the result of the passing of time. With immigration being at a minimum in this period, the ratio of the Canadian-born within the ethnic group naturally increased. Indeed, the new census found 22,929 second-generation Hungarian Canadians in the country. This was 42 per cent of the total, up from 28 per cent ten years earlier. Nearly half of these were natives of Saskatchewan. A quarter were Ontario-born, and the rest were divided among Alberta, Manitoba, and, to a lesser extent, Quebec, British Columbia, and Nova Scotia.[26] As might be expected, most of these second- and third-generation Hungarians lived in Saskatchewan (9,400, or 41 per cent of the Canadian total), in Ontario (6,900, or 30 per cent of the Canadian total), in Alberta (close to 3,000, or about 13 per cent), and in Manitoba (nearly 1,200, or 5 per cent of the total).[27] When comparing the ratios of Canadian-born and immigrant Hungarians, we find that Saskatchewan led the way. In 1941 that province's Hungarian population was 64.5 per cent native-born and only 35.5 per cent immigrant. Manitoba was next with its population being divided almost equally between Canadian-born and immigrant Hungarians (48 per cent and 52 per cent). With 22 per cent Canadian-born, Quebec stood last in this category.[28] It may also be of interest that, while only 35 per cent of urbanized Hungarian Canadians were Canadian-born, almost half (48 per cent) of those living in places with 10,000 or fewer inhabitants belonged to the second- and third-generation group. In Saskatchewan the percentage of the native-born in the countryside was especially high. There, a full two-thirds of Hungarian rural residents were natives of Canada.[29]

In 1931 the census had revealed certain marked anomalies in Hungarian-Canadian society's demographic structure. Ten years later some of these irregularities were still there. The "bulge" in the population curve of 1931, caused by the overabundance of people twenty-five to thirty-five years old, had moved over the ten-year period to the thirty-five to forty-five age bracket. By 1941, then, the bulk of Hungarian-Canadian society was entering middle age. But by this time another bulge had appeared on the group's demographic chart, caused no doubt mainly by the large number of offspring produced by members of the previous bulge. In fact, in 1941 children were so numerous in Hungarian-Canadian society that the census found 40 per cent of all Magyar Canadians to be less than twenty years old.[30] The national statistics were once again heavily influenced by conditions in Saskatchewan, whose relatively small Magyar population had raised some 6,800 children during the nineteen years before 1941. At the time of the census, this age group made up an incredible 47 per cent of the province's Hungarian total![31] But by then the period of abundant child-rearing seems to have come to an end, and the group's birthrate declined drastically. According to the new census, the fertility index for married Hungarian women in the fifteen to forty-four age bracket was around 60, down from over 150 ten years earlier. From being a group with one of the highest birthrates in 1931, Hungarians had become one with almost the lowest by 1941. Only the Finns and Jews had lower rates.[32] It was evident, however, that this state of affairs was a temporary one, and that in another decade the group would be on the threshold of still another "baby boom."

The appearance of this new generation of Hungarian Canadians during the 1930's considerably reduced that glaring imbalance between males and females that had existed within the group earlier. By 1941 women had made up 44 per cent of Canada's Hungarian society.[33] The improvement was not solely the result of the growth of the female population through natural reproduction. The fact was that a substantial majority, close to 60 per cent, of the new arrivals from Hungary during the 1930's were women. Nevertheless, in the over-thirty-five age bracket, the number of women remained considerably smaller than that of men. Among Hungarian Canadians forty to fifty-four years old, for example, men still outnumbered women by more than two to one.[34]

The passage of ten years also brought important changes in the Hungarian group's degree of integration as reflected by official statistics. For example, by 1941 66.3 per cent of immigrant Hungarians had become naturalized, a striking advance over the 1931 figure of 22.4 per cent. Similar advances were made in the knowledge of Canada's official languages. In 1931 close to 22 per cent of Hungarians in Canada had been unable to speak either English or French. Ten years later, the figure dropped to 3 per cent. In the meantime, those Hungarians speaking English or French as their mother tongue had increased from 4 per cent to over 11 per cent. Intermarriage, especially with British spouses, was also more prevalent than previously. While two-thirds of Hungarian Canadians were still married to members of their own nationality, other Canadian groups began to play a more prominent role in Hungarian intermarriage statistics.[35]

As far as Hungarian-Canadian society's demographic makeup is concerned, the 1930's had been a period of gradual maturation. By the early forties, the group was no longer that largely recent immigrant community it had been ten years earlier. The increased proportion of native-born Hungarians, the reduced imbalance between males and females, and the growth of the indicators of integration were all proofs of that process of aging which ethnic groups undergo in time unless they are "rejuvenated" through a massive influx of newcomers. Under ordinary circumstances this process is accompanied by a certain degree of transformation in the group's organizational and social life, as well as improvement in its economic and political situation. A decade in the development of ethnic groups composed largely of immigrants usually brings a strengthening of their organizations, an enhancement of the quality of their cultural and social life, an improvement in their financial position, and even perhaps a growth of their political influence. But these changes do not seem to have taken place in Hungarian-Canadian society during the 1930's. In fact, in many cases, even the meagre progress that had been made before the Depression was reversed. The "dirty thirties," with their instability, despair, and misery, blocked improvement in Hungarian-Canadian society's conditions and even caused some setbacks. For organized Hungarian life especially, the Depression was a period of trials and agonies whose after-effects would be felt for a whole generation.

ORGANIZATIONS AND POLITICS

Except for the organizations established in the pre-1914 Hungarian-Canadian centres, the foundations of most Hungarian institutions in Canada were laid in the second half of the 1920's. The weaknesses and problems of these new congregations, clubs, mutual-aid groups, and political associations have been outlined. The conditions of the 1930's prevented the solution of most of these problems, increased some of them, and even created a few new ones.

Religious Organizations

During the decade under discussion here, religious institutions continued to play a very important role in Hungarian-Canadian life. They displayed much vitality in trying to attend to the religious and, in many cases, the social and cultural needs of their members. But their effectiveness was hindered by a number of problems. Some of these have been alluded to. Geographic and social atomization made religious work difficult. Religious divisions, especially among Protestants, precluded the establishment of viable congregations in all but the largest Hungarian centres. Residential instability posed a constant problem to existing institutions and required unceasing organizational efforts. The Depression aggravated these troubles. The greatest difficulty, and the source of a host of irritants, was the drastic decline of revenues. The general despair which accompanied the Depression also took a toll: it provided fertile ground for the spread of ideologies hostile to organized religion. But it would be unfair to imply that nothing positive was achieved in religious life in the period under discussion. Adverse conditions not only created problems, they also brought people close together and induced them to co-operate. Many of Hungarian Canada's religious achievements, ranging from the establishment of still newer congregations to the acquisition of houses of worship, were attained precisely during these years of adversity.

The increasing geographic dispersal of Hungarian Canadians continued to hinder effective religious work in many parts of the country. When even some older colonies had trouble maintaining viable parishes or congregations, it is not surprising that most new settlements of the 1930's failed to establish religious organizations. A prominent exception was Abbottsford, where Roman Catholics organized themselves into a parish.[36] The scattered, older Hungarian settlements on the Prairies and in southern Ontario continued to be served by missionaries from larger Hungarian-Canadian religious centres. In Alberta, the most effective work of religious organization and missionary service was carried out by Hungarian Reformed ministers based in Calgary. They helped to establish Calgary's Presbyterian congregation and attended to the religious needs of their co-religionists in the southern half of the province.[37] In Saskatchewan, where missionary work had been a long-established tradition among Hungarians, Roman Catholic groups without priests were served from Stockholm and, on some occasions, from Kaposvar or Saskatoon. Important and wide-ranging missionary and social work was being done by the Sisters of Social Service, whose chief centre was also Stockholm.[38] The province's Protestants were not to be outdone when it came to serving a very scattered religious community. The needs of the smaller, older settlements in the southeastern parts of the province were attended to by ministers from Bekevar, Otthon-Halmok, and Yorkton. Much of the rest of Saskatchewan, including Regina, was looked after by Hoffmann from Saskatoon. To his flock, he was the "mounted minister" (*lovas pap*) who was deterred neither by distance nor by bitter cold when it came to making his rounds. To his church, the United Church of Canada, he was their "indefatigable" "missionary-extraordinary" to all Hungarians.[39] On many occasions during the 1930's, Winnipeg's Protestants also received their pastoral services from ministers stationed in Saskatchewan.

The practice of visiting pastors regularly taking care of several congregations had not been as widespread in central Canada as it had been on the Prairies, and it did not expand appreciably during the decade under discussion. Several of the larger Reformed and Roman Catholic congregations had resident Hungarian ministers. One (Toronto's Roman Catholic parish at the end of the decade) had an English-speaking priest. In Hamilton, Hungarian Catholics were organized into a non-Hungarian (German and English) parish. Under such circumstances only smaller denominations needed extensive missionary work. The Lutherans, for example, had some six or seven congregations that had to be served by two or three ministers. The Baptists were in a similar situation. From their two centres with resident ministers, Welland and Toronto, they were serving their brethren in about ten central Canadian localities.[40]

The increased missionary work sapped the resources and energy of most Hungarian-Canadian churches and religious leaders. In addition, the churches had to face growing disillusion with the teachings of religion and even some anti-religious propaganda from an increasingly bold and vociferous political left. It should be stressed that the conflict between the churches and leftist radicals was not new, but the bitterness of the struggle and the effectiveness of the anti-religious agitation turned this problem into an important issue during the 1930's. The attractiveness of the radicals' teachings is not surprising in view of the human despair created by the Depression. The young Lutheran minister Ruzsa, who toured much of Hungarian Canada at the end of the decade, repeatedly stressed the hardships the crisis had caused for all facets of Hungarian organized life. He explained the success of the anti-religious forces:

> The ruined plans, the unfulfilled dreams, the broken marriages, the (news) of misery in the o'country; the bitter, accusing, worried let-

ters (from home); the unemployment, the rapid passage of years which failed to bring relief, all kept increasing the numbers of those who moved further and further away from the House of God.[41]

While no comprehensive picture can be given of the malaise that ailed Hungarian-Canada's churches, it is possible to describe some of its symptoms. One of these was the difficulty of recruiting and retaining people for the task of religious work and leadership. Considering the fact that being a member of the clergy was virtually the only "white collar" occupation an immigrant ethnic could aspire to, the lack of candidates for this profession may seem inexplicable. But on closer examination of conditions under which priests and ministers had to work, the existence of this problem is not at all surprising. The fact was that the life of "ethnic" ministers was quite unattractive. The story of Jenő Ruzsa is not untypical and illustrates the point. Hardly out of college, he tried to look after as many as three small Lutheran congregations in Kitchener, Hamilton, and Toronto. Only during his Toronto stay did he receive some pay: $300 a year from his local congregation and a monthly stipend ($85 at first and much less later) from the United Church. Appeals by him for more support from his congregation resulted in nothing but empty promises. In his eight years of serving the Hamilton congregation, he received no salary. To support his wife and five young children, Ruzsa had to get a job in a factory.[42] Faced by such financial conditions, demanding work, disillusioned parishioners, and ϼ Hungarian community increasingly divided along ideological lines, priests and ministers could hardly maintain a high morale. Not surprisingly, the recruitment of new clergy proved next to impossible. Appeals to church authorities in Hungary rarely brought adequate results, as priests and ministers there were most reluctant to exchange a relatively comfortable life for the hardships and social isolation of Canadian service. A few men of the cloth were sent from Hungary, but their quality often left much to be desired. It has been suggested that Hungarian church authorities had assigned them to missionary work because their suitability for effective leadership at home was doubted.[43] A handful of Hungarian immigrants did enter theological training after arrival in Canada. They were put in charge of whole congregations without experience, often before they had a chance to finish their studies. Only a few met the challenge. Second-generation Hungarians were apparently not interested in becoming "ethnic" clergymen. In 1937 Father Sántha, and five years later the Reverend Steinmetz, could publicly complain that Hungarian Canada had yet to raise a single priest or minister of its own.[44]

As a result of the lack of new recruits, many parishes and congregations had to forgo the privilege of having a resident Hungarian minister. The situation was especially bad in the West. The real tragedy of Hungarian-Canadian religious life was the fact that while in some large central Canadian cities several ministers competed with each other in spreading the gospel, in western Canada vast regions were left without adequate religious leadership.[45] It was not only religion that suffered as a result; there can be little doubt that the real loser was Hungarian ethnic life.

At times, the scarcity of clergy was alleviated by the arrival of a few Magyar priests or ministers from the United States. But the traffic across the international boundary was certainly not one-way. In fact, there is every indication that far more clergymen were lost to the U.S. than were gained from it. The size and wealth of American-Hungarian religious centres were powerful attractions. Welland alone seems to have lost a total of four clergymen to the United States during the 1930's. In terms of numbers, Canada's 50,000 strong Hungarian community was never served by much more than two dozen ordained servants of God.[46]

The difficulties Hungarian Canada's churches were experiencing certainly did not result in a complete stagnation of religious life. Despite the problems, the organizational work started in the late 1920's in the group's post-World War I settlements continued, and not without success. For Roman Catholics, most success came in Montreal and Stockholm. In the former centre they managed to acquire a church and rectory of their own, and with the aid of a few members of the Sisters of Social Service they expanded their educational, social, and recreational activities. This type of work was also very much in evidence in Stockholm, but that community achieved the additional recognition of being the home of the priest (Paul Sántha) who was delegated by the Pope to represent all Hungarian Catholics at the 1937 Eucharistic Congress in Manila.[47] Very active Roman Catholic life was carried on also in Welland and Toronto. In the latter city, the 1930's witnessed the establishment of a Hungarian Roman Catholic parish. In Hamilton a similar attempt was blocked by the local Catholic hierarchy.[48]

For the Calvinists, also, the 1930's brought many successes. Their congregations in Montreal, Hamilton, and Toronto were especially active, with able, dedicated, and effective ministers. In the latter two centres they managed to acquire their own church buildings. This was a particularly praiseworthy achievement for the Toronto group, which had been the weakest of the three at the beginning of the decade. The feat was largely the work of Károly Steinmetz, a student minister the Toronto congregation had acquired in 1932. After completing his studies in 1937, Steinmetz turned his energies to the acquisition of a church. The decision was made to build one. Steinmetz managed the fund-raising campaign and acted as a draftsman, architect, construction foreman, and chief carpenter. The building was completed in 1938 and was consecrated in the following year. It was Toronto's first Hungarian house of worship.[49]

For Canada's Lutherans the 1930's were also a decade of feverish activity. Many attempts were made in this decade to establish independent Lutheran congregations. Some of these brought only partial or temporary success. But in Windsor, Lutheran organizational life was successful

153

as evidenced by the construction of a church complete with a rectory and a classroom. It was the first of its kind for Hungarian-Canadian Lutherans.[50] Another small Hungarian religious group to make its debut in the annals of Hungarian-Canadian history during the 1930's was the Greek Catholic. Early in the decade the members of this denomination started to make efforts to establish parishes independent of Hungarian Roman Catholics. Only in Hamilton were they successful. Here, their parish was served by a local Ukrainian priest and Hungarian Greek Catholic missionaries from the United States. In Port Colborne and Welland, Greek Catholics organized themselves into clubs rather than parishes. It is noteworthy that the one place they established an independent parish was in the only large central Canadian Hungarian centre without an "ethnic" Hungarian Roman Catholic congregation.[51] As a postscript to the achievements of Hungarian religious groups in the 1930's, it should be mentioned that it was not only in larger centres that some congregations led an active religious life and managed to erect houses of worship. Hungarian churches were built, often by volunteer labour, in such small places as Riverton and Langruth, Manitoba, and Mistatim, Saskatchewan.[52]

Lay Associations

Like Hungarian Canada's churches, its lay organizations had had their share of troubles even before the Depression. The 1930's brought new problems for all of them. Because of the differing structures of religious and ethnic lay organizations, they were affected differently by the difficult conditions. As far as leadership was concerned, for example, the leaders of lay associations did not require formal training or certification by authorities above and outside of the ethnic group. As a result, lay organizations did not suffer a lack of potential candidates for leadership. But there was another important way in which churches and lay organizations differed. The former were usually affiliated with and subordinated to religious organizations which transcended ethnic and even national boundaries. This type of affiliation imposed certain limitations on Hungarian Canada's numerous denominational institutions, but it often also brought support for them. One need only think of the extensive financial and moral support the United Church of Canada provided for its Hungarian congregations. The vast majority of Hungarian-Canadian lay organizations had no such external affiliation, and what was very significant in these years of trouble, they didn't have any outside help either. Naturally, there were a few exceptions. The *Canadian Hungarian News* continued to receive a subsidy from Hungary, and the Montreal and Winnipeg Magyar clubs often got advice and moral support from the local Hungarian consulates. Hungarian Canada's leftist associations received similar support from Canadian and international Communist sources. But all this did little to alter the fact that most Hungarian-Canadian lay associations lived a very independent and lonely existence.

In spite of these differences between religious and lay organizations, the particular problems confronting them during the 1930's were often very similar. The population shifts caused problems for many lay associations as their membership constantly fluctuated – leaders departed and newcomers had to be introduced to local social life. In many of the very recent settlements years passed before Magyar clubs could be formed. People had to get to know each other, and candidates for leadership had to gain trust and popularity before effective organizing could be undertaken. A second general problem was decreased revenues. When people hardly had enough money for themselves and could only spare small change for their churches, it is no wonder that they rarely gave to their lay organizations. Nevertheless, some clubs were still able to raise some money from dedicated members. They were also able to recruit volunteer workers from a large pool of unemployed and under-employed individuals. Many of Hungarian Canada's positive achievements resulted from such co-operation during the 1930's.

The Ideological Rift

The vast majority of the pre-1914 Hungarian immigrants to Canada had been highly religious and conservative people. Among the post-World War I arrivals there were some radicals, individuals who had been exposed to leftist revolutionary ideas before their emigration or who had actually taken part in Hungary's post-war political upheavals. There is every reason to believe that they were in a minority among the new immigrants. Nevertheless, it is also evident that many of the newcomers were disillusioned, disgruntled people. They were dissatisfied with conditions in their homeland but, rather than joining radical movements, they sought solution to their economic or political grievances through emigrating to Canada. The hopes of these people for a better life were disappointed. Instead of finding economic security and human dignity, most of them probably found life in Canada of the 1930's in some respects more inhuman than that which they had left behind.

Having found "capitalist" Canada no better than their "semi-feudal" old country, many of these people came to the conclusion that the only salvation for them was the new world order preached by Marxist radicals. Accordingly, many of them began paying attention to the propaganda of Canada's increasingly vociferous Communist movement. At the same time they became alienated from the old, conservative Hungarian associations and even turned against their own ethnic churches. In time they became active members of Communist or Communist-inspired organizations.

The influence of the Communists in Hungarian-Canadian organizational life had started already in the late 1920's. It resulted in the launching of the *Canadian Hungarian Worker* and the development of the Hamilton-based sick-benefit federation into an influential political organ. The fate of these institutions will be outlined below; the present discussion will be confined to an explanation of the ideological rift's general impact on Hungarian-Canadian organizational life.

For Hungarian Canadians the growth of ideological dissension was a traumatic experience. In Hungary the struggle between Communists and their opponents in 1919 had been a vicious, bloody affair. The conflict left a legacy of bitter hostility between the Christian, nationalist elements and the radicals. The former considered the latter as godless traitors, while the latter denounced the conservatives as reactionaries, chauvinists, and agents of the "white-terrorist" regime of Horthy. The bitterness existed wherever Hungarians of rightist and leftist persuasion existed together, and it was greatly accentuated by the human misery caused by the Depression. No one could mediate in the war of recriminations. The churches were committed to the conservative side and had little if any influence on the radicals.

The spread of Communist influence caused problems for many Hungarian-Canadian organizations. In some cases the converts to revolutionary ideas simply left the existing conservative clubs. In others, they made attempts to gain control of their executives in order to turn them into organizations of the left, members of the growing federation of workers' associations. When frustrated in their plans, these people often resorted to obstructionism, and to slandering their opponents.[53] The results were unfortunate. The departure of disillusioned members from existing organizations was only a minor loss. Far worse was the impact of the quarrels and struggles that took place within many organizations. These, no doubt, sapped the morale of both leaders and members. The wrangling and acrimony probably made many people disillusioned with organized ethnic life and caused them to stay away altogether. One wonders how many second-generation Hungarian Canadians, who had no particular feeling about ideology, shied away from Hungarian ethnic functions simply because they were tired and ashamed to see so much bickering and animosity within their ethnic community. There can be little doubt that in this struggle between the radicals and the conservatives, the real loser was neither the left nor the right but the Hungarian ethnic group as a whole.

The damage caused by the ideological division of Hungarian-Canadian society during the 1930's can never be assessed with any degree of accuracy. It can never be determined, for example, to what extent the setbacks of some ethnic organizations and the slow progress of others can be blamed on this particular problem. Nor can it be stated with certainty that the results of the split were entirely negative. Divisions within ethnic groups often cause many of their members to redouble their efforts in serving the causes they believe in. In other words, competition can be a boon to activity and can act as a catalyst to achievements in many situations.[54] But it is doubtful that the impetus given to Hungarian organizational life by the increased left-right rivalry outweighed the severe damages that the split had caused and continued to cause for decades to come.

Activities and Achievements

The progress made by Hungarian-Canadian organizations in the 1930's is also difficult to measure. No accurate records exist indicating the quality of social life carried on in the various Hungarian colonies across the country. From a few contemporary accounts, newspaper reports, and recollections of a handful of individuals we gain the impression that many clubs and associations had a very active and satisfying social life.[55] A somewhat more precise account can be given of such manifestations of organized ethnic life as the acquisition of "Hungarian houses" and similar recreational facilities.

There must have been hundreds of social and cultural associations by the end of the 1930's. From Montreal in the East to Vancouver in the West, all but a few small or very recent Magyar centres had at least a few clubs, circles, or societies. Most of them catered to a wide variety of social and recreational needs. By the 1930's there were also more Hungarian associations with very specialized functions. For example, in Winnipeg there was a fencing club, known to be the only one of its kind in North America at the time; in Toronto there was a club for chess enthusiasts; and, in Regina, Hungarian supporters of the Liberal Party had formed a club.[56] Not much reliable information exists on the size of these and other associations. Some probably had only a handful of members; others, several hundred. Most of them seem to have functioned independently, but many ventures or functions too large for any one association to undertake were carried out jointly. Once in a while, a host of these lay organizations joined forces in the holding of a mammoth event designed to demonstrate to the outside world the size and importance of the Hungarian community. An example of this was the Hungarian Day held in 1935 in Welland, where some 3,000 people gathered from all over Ontario and from American border states.[57]

Some of the more important efforts of Hungarian-Canadian clubs in the years discussed here were aimed at the attainment of Hungarian-owned and -managed centres of recreation and culture. Only two of these "Hungarian house movements" (*magyar ház mozgalmak*) succeeded in this age of adversity. In Abbotsford a "house of culture" (*kulturház*) was built in 1936-37, and in Hamilton a building was bought and converted into a Hungarian "home" (*otthon*) during the following year. In Montreal, a campaign by the Hungarian Social Club failed to yield sufficient funds, and the association had to be satisfied with being able to move to more spacious rented premises.[58] In Toronto, the story was somewhat more complicated. There, a movement aimed at uniting all "patriotic" Hungarians and acquiring a Hungarian house was started in 1938. From the very beginning, the group's efforts were opposed by factions of both the left and right of the city's Hungarian community. Early in 1939 representatives of the city's Hungarian churches and conservative clubs also met and launched their own campaign aimed at achieving the same purpose. The "progressive" organizations, although invited to participate, remained opposed to the undertaking; and by the time the city's two Hungarian house movements had joined forces late in 1939, some of the very same religious and worldly organizations that had endorsed the cause so enthusiastically early that year lost heart and withdrew their support. The continued opposition of the left, the lack of support by the right, and the outbreak of World War II dashed any hopes of Toronto's Hungarian community acquiring a home of its own in the near future.[59]

The Sick-Benefit Federations and the Press

In discussing Hungarian Canada's lay organizations during the Great Depression, special mention must be made of two rival sick-benefit federations that emerged at the end of the 1920's. The Brantford group, which adhered to what might be called "patriotic-Christian" principles, continued to function during the 1930's despite the increasingly intense competition from the progressive federation based in Hamilton. By the second half of the decade the Brantford federation had branches in a half dozen Ontario cities and two Nova Scotia industrial centres and collected about $2,000 a year in fees.[60] For two basic reasons, the Brantford group did not grow as fast as its rival: first, it could attract members only in centres not served by a strong Hungarian association with its own sick-benefit scheme; second, it was not considered to be an important arm of the conservative camp of the Hungarian-Canadian community, i.e., there were no political reasons for joining it.

In contrast, the Hamilton group had been the main gathering place of leftists even before the Depression. The coming of bad times boosted rather than diminished its ranks by creating fertile grounds for radical propaganda. The opportunities provided by the Depression were exploited to the fullest. The first massive membership recruiting drive was started in the spring of 1931, when the group's central organizer visited Winnipeg, Regina, Saskatoon, Edmonton, and many of the mining and industrial centres of southern Alberta and northern Ontario. The drive was accompanied by a subscription campaign for the *Hungarian Canadian Worker*, with a free trip to the U.S.S.R. being offered to whomever collected the most new subscribers.[61] The recruiting campaigns were repeated several times during the 1930's. As Slovaks and Germans were also attracted, the federation gradually lost its basic Hungarian character. In 1933 the "Hungarian-Canadian" was dropped from the federation's name and was replaced by the word "Independent." In 1940, the numerous Hungarian branches of the Independent Sick-Benefit Federation merged in the Kossuth Sick-Benefit Association, forming a kind of a federation within the federation. This association would remain the principal organization of Hungarian-Canadian Communists for a whole generation. Attached to most of its local branches would be a "workers' club," which catered to the entertainment needs of the membership.[62]

Still another important institution of the Hungarian-Canadian left was the *Canadian Hungarian Worker*. It was started on a shoestring budget, and during 1930 and 1931 it had to reduce its bulk and skip an issue now and then because of financial difficulties. But as the Depression deepened, the *Worker's* lot improved. It received the blessing of the Communist Party of Canada. Moreover, its bold attacks on Canada's and Hungary's establishments, and its vulgar language, met the approval of a great number of bitter and angry people. By the early 1940's the paper had attracted about 2,000 subscribers.[63]

Among the other, non-radical Hungarian-Canadian newspapers only a handful seem to have survived the Depression without setbacks. Foremost among these was the *Canadian Hungarian News* of Winnipeg. Despite the economic crisis, this paper managed to reduce its subscription rates and double its frequency of publishing by becoming a semi-weekly. Under the editorship of the dedicated and hard-working Bácskai-Payerle, the *News* fought to maintain the morale of Hungarian Canadians and to keep them from being seduced by revolutionary ideologies. An ally in this struggle was the *Little Hungarian News of Canada*, which under various names and formats continued to publish throughout the period.[64]

The middle of the decade witnessed the launching of still another paper for the non-radical Canadian-Hungarian reading public in central Canada. The paper, titled the *Hiradó* (Courier), was started by Kálmán Koynok in Toronto. When the Canadian Hungarian National Federation was established in the same city in 1936, Koynok turned it over to this new umbrella organization. Despite its high quality, the *Courier* did not attract enough subscribers to become financially viable. To the disappointment of many of its supporters, it had to fold. In 1939 Koynok gave it another try when he and an associate, L. Szabó of Hamilton, launched the *Magyarság* (Hungarians). The new paper proved even more short-lived than its predecessor.[65]

A somewhat longer-lived and unusual experiment in the history of Hungarian Canada's press also took place during these years. It was the publication of an English-language monthly paper, the *Young Magyar American*. Launched in 1937 by Bácskai-Payerle in Winnipeg, the paper tried to appeal to second- and third-generation Hungarians in North America. It contained world news and feature articles, as well as information on Hungarians in Canada, the U.S., and elsewhere. After publishing for a few years, this attractive and unique publication also had to fold.[66] The 1930's also witnessed the first experiments in Hungarian-language radio broadcasting in Canada. In western Canada the attempt was sponsored by the *News* of Winnipeg, while in the East, a Hungarian Radio Club organized a daily program of half-hour broadcasts from Port Colborne in the Niagara Peninsula.[67]

Political Ventures

In discussing Hungarian-Canadian political history in the 1930's it is difficult to separate the story of the group's institutions from that of its Canada-wide affairs. As has been seen, both the sick-benefit movement and the press were involved in an ideological struggle that transcended local, purely institutional politics. Yet there were organizational efforts and political undertakings with undeniable implications for the whole ethnic group. These can be classified into two categories: attempts to establish umbrella organizations, and active involvement in national or international politics.

The demise of the Canadian Hungarian Federation in the early 1930's left Canada's Magyars without any leading organ to co-ordinate their political activities and to speak for them in Ottawa and elsewhere. The disappointment caused by the CHF's failure and the shock of the first years of the Depression prevented Hungarian Canadians from making new efforts at establishing a national umbrella organization for a few years; but the work was resumed during the second half of the decade. In 1936 the Canadian Hungarian National Federation (Kanadai Magyar Nemzeti Szövetség) was brought into being by a group of leaders concerned about the spread of leftist ideology among Hungarian Canadians. Significantly, the new federation was based in Toronto, one of Magyar Canada's more recent centres. Although, unlike its predecessor, the new federation did acquire a press organ of its own, it had to end its work after about a year. It seems that it had limited funds and could muster only little support outside of Toronto.[68] Somewhat more successful were a few umbrella organizations that tried to co-ordinate Hungarian social and political life in a single city. During the 1930's such "steering committees" existed at one time or another in Winnipeg and Toronto.[69]

If the attempts at the creation of regional or national organizations had implications for the whole ethnic group, a few of Hungarian Canada's activities during the 1930's transcended ethnic affairs and even assumed international significance. The background to the most outstanding of these undertakings was the campaign – conducted by Hungarians virtually everywhere during the interwar years – for the revision of the Treaty of Trianon. The campaign was orchestrated from Hungary. Hungarian Canadians were first aroused to its importance when Count Albert Apponyi, one of Hungary's most respected statesmen, toured Canada in 1923. In 1929 further efforts were made by the World Federation of Overseas Hungarians to get leading Hungarian-Canadian organs to champion the cause of treaty revision.[70] On the whole, Hungarian Canadians responded to such efforts positively, but it was the result of a quirk of fate that Hungarians from Canada managed to contribute to this campaign substantially. The fact was that after the Great War a handful of Hungarian ex-pilots had immigrated to Canada. One of these was Sándor Magyar, a man with a flair for aeronautical stunts. 1929 found him chafing in Windsor. It was there that the idea was suggested to him that he should do something stunning, that he should better Charles Lindbergh's flight across the Atlantic by flying not to Paris but to Budapest. The unprecedented feat could be used to bring world attention to the injustice of the peace settlement with Hungary.[71] It was in this manner that the idea of the famous "Justice for Hungary" trans-oceanic flight was conceived.

Soon, a campaign to collect money for the venture was started in Windsor and was extended to the whole of Canada and the United States. It could hardly have succeeded had it not been for a rich Hungarian American, Emil Szalay of Chicago, who gave $28,000 for the cause. With the aid of Szalay's donation, Magyar and his associates could purchase a plane and equip it with extra gas tanks needed for the planned non-stop flight from Newfoundland to Budapest. The Hungarian government also contributed to the undertaking by sending a pilot with better training than Magyar, György Endrész. Finally, on August 15, 1931, the Justice for Hungary flight left Grace Harbour with Endrész at the controls and Magyar as his "navigator." The plane lost precious fuel in a storm, which blew it off course over the eastern Atlantic, and was forced to land in a cornfield only a few minutes' flying time from Budapest. Despite this anticlimactic ending, the venture proved a success. Endrész and Magyar had crossed the Atlantic in record time and had set a new record for non-stop long-distance flying. They had also attracted worldwide attention to the Hungarian campaign for treaty revision.[72]

In many ways, the Justice for Hungary flight was typical of Hungarians. All it took was a bit of imagination, enthusiasm, and a lot of bravado. It is perhaps symbolic that it was conceived in 1929 and was carried out two years later. It may be recalled this was almost the lifespan of the Canadian Hungarian Federation. Just when Magyar Canada's most promising national organization was going through its death throes, plagued by lack of finances and apathy, two dashing Hungarians were crossing the Atlantic at a monetary cost unprecedented in the group's history. No doubt, there was more glory to world publicity than to keeping an organization alive. But the flight tells much about Hungarian-Canadian priorities. Doing something for the good of Hungary must have seemed far more important than the well-being of a Canadian ethnic organization. It is most doubtful that the money collected for this daring venture could have been collected for any cause limited in its implications to Hungarians in the New World alone. The feat of Endrész and Magyar was a symbolic gesture in which Hungarians who had been cast adrift in the world came to the aid of their only true homeland. As such, it was an expression of that common subconscious attitude which considered immigration as a sojourn whose expected end was a return to a prosperous and proud Hungary.

While the Justice for Hungary flight was typical of Hungarians who believed in the liberation of their homeland from the shackles of the post-war peace settlement, it was quite untypical of Hungarian-Canadian society's history during the 1930's. It contrasted sharply with the everyday life of an ethnic group that neglected its schools, paid pittance to its religious leaders, and failed to sustain an organization to look after its collective interests. True, the great "ocean flight" did not belong to the 1930's. It was conceived in an era of optimism, the late 1920's. It was the deed of an ethnic society still possessing a youthful dynamism and a great deal of loyalty to the country of its origin as well as to that country's regime. It was the accomplishment of a group still unbroken by the hardships of immigrant life and the ravages of the Depression. Few of those campaigning for the flight would have believed that in a half-decade their Hungarian-Canadian society would be so demoralized, confused, and split that many of its members would be leaving Canada to risk their lives not for the Christian, neobaroque Kingdom of Hungary, but for a leftist, republican Spain.[73]

Nothing symbolizes the political and ideological division of Hungarian-Canadian society more than the stark contrast between the ardent revisionism of its right and the relentless internationalism of its left. By the end of the 1930's, this split had permeated nearly all aspects of Hungarian-Canadian existence. It had politicized the group's affairs to an unprecedented extent. From the smallest local club to the ephemeral national federations, all were affected and preoccupied by this division. And just as the main cause of this problem, the Depression, began to lift, another development came that not only made reconciliation difficult, but further widened the rift. That development was the outbreak of the Second World War.

NOTES

1. The best fictionalized account is John Marlyn, *Under the Ribs of Death* (Toronto, 1957). See also Chapter Four, note 61.
2. Consular Records, Memorandum by Schefbeck (Petényi), 28 May 1930 (see Chapter Four, note 62).
3. For a general introduction to conditions in Canada during the 1930's, see H.B. Neatby, *The Politics of Chaos, Canada in the Thirties* (Toronto, 1972), Chapter 2. For conditions among Hungarians in northern Saskatchewan, see an interview with Sister Mary Schwartz, reported in *KMU*, 17 September 1931.
4. Consular Records, Memorandum by Schefbeck (Petényi), 11 June 1930.
5. According to the Reverend László Borsay, one-time Calvinist minister in Delhi, Ontario, many of the prosperous Hungarian tobacco farmers in that region had purchased their farms during the Depression for less than a thousand dollars. Borsay, "The Origins of the Tobacco District Hungarian Presbyterian Church" (1977), in my possession.
6. Interview with Sister Mary. Cf. *KMU*, 4 June 1931, 3 and 17 September 1931, 24 December 1937.
7. The regulations against poor immigrants bringing out their families were

circumvented in some Hungarian circles. In Montreal there was something akin to a "travelling fund," donated by a generous benefactor of Hungarians, which was deposited in the name of a person who wished to bring out his family. Once the sum had served its purpose, it was transferred to the bank account of another immigrant. The scheme had the covert approval of the local Hungarian parish. Interview with Sister Mary. For a brief discussion of immigration regulations in the 1930's, see Gerald E. Dirks, *Canada's Refugee Policy* (Montreal, 1977), p. 55.

8. PAC, "Fiscal statements on deportations," in Records of the Department of Citizenship and Immigration, RG 26, vol. 16. According to official Hungarian statistics, 743 people returned from Canada to Hungary in 1932, 444 in 1933, 246 in 1934, 229 in 1935, and 200 in the next year. Thereafter the number of returnees declined. No statistics are available for the pre-1932 period. Egon Szabady *et al.* (eds.), *Magyarország népesedése a két világháború között* [Hungary's Population between the Two World Wars] (Budapest, 1965), p. 328.

9. *KMU*, 31 October 1933.

10. Bácskai-Payerle, "A Kanadai," p. 221. Cf. *KMU*, 4 June 1931.

11. *Census of Canada*, 1931, II, Table 33, pp. 482-93, *Census of Canada*, 1941, II, Table 32, pp. 498-507. No statistics exist to indicate where British Columbia's Hungarian-Canadian population resided before coming to the province, but there are figures which tell where the province's Magyar residents were born:

British Columbia *607*
Saskatchewan *546*
Alberta *136*
Manitoba *32*
the rest of Canada *21*
Hungary and other
    European countries *1,491*
United States *59*

These figures suggest a very heavy contribution to the growth of B.C.'s Hungarian population by the Prairie Provinces, particularly Saskatchewan.

12. Paul Sántha, who visited Abbotsford in 1937, estimated that a quarter of the local residents were from Stockholm. *KMU*, 19 December 1937. Cf. Ruzsa, *A Kanadai Magyarság*, pp. 38ff.

13. Ruzsa, pp. 38-42; *KMU*, 22 January 1937; John Norris, *Strangers Entertained: A History of the Ethnic Groups of British Columbia* (Vancouver, 1971) p. 168; Peter Duschinsky, "The Hungarian Community of British Columbia," ms prepared for the author in 1972, p. 2.

14. Norris, *Strangers*, p. 168; Duschinsky, "Hungarian Community," pp. 2ff.; *Census of Canada*, 1931, II, Table 33; *Census of Canada*, 1941, II, Table 32.

15. Ruzsa, *A Kanadai Magyarság*, pp. 44-7; Norris, *Strangers*, p. 169; *KMU*, 27 December 1935.
16. *KMU*, 7 September 1933.
17. *Census of Canada*, 1941, II, Table 32, pp. 624-6; Ruzsa, pp. 204-7; Dégh, *People in the Tobacco Belt*, pp. XVII-XVIII.
18. For the exact data, see *Census of Canada*, 1941, IV, Table 26, p. 692.
19. The decline in the number of Romanian Canadians between 1931 and 1941 (from 29,056 to 24,689) lends some support to this hypothesis. The main reason for the equally dramatic decline in the number of German Canadians in the same period is believed to be the decision of many Mennonite groups to become "Netherlandese" for the purposes of the census of 1941. For some speculations on the results of the 1941 census for Hungarian-Canadian society, see Pál Sántha, *Kanada Magyarsága* [The Hungarians of Canada] (Winnipeg, 1946), especially pp. 1-9.
20. See the data given in the 1931 and 1941 censuses, Tables 33 and 32 respectively.
21. *Ibid*. The 1941 data for the main Ontario centres are: Hamilton and environs, 2,628; Metropolitan Toronto, 2,511; Welland and Crowland, 2,407; Windsor and environs, 2,052; Port Colborne, 883; Brantford, 593; Kitchener, 466; Niagara Falls, 451; Oshawa, 351. See also *Census of Canada*, 1941, II, Tables 33, 34.
22. According to Paul Sántha, in the Stockholm area some young Hungarians abandoned farming and moved to other parts of the country with plans to return to Stockholm when economic conditions improved. Most of the old settlers stayed, and the total number of families did not change during the years of adversity. (Letter, Sántha to Béla Eisner, 6 November 1942. Béla Eisner Papers, kindly put at my disposal by Mrs. A. András.) See also Sántha, *Three Generations*, pp. 30ff.
23. *Census of Canada*, 1931, II, Table 33; *Census of Canada*, 1941, II, Table 32.
24. Hurd, *Racial Origins* (1941), p. 61. The decrease in urbanization rates meant that from being the thirteenth most urbanized group in Canada in 1931, Hungarian-Canadians dropped to seventeenth a decade later.
25. Figures based on data provided in *Census of Canada*, 1931, II, Table 35, pp. 500ff., and *Census of Canada*, 1941, II, Table 32. British Columbia's urbanized rate also increased, from 33.4 per cent in 1931 to 37.9 in 1941.
26. *Census of Canada*, 1941, IV, Table 28, pp. 334ff. Statistics for the various provinces are as follows: Nova Scotia, 282; Quebec, 967; Ontario 5,617; Manitoba, 1,263; Saskatchewan, 11,221; Alberta, 2,859; British Columbia, 659.
27. *Ibid*.
28. Calculations based on figures provided in *ibid*. The percentages of the Canadian-born Hungarians in the Hungarian populations of Canada's various provinces are as follows: Quebec, 22; Ontario, 31.3; Manitoba, 48; Saskatchewan, 64.5; Alberta, 37.2; and British Columbia, 46.2.

29. The proportions of the Canadian-born and immigrant urban and rural Hungarian populations were not imbalanced everywhere in the country. In Ontario, there was hardly any difference: here, 32 per cent of the rural and 31 per cent of the urban populations were native-born. Figures based on statistics provided in *ibid.*

30. *Ibid.*, Table 2, pp. 4ff.

31. *Ibid.*

32. Hurd, *Racial Origins* (1941), p. 168.

33. *Ibid.*, pp. 2ff. Official statistics establish the rate of males as a percentage of females in 1941 as 148. Ten years earlier the figure had been 193. Hurd (1941), p. 77; Hurd, *Racial Origins* (1931), p. 58.

34. *Ibid.*, Table 2, pp. 4ff.

35. *Ibid.*, Part II, Table 1.

36. Ruzsa, *A Kanadai Magyarság*, p. 39. On the lack of religious organizations in the tobacco belt, see *ibid.*, p. 206.

37. Alberta's other Presbyterian congregation, in Lethbridge, had no resident minister for long periods during the 1930's. Ruzsa, pp. 19-23, 30, 34; *KMU*, 30 March 1933.

38. Ruzsa, p. 118; Sántha, *Three Generations*, pp. 79-81; interviews with Sisters Mary and Columba; *KMU*, 21 and 24 December 1948.

39. *United Church of Canada Year Book*, 1932 (Toronto, 1933), p. 153. Ruzsa, pp. 106-7. For some time Hoffmann's missionary work was shared by Imre Csendes, who at one point operated out of Rothenmere, Saskatchewan. (Ruzsa, p. 121).

40. Ruzsa, pp. 167, 306, 342-52, 375-8; *KMU*, 3 March 1932.

41. Ruzsa, p. 335. On conditions in the Depression and some of the political conflicts see pp. 114, 160, 180, 211, 261. Cf. Fehér, *Montreáli*, pp. 52ff.

42. Ruzsa, pp. 172, 217.

43. *Ibid.*, p. 335.

44. *KMU*, 7 December 1937, 4 September 1942. Actually, by 1942 Hungarian-Canadian society had produced a native-born priest, Father John Oroszkovits of Winnipeg, who was serving in the Canadian Army's Chaplain Corps at the time.

45. Bácskai-Payerle, "A Kanadai," p. 222.

46. According to Ruzsa, p. 251, the following priests and ministers left Welland in the 1930's: Jeromos Hédly (R.C.), Olivér Horváth (R.C.), István Csutoros (Reformed), Ferenc Nagy (Reformed). A probably incomplete list of those who had left the Canadian West for the Republic, also from Ruzsa (pp. 30, 58, 60, 355), is as follows: Dezsö Parragh (Presbyterian), Zsigmond Balla (United Church), József Rácz (R.C.), Vilmos Tátter (Baptist).

   According to Bácskai-Payerle, p. 222, in 1933 there were six Hungarian Roman Catholic priests and eleven Protestant ministers in Canada. In 1940, Ruzsa (p. 336) reported sixteen ministers (six United Church, four Presbyterian, three Lutheran, and three Baptist) and nine Roman Catholic priests.

47. *KMU*, 25 January 1935, 3 December 1937, 4 March 1941; Ruzsa, pp. 114-18, 305.

48. Interviews with the late Father István Király, 30 December 1975, and with Sister Mary and Sister Columba; Minute book of the Hungarian Roman Catholic Club of Toronto, for the 1930's; *50 Years: St. Elizabeth of Hungary Church* (Toronto, [1978]), pp. 9-13; Ruzsa, pp. 114-18, 159-61.

49. The ministers in Hamilton and Montreal were Ferenc Kovács and Mihály Fehér respectively. On the Hamilton congregation, see Ruzsa, pp. 211-16. On the Montreal one, see Fehér, pp. 43-56 *passim*. Also, *Hungarian United Church, Montreal, Quebec, 1926-1976* (Montreal, 1977), pp. 37ff. Also, the annual reports on this congregation in the *United Church of Canada Year Book* for the 1930's. For a brief history of the Toronto congregation (by Steinmetz), see *KMU*, 14 February 1941: and Ruzsa, pp. 163ff. Also, interview with Steinmetz.

50. Ruzsa, pp. 375-8.

51. On Canada's Hungarian Greek Catholics, see György Papp, "A Magyar Görögkatolikus Egyház Kanadában" [The Hungarian Greek Catholic Church in Canada], ms, n.d., in *CHN* Records, Box 30a. Also, Julian Beskyd (ed.), *In the Vineyard of Christ: Yearbook of the Eparchy of Toronto* (Toronto, 1964), pp. 520ff.

52. The Manitoba churches were erected with the moral support and advice of Father István Soós; the Mistatim church was erected under the direction of Hoffmann. *KMU*, 16 and 19 June 1942; *United Church Year Book 1932,* p. 153.

53. Ruzsa's dislike of the left prevented him from analysing their actions in detail. Only from his scattered and often obscure references (aside from the contemporary press) can we gain a glimpse of the ideological rift's impact on Hungarian organized life. See Ruzsa, pp. 31, 103, 180, 211, 361, 369.

54. Geraldine Vörös, in "Formal Institutions," has argued that the main driving forces of Hungarian ethnic activity in Welland have been religious and ideological divisions and rivalries.

55. Interviews with Mrs. Andras, the Reverend Steinmetz, Sister Mary, Sister Columba, and Kertész, Jakus, and Nemes; Ruzsa, p. 359; Fehér, p. 52.

56. Ruzsa, pp. 66, 103, 188.

57. *KMU*, 13 September 1935. The involvement of Hungarian-American organizations in Hungarian-Canadian undertakings in this period does not seem to have gone beyond participation in such gatherings. In fact, according to Ruzsa, links between the lay organizations of American and Canadian Hungarians were non-existent. (Ruzsa, pp. 385ff.)

58. *Ibid.*, pp. 40, 223, 308ff. *KMU*, 22 January 1937.

59. Ruzsa, pp. 179-86.

60. *KMU*, 9 April 1935, 30 July 1937, and 18 February 1938. Monthly fees ranged from 50¢ to $1.30, weekly payments to the sick from $3.50 to $9

(according to the monthly fees paid); death benefits ranged from $62.50 to $150 (*KMU*, 3 March 1938).

61. *Az Uttörö* [The Pioneer], 11 June 1931; *Kanadai Magyar Munkás* [Canadian Hungarian Worker, hereafter *KMM*], 29 April 1931.

62. *Az Uttörö,* 10 April 1958; Ruzsa, pp. 373ff.; Andrew Durovec, "Harmincöt éves a Kanadai Kossuth Betegsegélyzö Egylet" [The Canadian Kossuth Sick-Benefit Association is Thirty-five Years Old], text of speech, Durovec file, Multicultural History Society of Ontario Archives. During the Second World War, the Workers' Clubs were banned by Canadian authorities. They reconstituted themselves into the Canadian Hungarian Democratic Federation and continued functioning.

63. *KMU*, 16 July 1929; Eisner to E. Duha (ca. December, 1942), Eisner Papers; Ruzsa, pp. 369-71; Watson Kirkconnell, "A Canadian Meets the Magyars," *Canadian-American Review of Hungarian Studies*, 1, 1-2 (1974), p. 8.

64. *KMU*, 17 August 1933 and 29 November 1974; Ruzsa, pp. 364-7; interview with Nemes; Duncan McLaren (comp.), *Ontario Ethno-Cultural Newspapers, 1835-1972* (Toronto, 1973), pp. 81ff. For some time the *Little Hungarian News* was published in Hamilton under the title *Canadai Magyar Népszava* (Canadian Hungarian People's Voice). It was sponsored by the Hungarian Sick-Benefit Federation of Brantford.

65. *KMU*, 27 April 1937. The *News* took over the *Courier's* subscriptions. Ruzsa, pp. 363ff.; McLaren, *Newspapers,* pp. 83, 87; and interview with Steinmetz.

66. *KMU*, 1 June 1937; a few samples of this paper can be found in the *CHN* Records.

67. *KMU*, 27 December 1935 and 9 July 1937.

68. Ruzsa, p. 186; interview with Steinmetz.

69. *KMU*, 9 January 1930; Ruzsa, pp. 179ff.

70. *CHN* Records, Box 42, Imre Josika-Herczeg, President, World Federation of Overseas Hungarians, to the executive of the Canadian Hungarian Federation, 16 February 1929.

71. Grob, "Recollections," pp. 19ff.; Lajos Veress de Dálnok (ed.), *Magyarország Honvédelme 1920-1945* [The Defence Policies of Hungary, 1920-1945] (Munich, 1972-73), I, p. 212. It appears that the principal promoters of the project were the Reverend Jenö Molnár, Hungarian Presbyterian minister in Windsor at the time, and his wife Rózsa. (Information obtained through the kindness of the Reverend Kálmán Toth of Ottawa.)

72. Letter, Grob to Kohári, 2 April 1974, copy in my possession; contemporary clippings collected by Mr. Grob; Grob, "Recollections," pp. 19ff. All placed at my disposal by Mr. Grob. Veress de Dálnok, *Magyarország,* I, p. 212; Szántó, *Magyarok a nagyvilágban,* pp. 135ff.; Ruzsa, pp. 274ff. Mr. Grob handled the campaign to collect money for the venture in Saskatchewan.

73. According to one source, "over one hundred" Hungarian "workers" volunteered to fight for the loyalist cause in the Spanish Civil War. See István Toth, *23év Kanadában* [23 years in Canada] (Budapest, 1961), p. 159. Victor Hoar, in his *The Mackenzie-Papineau Battalion* (Toronto, 1969), lists the Canadians killed and missing in the Spanish Civil War (pp. 241-9). The list contains several obviously Hungarian names.

SIX

The End of an Era: The 1940's

N. F. Dreisziger

ETHNIC AFFAIRS DURING THE WAR

Wedged between the end of the Great Depression and the coming of the post-war waves of immigration, the 1940's constitute another fairly well-defined and important chapter in the history of Hungarian-Canadian society. It is a period characterized by limited growth, caused mainly by the absence of immigration particularly between 1941 and 1948. In economic, political, and social affairs, it is an era of uncertainty and change. The decade saw the return of better economic conditions and brought continued political turmoil prompted partly by the impact of the Second World War on Canada and partly by the dramatic and often un-settling events in Hungary. Above all, the 1940's constitute the last phase of the epoch in Hungarian-Canadian history that had started with the mass immigration of the 1920's. Although the immigrants of that era would long remain on the scene, the post-1950 years were to be dominated more and more by new people and different issues.

As far as Hungarian-Canadian society was concerned, the single most important event of the 1940's was the war. In Magyar Canada's history the war years can be divided into three more or less identifiable periods. The war's preliminary phase lasted from the fall of 1939 to the summer of 1941. During this time Hungary was a neutral power. This was also the period of the Nazi-Soviet Non-Aggression Pact, which meant that Hungarian-Canadian Communists were expected to oppose Canada's war effort. In doing so, they found still another issue on which to disagree with the mainstream of Hungarian-Canadian society. The next period began with the Axis invasion of Russia in June of 1941 and ended with the Russian occupation of Hungary during the winter of 1944-45. These three and a half years were most eventful for Hungarian Canadians because Hungary was at war with Canada and her allies. The Canadian government became involved in Canadian-Hungarian affairs on an unprecedented scale. In addition, this period during the war brought a marked expansion of economic opportunities for Magyars in Canada. The last of the three periods, coinciding with the end of the war in Hungary and the immediate post-war period, was characterized mainly by relief work on behalf of war-torn Hungary and her suffering people.

Throughout the war years, political discord seems to have dominated the history of Magyar Canada's development. In this respect, the war period was not unlike the 1930's. As shall be seen, it was not very different from the subsequent era either. Issues, organizations, and leaders would change, but the high degree of Hungarian-Canadian society's politicization, so evident by the 1930's, would continue unaltered.

The Coming of the War

Not much is known about Hungarian-Canadian public opinion regarding European affairs on the eve of World War II. One contemporary observer reported that during the late 1930's international developments in Europe aroused the hope in many Hungarian Canadians that their home country would be able to break the shackles imposed on it by the peace settlement. When lost territories were returned to Hungary in 1938 and 1939, there was rejoicing in Magyar-Canadian circles. Nevertheless, when the war broke out in the late summer of 1939, many Hungarian Canadians were willing to pledge their support for the war against Germany. They had no conflicts of loyalty, for as far as they knew Hungary had maintained complete neutrality in the events leading to the outbreak of the war and had no special ties with Germany. Only some left-wing Hungarians were in a predicament: as residents of Canada they were supposed to support her war effort, while as good Communists they were expected to oppose an "imperialist war" against a country on good terms with the Soviet Union.

As events in Europe unfolded, the situation of Hungarian Canadians became more complicated. By 1940 it must have been increasingly evident to many that Hungary's policy aimed at recovering lands lost as a result of the peace settlement could lead to an alliance with Nazi Germany. This was a price some Hungarian Canadians were not happy to see paid for their native land's prosperity. Instead of treaty revision, they would have preferred to see the creation of a more progressive Hungary at peace with her neighbours. This kind of thinking was current not only among Communists, but among more moderate people. Czakó's journal, the *Tárogató*, espoused these ideas repeatedly.[1] But there is reason to believe that Czakó and his fellow progressives were in a minority.

Most Hungarian Canadians, either not realizing the implications of a revisionist policy on Hungary's neutrality or not caring much about it, seem to have approved Budapest's foreign policy. But when Hungary did become involved in the war, most Hungarian Canadians probably realized that their loyalty had to be with Canada. Their foremost press organ, the *Hungarian Canadian News*, endorsed the idea. It regretted the fact that Hungary had entered the war. As far as the *News* was concerned, it all happened because of the "unprovoked" attack on Hungary by Russia.[2] There is also evidence that while many Hungarian Canadians were deeply concerned by these and other wartime developments, a few of them cared very little. One clergyman complained that many simple, peasant-stock members of his congregation were uninterested in the flow of events in Europe, saying that wars were the "concern of gentlemen."[3]

A New Attempt at Unity

While Canada's Central and East European immigrants grappled with their aroused emotions and concerns over events in their native countries, the Canadian government was slowly developing a policy toward these ethnics. Ottawa's primary concerns were, of course, Nazi sympathizers and Communists opposed to the prosecution of the war effort. There is no evidence to suggest that there were converts to the German brand of national socialism among Hungarian Canadians. Communists were numerous, and the government moved to restrict the flow of their literature, banned some of their organizations, and began to keep a very close watch on their publications and activities.[4] While the activities of ethnic radicals were to be curbed, a different approach was formulated toward the masses of loyal new Canadians. The strategy adopted was basically novel for a wartime Canadian government. It was one of confidence and co-operation rather than distrust and confrontation. The roots of this policy can be found in the attempts during the 1930's by certain elements of Canada's Anglo-Saxon elite to establish closer rapport with the country's immigrant masses.[5] After the outbreak of the war, these efforts were continued with government blessing, but not as a part of a systematic, co-ordinated policy. The development of a Canadian strategy regarding the war effort was a slow process, and the birth of an approach to immigrant minorities was even slower. In July of 1940, Ottawa established a new ministry, the Department of National War Services. Sixteen months later a Nationalities Branch was created within this ministry to handle relations with ethnic communities. Soon thereafter an advisory body, the Committee on Co-operation in Canadian Citizenship (CCCC), was constituted within this branch. The CCCC was made up of prominent individuals, mostly academics, who had an interest in and had good relations with recent European immigrant groups.

Under the CCCC's auspices a great many projects were undertaken to promote mutual understanding between immigrant ethnics and native-born Canadians.[6] Most of these were aimed at Central and East European groups in general and were social or cultural in character. But a few were political and aimed at particular ethnic groups. One of the latter types of CCCC undertakings was an effort to help Hungarian Canadians to achieve that unity which had eluded them ever since the days of the short-lived Canadian Hungarian Federation.

Not much is known about the origins of this effort. In 1940 an umbrella organization of Montreal Hungarian clubs and congregations was formed under the name Grand Committee of Hungarian Churches and Associations of Montreal. Soon, contacts were established between its leaders and CCCC officials. The latter decided to use this organization as a model to be emulated by Hungarians elsewhere in Canada. The ultimate aim seems to have been the union of Hungarian-Canadian organizations into a nation-wide federation of local co-ordinating committees.[7] Since the two most important leaders of the Grand Committee, Father Miklós Horváth and Reverend Mihály Fehér, were tied down with their religious duties, the CCCC's contact man became Dr. Béla Eisner, a Sun Life Insurance Company employee with a long record of organizational work among Montreal's Hungarians. Eventually Eisner was "borrowed" from his employer and was commissioned to carry out the CCCC's plans. He was to do the work throughout Canada, except in Toronto, where the task of organizing was given to another dedicated Hungarian leader, Nicholas (Miklós) Hornyánszky, the noted artist.[8]

Eisner went to work in June of 1942. First he approached Hungarian clergymen and newspaper editors asking for publicity for the CCCC's cause and advice regarding organizational work. Next, Eisner embarked on a tour of Ontario's Hungarian centres. No sooner did he start his tour than difficulties began to emerge. The most influential ethnic leaders, usually clergymen, were too busy to assist Eisner. The people at large could not be brought together for public meetings because some were working on shifts while others were putting in many hours of overtime. Eisner had his share of problems with Communists as well. He had instructions not to approach their organizations but to appeal only to individual members, but his contacts even with the latter were resented by non-Communist Magyars.[9] The Hungarian left's attitude to the CCCC's efforts soon became known when Eisner's activities came under bitter attack in the *Worker*. Undaunted, Eisner continued his tour, this time concentrating on western Canada. His message remained the same: the Canadian government wanted co-operation with all immigrants in the war effort, and ethnics should band together in order to make their voice felt and to combat discrimination against them by employers. Only Eisner's method had changed. He no longer sought public meetings; instead, he just talked to influential ethnic leaders. After visiting most of the larger western centres, Eisner was satisfied by his progress. His ideas were well-received everywhere but in Calgary. It seemed, at long last, that some order and unity could be achieved in Hungarian-Canadian politics at least on the local level.[10]

But it was not to be. No matter how enthusiastically Eisner's scheme and ideas were received by leaders in a particular centre, putting them into effect proved difficult. In many places misunderstandings and dissention developed in the wake of his visit. Some people who had approved his schemes earlier began to have second thoughts about them. Organizing meetings were poorly attended or could not be held – people were more concerned about making up for wages that had been lost during the Depression than about constructing an effective Hungarian lobby. In some northern regions, organization work could not be carried on in the middle of winter. Some people wondered why the "War Department" (*Hadügyminisztérium*; a mistranslation of "Department of National War Services") was the sponsor of Eisner's activities. They feared that his tour was just a prelude to a recruiting campaign for men to fight in Europe. One Hungarian miner wrote to Eisner from Sudbury that no committee of Hungarians could be established there because not one "schooled gentleman" lived in the city who knew how to run an organization.[11] But Eisner's efforts were not entirely without results. In a few places local co-ordinating committees were formed. The most notable was the Hungarian Canadian Cultural Council of Winnipeg. It embraced all but one of the non-radical Magyar organizations in that city. Montreal's Grand Committee also continued to function; in fact, it is still active today.[12]

Apart from the formation of a few local co-ordinating committees, the CCCC's intervention in Hungarian-Canadian affairs achieved little that was visible. The reasons for this lacklustre performance were obvious. Some of them have been mentioned: the opposition of the left, suspicions about Ottawa's motives, and general apathy. During the Depression organized life suffered because of economic adversity, but in the relatively prosperous 1940's it suffered because people were too busy working and had no time for "ethnic" politics. But the CCCC venture's biggest problem had been the fact that no preparations had been made in advance. It was a typical government measure: it had a deadline and a very limited budget. Not surprisingly, it was received with suspicion. An ethnic group that had lived for decades in total governmental neglect could hardly be convinced that Ottawa's new interest in its affairs had no ulterior motives.

Wartime Conditions: The Eisner Report

Nevertheless, the Eisner tour bequeathed us with one concrete piece of legacy, a detailed memorandum on contemporary Hungarian-Canadian society that Eisner wrote for the Department of National War Services. The report's first part deals with the situation of Hungarians in the industrial centres of southern Ontario. The picture it paints differs radically from what had prevailed in this region during the 1930's. Now there were jobs for all able-bodied men. Factories were operating twenty-four hours a day and most workers could put in as much overtime as they wanted. Hungarians were eager to take advantage of the opportunities presented by the economic boom created by the war. They were keen to make up for wages lost during the Depression. An aura of prosperity filled the Hungarian centres of southern Ontario. Working people were buying cars and houses, investing in real estate, and even sending their children to college. But the dramatic improvement in their financial

173

situation had not brought an end to worry and fear. Most of them were concerned about the future. They were afraid that devaluation and depression would follow the war and that they would lose their jobs as soon as the special economic conditions ended. In fact, much of the feverish drive to make as much money as possible, and to invest it in houses, farms, small businesses, or in the education of children, can be explained in terms of this uncertainty about the future.[13]

Closely linked to the economic situation was the political one. The fact was that, despite the prosperity, the union movement was becoming popular among Hungarians. Eisner found two reasons for the unions' popularity. Many Hungarian-Canadian workers believed that unions would help them to retain their jobs after the wartime employment boom was over, that they would bring a recognition of the seniority principle in lay-offs, making discrimination on the grounds of ethnic origin difficult. But one political phenomenon had little relation to the general situation of 1942. This was the continued adherence of many Hungarian Canadians to Communist ideas. The explanation, according to Eisner, lay in the immigrants' backgrounds. Most of those who became Communists had been people who had left Hungary bitter and disappointed. They had great hopes in Canada but their expectations were dashed by the Depression. They were converted to Communism without really knowing what it stood for. The majority of Hungarian Canadians despised these people and considered them godless traitors. Relations between Communists and non-Communists became bitter and remained so even after the bad economic conditions, which had brought about the split in the first place, had disappeared. Times had changed, but the "enmity remained." Eisner estimated that in five Ontario centres more than half of Hungarian-Canadian workers belonged to the extreme left.[14]

In the West the general situation was somewhat different. First of all, radicalism had fewer converts there and was confined to the urban areas. The rural Hungarian-Canadian population adhered to a middle-of-the-road political position. This did not mean that everyone was happy. Most people had suffered much during the Depression and some never recovered from the hardships. Many farmers were still paying debts incurred earlier, and very few had money for other than immediate needs. They also found it difficult to hire help because of general labour shortage caused by the war. Despite these problems, most Hungarian farmers were pleased with their adopted land, and Eisner noted that none of them planned to return to Hungary on a permanent basis. In the cities there was more dissatisfaction. Almost half of the Hungarian population of places like Winnipeg and Regina were Communists or leftist sympathizers. Wages and job opportunities there were not as plentiful as in Ontario, and there was a particular group of people whose lot was wretched. These were the seasonal workers, mainly unmarried men or men whose families were still in Hungary. They worked hard when there was work for them, had substandard housing, hardly ever ate a decent meal, and squandered their money at the end of the season when they got paid. Then, until their next job, they lived on credit. According to Eisner, these were unfortunate, unhappy, and in many ways undesirable people. They should not have been allowed to come to Canada alone.[15]

The last part of the report was devoted to the issue of discrimination. From what Eisner heard from people from Ontario to Alberta, the problem did exist for Hungarian Canadians. He admitted that the situation had improved a great deal during the last two years, yet he stressed that Hungarian Canadians believed the decline in discrimination to be a temporary phenomenon expedited by government concern about the war effort. Discrimination against Hungarians manifested itself in many ways. It could range from mere name-calling to the denial of promotions by employers. Hungarians could be called "bohunks," "hunkies," or, at best, "foreigners." Sometimes they would be told that they were not "white men." At work, they would get the toughest, dirtiest jobs, the "soft" ones being reserved for native-born or other English-speaking Canadians. Promotions were rare for Hungarians, even though many of them were well-trained, "first-class" workers. Furthermore, they could be dismissed by employers on grounds of "radicalism," a charge that would stick to a worker and make it difficult for him to find another job. Others could be dismissed because their health had deteriorated as a result of working in an unsafe environment. For these people there was no recourse. In his recommendations Eisner strongly urged that everything possible should be done by the government to combat discrimination.[16]

Contributions to the War Effort

During his tour, Eisner paid visits to officials of several factories involved in war production and asked about the performance of Hungarian employees. The answers he received were laudatory: every manager interviewed had only praise for his Hungarian workers. Eisner learned also that many Hungarian Canadians were buying wartime savings stamps and were subscribing to war loans. They did so "as good Canadian citizens . . . and also in the interest of their own future."[17] More important still was the direct involvement of Hungarian Canadians in the struggle against the Axis powers. Eisner could collect only partial data in this connection, mainly lists of Hungarian parishes' or congregations' members serving in the Canadian Armed Forces. One of these gives the names of sixty-four Hungarians from Regina.[18]

Government statistics on this subject, while also incomplete, are more enlightening. A check of somewhat less than half of the cards that had been kept on Canadians enlisted in the Armed Forces during the war revealed nearly 1,100 Hungarian-speaking persons. The vast majority of these, 982 to be precise, were in the Army, seventy-four in the Air Force, and the rest in the Navy. Nearly three-quarters of these recruits came from Ontario and Saskatchewan, the two provinces most populated by

Hungarian Canadians.[19] Unfortunately, there seem to be no records that tell the total of Hungarian-speaking participants in Canada's wartime military, nor any that reveal how many English-speaking, i.e., predominantly second- and third-generation, Hungarian Canadians had enlisted in Canada's Armed Forces.

Toward Wartime Co-operation

As has been mentioned, Eisner's efforts to inspire Hungarian Canadians to unity brought only limited success. During 1942 not much more luck accompanied the work of Hornyánszky, the CCCC's contact in Toronto. But, during the summer of the next year, the city's Hungarians finally succeeded in buying a building of their own on Spadina Avenue near College Street. Hornyánszky, who was one of the house's trustees, expressed the hope that the new home would serve as a "second home" to every Toronto Hungarian who did not belong to a church or a political party, and that it would help to keep second-generation Hungarian Canadians "Hungarian."[20] Soon the Spadina property proved too small, and toward the end of 1945 another building was purchased. Once again a site was selected close to Toronto's Hungarian section, this time on College near Spadina. The new building was roomier. Its purchase price of $33,000 was defrayed from the sale of the older property ($12,000) and by donations from Hungarians in Toronto and elsewhere. One generous Albertan sent $250. The move to new quarters gave rise to much optimism. There was talk of greater fund-raising efforts in the future and the establishment of a home for the aged, an orphanage, and scholarships for Hungarian youths.[21]

The success of the Hungarian House movement in Toronto was no doubt partly the result of a marked improvement in the group's economic condition, as well as of a more optimistic state of mind that manifested itself in growing centres such as Toronto by the end of World War II. Despite these changes, effective organizational unity continued to elude the Hungarian-Canadian community. But the absence of a national umbrella organization did not mean that Hungarian Canadians could not achieve a large degree of unity and act in unison under exceptional circumstances. In fact, the immediate post-war era witnessed a period of unusual intra-ethnic co-operation among Hungarian-Canadian society's many groups.

The focal point of this unity was a relief effort aimed at providing help to Hungarian victims of World War II. The campaign had rather inauspicious beginnings. In June, 1944, the *Canadian Hungarian News* of Winnipeg, in collaboration with Montreal's Grand Committee, announced the launching of a campaign to collect funds to aid war victims in Hungary. The movement was almost derailed right at the start by the launching of another collection campaign to help a Hungarian widow in Saskatchewan whose son had been condemned to death. As donations poured in to defray this unfortunate mother's legal expenses, the war-relief campaign stalled. After four months, its contributions totalled only $200.[22] But the campaign gained new momentum in the spring of the following year. No doubt, the news of devastation, hunger, and suffering in Hungary during that tragic winter of 1944-45 stressed the need for vigorous and urgent action.

In April, 1945, Toronto's Hungarians officially embraced the cause. On April 19, representatives of the city's Hungarian churches, clubs, and newspapers met and established a Grand Committee (Nagybizottság) to spearhead the relief movement in the city. There were no dissenters at the meeting, a fact all the more remarkable because representatives both of the conservative churches and clubs and of left-wing associations were present.[23] As no policy was decided on this day, a further meeting had to be called. It took place on May 3, and resulted in the election of an executive comprised of lay and religious and conservative and progressive elements. The meeting called also for the establishment of similar councils in other Hungarian-Canadian centres and for the start of a nation-wide relief campaign.[24] In the meantime efforts were made to find out the federal government's attitude to the planned fund-raising action. The reply apparently made official sanction for the campaign conditional on a united effort by the Hungarian-Canadian community.[25]

The government's call for unity reinforced a trend toward united action that had been growing within the group. As a result, an all-Canadian conference to get the relief movement officially launched was called in August. Its sponsors included some of Hungarian Canada's most influential organizations: the already functioning local relief committees, the two largest newspapers, and the chief progressive associations. The meeting was held on August 12 in Hamilton's Royal Connaught Hotel and seems to have been the largest Hungarian-Canadian gathering of its kind to that day. A total of 222 delegates attended, representing twenty-seven parishes and congregations, as well as over seventy lay organizations. The left was amply represented. The twenty-one clubs associated with the Canadian Hungarian Democratic Federation had forty-three delegates present, while the thirty-two chapters of the Kossuth Sick-Benefit Federation sent fifty-four people. The meeting established the United Canadian Hungarian Relief Committee (UCHRC) with headquarters in Toronto. There had been disagreement over the composition of the organization's national executive committee, but it was resolved. In the end equal representation (ten seats) was allocated to each of the following groups: the Catholic parishes, the Protestant congregations, the progressive associations, the conservative organizations, and the two sick-benefit federations. Additional seats were assigned to the two most prominent newspaper editors. Next, an executive was elected. Its composition also reflected a spirit of unity. The churches, lay associations, and conservative and radical elements all had members elected. Bertalan Török of the Toronto Hungarian House became president and Ambró Czakó the co-president. Among the numerous vice-presidents were some of the Hungarian-Canadian community's most respected and most active pastors (Sántha, Ruzsa, and Steinmetz) as well as radicals such as István Szöke, the *Worker's* editor.[26]

The fund-raising campaign began to bear fruit by the spring of 1946. In May of that year, it sent $30,000 worth of medicine and food to Hungary through the Canadian Red Cross. Although officially the campaign was headed by the UCHRC, by early 1946 most of the actual fund-raising had passed into the hands of the local co-ordinating committees. Moreover, some Hungarian organizations, such as the Hungarian House in Toronto, had their own independent relief campaigns.[27] Nevertheless, the national organization continued to function. Its second congress, held on June 16, 1946, in Hamilton, attracted 246 delegates and about 100 non-voting dignitaries and guests. It passed numerous resolutions, many of which had nothing to do with the relief campaign but did have distinct political overtones. The congress also effected a few changes in the UCHRC's executive, the most important being the replacement of Czakó by Steinmetz as co-president and the co-opting of Canadian politicians Paul Martin and Senator A.K. Hugessen as "Honorary Presidents."[28]

The Demise of the Relief Movement

The fund-raising continued. By November over $61,000 had been collected. It was spent on shipments of baby food, medicine, and medical instruments. By April, 1947, a total of nearly $83,000 had been collected,[29] but within six months the campaign closed. Dissension seems to have arisen between leftist and conservative elements, and the two sides went their own way. In October the "democratic" clubs, the Kossuth Sick-Benefit Federation, and two non-radical organizations from Toronto established their own Hungarian Relief Committee, while the rest of the conservative churches and associations of central Canada made preparations for a meeting of their own to deliberate over the future of their relief efforts.[30]

The disintegration of the "united" relief movement did not come as a surprise. The movement had grown out of unusual circumstances. At the end of the war Hungarian Canadians for once could unite in a cause that transcended all ideological boundaries. The unity was reinforced by Ottawa's refusal to sanction the fund-raising unless it was a united effort. At first there were no grounds for dissension, but as time passed circumstances changed. Most unsettling were events in Hungary, particularly the efforts of the Communists to turn the country into a Soviet-style people's democracy. Aid to Hungary then might fall into "wrong hands" and might be used for partisan purposes. The change in Hungary's political fortunes was brought to the attention of Hungarian Canadians when their largest paper, the *News*, was put on the forbidden publications list by Hungarian authorities. Almost simultaneously, the *Worker* broke the truce and accused the *News* of having accepted subventions from Hungary's wartime pro-Axis government.[31] Under these circumstances, it is not surprising that Hungarian Canada's new-found unity did not last very long. Indeed, the 1945-47 relief movement seems to have been a brief interlude, an aberration from the normal state of affairs in Hungarian-Canadian political history. Moreover, the left-right split was not the only problem that plagued the relief campaign by 1947. By then there was dissension within the "patriotic" camp itself. The trouble arose from the Toronto Hungarian House's campaign to send relief parcels to Hungary. Apparently, some of the money collected for this purpose was retained for the House's own use and the use of two members of its executive. The action was not illegal, but it offended many Hungarians' sense of fair play and led to bitter recriminations.[32]

In view of the relief movement's experience, it is not surprising that lasting and effective organizational unity continued to elude Hungarian Canadians in the early post-war era. This fact should not obscure the campaign's positive achievements. Close to $100,000 had been raised to help people in war-torn Hungary. No figures exist to tell how much more was sent by individual Hungarian Canadians to relatives and friends in East Central Europe, but the results of the official campaign alone are impressive. Never before had Hungarian-Canadian society raised so much money for a single cause. The large sum was a reflection both of the generosity of Hungarian Canadians and of their much improved economic position. The ravages of the Depression were slowly being overcome; for some time, at least, the group was once more capable of united action, and its members were willing and able to contribute more than just minimal amounts to an important cause. But truly effective political and economic action, the kind that required considerable finan-cial support and more than temporary unity on more than a single issue, was still beyond the realm of the possible. It would remain so for many years to come.

SOCIETY AND CULTURE ON THE EVE OF THE 1950's

The united relief campaign of the mid-1940's was the last major organizational effort of the Hungarian-Canadian society of the post-World War I immigrants. The next important event in Hungarian-Canadian political history, the founding of a national umbrella organiza-tion during the early 1950's, was to take place under rapidly changing conditions and would mark the beginning of a new period of historical development. Before examining the great changes the opening of the sec-ond half of the century would bring, a few more aspects of the interwar Hungarian-Canadian society deserve analysis.

Organized Religion in the 1940's
During the 1940's religion and religious institutions continued to play an important role in Hungarian-Canadian affairs. The decade, however,

brought mixed blessings. While some religious organizations made definite progress in this period, many of the problems prevalent prior to 1940 remained, or were accentuated by conditions created by the war and the passing of time.

The most remarkable advances in the life of the Hungarian Roman Catholic community seem to have come in Toronto. In 1939 the city's Hungarian parish had received a new priest, Father Leo J. Austin. His was to be a stop-gap appointment, intended to last until a Hungarian-speaking clergyman could be recruited from Hungary. Importing pastors from Central Europe proved impossible during the war, and young Austin's tenure became the longest lasting in the parish's history. It was an eventful one. First, the organization's rented premises were enlarged and renovated. Next, in 1942, the Sisters of Social Service were invited to extend their services to Toronto. More important still was the purchase of a church building at the corner of Dundas Street and Spadina Avenue, close to the city's Hungarian section. The purchase of the property was preceded by a continent-wide fund-raising campaign which yielded $10,000. The amount was matched by the Archbishop of Toronto. The St. Elizabeth of Hungary Church was blessed by Archbishop James C. McGuigan on March 19, 1944. The church soon became the centre of active religious, cultural, and social life, some of it directed by the two Sisters of Social Service who had joined the parish from Stockholm, Saskatchewan.[33]

The Torontonians' success gave inspiration to the Hungarian Roman Catholics in Hamilton. Under the guidance of a member of the Sisters of Social Service, they started a movement aimed at the establishment of their own ethnic congregation and the acquisition of a church building. Their dedication and determination impressed the local Catholic hierarchy and led to a reversal of its earlier opposition to the creation of a separate Magyar parish. The Hungarian Roman Catholic church of Hamilton, named after St. Stephen of Hungary, became a reality in 1949.[34]

The highlight of the Hungarian Protestant group's evolution during the 1940's was probably the continued success of the United Church congregation in Montreal. In January, 1942, the congregation ceased to be a mission and became self-supporting in all aspects of its work except the use of a place of worship, which continued to be provided by the United Church of Canada. Soon, this situation also changed when the congregation bought an old, neglected building on St. Urban Street. The purchase and subsequent remodelling were financed by a series of fund-raising drives. Many people gave money, others offered loans, still others contributed their own labour. The church was completed in April, 1943. The building was to serve as the centre of the congregation's religious, cultural, and social life for the next twelve years.[35]

While a few Hungarian parishes and congregations prospered, the religious life of Hungarian-Canadian society continued to be troubled by problems. The situation was most acute in the Canadian West, and the cause of the difficulties was an increasing shortage of Hungarian-speaking clergymen. As existing pastors moved away or retired, more and more congregations were left with little or no pastoral care. The story of the United Church in Saskatchewan illustrates the point. In 1941 the Reverend Balla left Yorkton, from where he used to serve a number of Hungarian congregations in the province as well as one in Winnipeg. He was replaced by the Reverend Imre Csendes, formerly the minister in Rothmere. The Rothmere congregation in turn was transferred to Hoffmann's already over-extended pastoral territory. Four years later Hoffmann also had to retire, leaving one elderly minister to the province's widely scattered 1,130 Hungarians belonging to the United Church. A few years later Csendes was also to leave to serve first in Winnipeg, and then in Toronto.[36]

The causes of this shortage of pastors were many. Serving ethnic congregations was a difficult and very poorly paid proposition. It was not respected by fellow clergymen and precluded chances of advancement. One United Church internal report admitted that there was open prejudice against work with ethnic congregations in the Church's Presbyteries, a fact which probably deterred many second-generation would-be ministers from embarking on careers serving their own peoples.[37] At the same time, the recruitment of pastors from Central Europe was impossible for the time being. As a result, the 1940's proved to be sad times for many of the older Hungarian-Canadian organizations and parishes. The situation was to improve only in the 1950's with the arrival of many refugee priests and ministers from Hungary. Many existing Roman Catholic Hungarian parishes made the difficult transition to the better days of the post-war era with the help of English- or (as in the case of Montreal) French-speaking priests.[38]

Schools and the Press

Closely linked to the churches were the ethnic schools. These also had their share of problems during the 1940's. Although they suffered from the effects of economic problems during the Depression, after 1941 they were increasingly plagued by a lack of support from the old country, and by a decline in enrolment. The former condition was the direct result of the war. After 1941 it became impossible to obtain aid from Hungary. The decline in enrolment probably had many causes. The dramatic increase in employment during the war may have resulted in increased apathy toward the schools. Parents who were constantly working overtime had little time or energy left for taking children to after-school or weekend classes. Moreover, by the second half of the decade, the size of the school-age population shrank as a result of the Hungarian-Canadian group's peculiar age distribution. Indeed, those knowledgeable on the subject regard the 1940's as a sad period, an age of decline in the history of Hungarian-Canadian schools.[39]

The 1940's were equally disheartening for the Hungarian-Canadian press. Here, too, the war had caused some setbacks. It brought an end to the subsidy the *News* of Winnipeg had enjoyed since the 1920's. As a result, the paper got into financial trouble. Its new owner-editor, Gusztáv Nemes, had to publish it with the aid of a single helper, a formidable task considering that the paper appeared twice a week and was mailed out to about 4,000 subscribers. Almost in contrast, the *Worker*, which by this time had become the *News'* chief Canadian rival, seems to have prospered. It published a relatively bulky issue each week and had an estimated 2-3,000 subscribers. While the *News* was popular in the West, the *Worker* had its largest support in central Canada. The only other periodical worthy of note during the war and the immediate postwar era was Czakó's *Táragató*, published monthly with the support of the United Church. Its highbrow approach and overt support for Count Michael Károlyi did not make it popular with many Hungarian Canadians. Under these circumstances it is not surprising that many Magyars in Canada, especially central Canada, subscribed to the often larger, better edited, and less partisan newspapers from Cleveland and New York.[40]

Community Life in Decline

A comparison of Hungarian-Canadian society's political and cultural efforts during the 1940's leads to the conclusion that, while the former continued to receive much attention, the latter tended to suffer from increasing neglect and apathy. The return of economic prosperity had salutary effects on the financial affairs of political organizations, even of some social clubs and religious institutions, but it did not have similar results for certain cultural aspects of Hungarian-Canadian life. Increased wealth did lead to the acquisition of recreational centres and houses of worship, but it did little or nothing to alleviate the problems of the schools and the press. It failed to fill the benches of the ethnic schools, and it could not end the financial troubles of the largest Hungarian-Canadian newspaper. Despite the increased earning power of Hungarian Canadians, their schools were fighting a losing battle against the forces of assimilation, and even their largest newspaper had to survive on a shoestring budget.

The spirit of enthusiasm and passion for community life that characterized Hungarian-Canadian society in the wake of the great migration of the 1920's declined and, in fact, hardly extended beyond the realm of ethnic politics. If it is possible to estimate Hungarian Canadians' priorities during the 1940's, one would have to say that their foremost concern was the economic welfare of their families. The fate of their political causes came second, the churches third, and cultural institutions fourth. There is even evidence suggesting that the new prosperity tended to hinder rather than promote a more vigorous community life and weakened ethnic solidarity. The new wealth caused or reinforced socioeconomic divisions within Hungarian-Canadian society. In certain urban concentrations it led to increased residential mobility and physical dispersal. As some members of an urban Hungarian-Canadian community became richer, they abandoned the ethnic ghettoes and settled in "better" districts. During the 1940's, for example, many Hungarians left Toronto's Beverley Street neighbourhood and bought homes in the more prestigious Madison Avenue-Bedford Road-Huron Street area north of Bloor Street. Montreal's rather compact Hungarian colony had also broken up by the end of the decade.[41]

As concerns over material advancement grew, the desire for the preservation of ethnic values and institutions seems to have lessened. And as geographic dispersal of individual urban communities increased, the maintenance of meaningful cultural life became more difficult. By the end of the 1940's, the Hungarian-Canadian society that emerged in the wake of the immigration of the 1920's was showing signs of fatigue and age. It was doubtful whether it could continue to sustain an active Hungarian-Canadian cultural life without the infusion of new blood in the form of a new wave of immigrants. Despite the signs of decline in the group's dynamism, the Hungarian-Canadian society of the pre-1950 era had numerous unique and remarkable qualities. Before the renewal of Hungarian-Canadian ethnic life through the immigration of tens of thousands of Hungarians during the 1949-1959 period is discussed, it is important to look at some hitherto unexplored features of the "old" Hungarian society.

Sib System, Social Stratification, and Marriage and Family
No truly comprehensive study has ever been written on the mores, customs, social values, and structure of this society. Fortunately, during the early 1950's one survey had been done on several aspects of this subject. It is John Kósa's *Land of Choice: The Hungarians in Canada*, a sociological analysis based on interviews with 112 members of what by then was called the "old Hungarian stock." As Kósa's sample group was small and all of its members were selected from the Hungarian communities of the Toronto and Delhi regions, his study hardly warrants generalizations for the whole of the "old" Hungarian-Canadian society. Nevertheless, many of its observations are useful.[42]

Kósa found that the cornerstone of the Hungarian-Canadian social order was a kinship or sib system regulated by myriad unwritten customs and mutual obligations. This social institution was common to all classes in Hungary, and it was brought to Canada apparently unaltered by the transfer to the new social environment. The tradition of mutual help among members of a sib was particularly strong among Hungarian Canadians. Out of Kósa's 112 respondents, eighty-seven had been helped by relatives in their immigration to and settlement in Canada. Furthermore, 106 of them had in turn helped or tried to help still other relations in their attempt to migrate and establish themselves here. Such help

183

ranged from advice and encouragement to long-term support and outright financial assistance. Those relatives who didn't come to Canada and were needy were helped through gift parcels or money orders. As time passed, ties with these members of the sib weakened, but the sib in Canada "stuck together." Kósa concluded that the "immigrant generation rigorously maintained the sib organization." In contrast, the second generation, influenced by North American traditions and values, rejected the system and broke the special ties with all but the most immediate members of their sib. Kósa believed that this step was an important stage in the process of assimilation. "When saying farewell to the sib," the second-generation Hungarian Canadians said "farewell to the Hungarian ethnic group as well."[43]

Through determination, hard work, and the help of their sib, many Hungarian Canadians had been able to establish themselves financially. Kósa found that his 112 respondents owned real estate worth over $3.5 million, an average of $31,000 for each family unit. The wealth was not distributed evenly. A third of the group had assets over $35,000, while a fifth had less than $15,000. Eleven members of the group owned real estate worth over $100,000 each.

Beyond perseverance and help from sib relations, the wealthiest of Kósa's respondents were driven by a competitive spirit. The in-between class, those with assets from $15,000 to $35,000, was further divided into two categories. The members of the first were motivated by the same spirit of competition as their wealthier fellow immigrants, but had not yet attained the same economic status. The members of the second category were not interested in further material advancement. They had achieved a comfortable life, saved enough for their old age, and were content to enjoy life in a quiet, unostentatious way. The poorer members of Kósa's sample included families with modest homes and bachelors who did not own real estate and did not seem to have had an interest in acquiring any. Those who had achieved striking or moderate financial success did so mainly through family enterprises such as tobacco farming, small business, or the keeping of rooming houses. Common to all successful families was thrift, a practice that was abandoned as soon as the desired economic status was reached.[44]

Economic stratification had considerable effects on the social attitudes and practices of Hungarian Canadians. The poor immigrant who had "made it good" in Canada no longer accepted unquestioningly the leadership of his social betters from Hungary. He felt equal to them, a fact that shocked many aristocratic and gentry arrivals during the postwar influx of 1948-51. At the same time, rich Hungarian Canadians felt superior to their poorer fellows, even if they had all hailed from the lower strata of Hungarian society. Kósa's rich respondents considered their poor compatriots lazy, shiftless good-for-nothings. The poor in turn described the rich as haughty and money-grubbing, and some of those in the middle scoffed at both the wealthy and the poor. Interestingly enough, the various, newly emerged "classes" kept very much to themselves, rarely mixing with each other unless they happened to be relatives.[45]

The family situation of many of Kósa's informants had been forged by circumstances surrounding their immigration. Slightly more than half of the married men in the group had taken a wife before coming to Canada, but only seventeen of them were accompanied by their spouses on their journey here. The majority of the rest were joined by their wives later. Often the process took years, if not decades; and in the case of six men, it never happened. Other men immigrated during their engagement and were followed by their brides later. In their case, too, the plans for union were delayed by the Depression and the war. Kósa estimated that over two-fifths of the group were "unable to establish a normal family life within a reasonable time after immigration." Those who came with the hope of marrying in Canada encountered many problems. Since male immigrants greatly outnumbered females, only a few of these newcomers could find Hungarian wives; and cultural and linguistic barriers made it very difficult for them to find non-Hungarian ones.[46]

Family traditions and patterns of child-rearing were also affected through the transplantation of the Hungarian family to a Canadian environment. Most noticeable was the increased importance acquired by women as administrators of family finances. As more and more Hungarian-Canadian women assumed functions beyond being homemakers, they learned the handling of money. Since they often knew as much English as their husbands, they gradually took over such tasks as shopping and banking. While they did not wish to emulate Canadian women, by social and economic circumstances they were forced to do so. It was somewhat different in the case of their children, who tended to follow behaviour more in tune with Canadian customs. They did so not as a result of economic pressures but out of their desire to conform to norms accepted by their Canadian friends and schoolmates. Conflicts arose between parents and children over such issues as allowances, dating, and leaving the family, but these were usually resolved through compromises. Kósa concluded that the Hungarian-Canadian family was constantly changing in its new Canadian environment, but it was not disintegrating under the impact of social change.[47]

Second-generation Hungarian Canadians tended to marry among themselves. Only about a third of the Canadian-born children of Kósa's sample group married outside of the Hungarian ethnic group; and very few married first-generation immigrants. The courtship and marriage rites (bridal and baby showers, receptions, etc.) of these children were thoroughly Canadian. In contrast to the usual Canadian tradition, however, after marriage the newlyweds often moved in with the bride's parents and stayed there until they saved enough money to buy a home of their own. While in the parental residence they adhered to Hungarian customs, but these were gradually abandoned after the couple moved to their own home.[48]

Adjustment and Assimilation

The growing economic power of women in marriage, the greater freedom granted to children, and the abandonment of the sib system's traditions by the second generation were all parts of the gradual but irreversible process known as immigrant adjustment and assimilation. Family traditions gradually were Canadianized. In the case of the post-1920 Hungarian newcomers, this process had often started soon after arrival in Canada. The first manifestation of it was the abandonment by the newcomers of the clothes they had brought with them from Europe. On the farms this shedding of the old garments often took place quite some time after arrival, as many newcomers cherished the clothes they had brought from the old country and kept them for special occasions. In the city, however, where peer pressure was greater, the immigrant often got rid of his strange-looking outfits as soon as he could afford to buy Canadian ones.[49]

Less rapid was the abandonment of culinary habits. The immigrants continued to cherish and relish their traditional dishes, but often finances and the lack of time (most Hungarian meals require elaborate preparations) forced Hungarian-Canadian families to adopt North American cooking habits on all but special occasions and holidays. Some changes came even in the attitudes to housing. While most Hungarian immigrants aspired to owning a family home, a tradition common to all but the lowest classes in Hungary, the home they acquired in Canada was not looked upon in a Hungarian way: it was not seen as a possession to be passed on to the children but was considered as a piece of real estate that served as residence but could be kept or sold as the family's economic and social interests dictated.[50]

Changes also came about in the immigrants' normative values and behaviour. From the stories told by his respondents, Kósa concluded that the tradition of fighting, a kind of primitive duelling common in many villages in Hungary, was on the wane among the old immigrants to Canada. Even drinking habits had changed, although very slightly, when such alcoholic beverages as whisky came to be consumed by the traditionally wine-drinking Hungarians. Kósa found also that families that had "made it good" in Canada began practising birth control even though this was usually not done by the members of the lower classes from which most Hungarian Canadians hailed. In accepting birth control, the immigrants were really adopting the behaviour patterns of another Hungarian class, the well-to-do peasants. On the whole, however, changes in normative values seem to have been few, and Kósa concluded that while the Hungarian immigrant readily accepted Canadian patterns in his "external forms of life," in his "normative attitudes" he strongly resisted Canadian influences. Nevertheless, the pace of adjustment and assimilation shown by the sample group seems to have been more rapid than that of some other, earlier immigrant groups, a fact Kósa attributed to the accelerating pace of social change, both in the mother country and in the country of immigration.[51]

The "Old Stock" in Census Statistics

Kósa's conclusions cannot be tested through an analysis of the 1951 census results. Unlike previous censuses, which usually identified Hungarian Canadians as a separate group, the 1951 census often lumped them together with a number of other immigrant minorities under the heading "other Europeans." Nevertheless, much statistical information exists on the "old" Hungarian stock, especially concerning its geographic distribution.

According to the census, in 1951 nearly 22,400 pre-World War II Hungarian immigrants lived in Canada. Some 12,400, or 55 per cent of them, resided in Ontario. About 3,400 lived in Alberta, 2,900 in Saskatchewan, 1,450 in British Columbia, and 1,400 in Quebec.[52] Noteworthy are the predominant position of Ontario and the gains made by Alberta. Given this provincial distribution, it is not surprising that the largest concentrations of these people were in the cities of southern Ontario. Hamilton was in the lead with slightly more than 1,500 residents; Toronto was a not-too-distant second. It is interesting that, as a centre of residential concentration for the "old immigrants," Toronto had surpassed Montreal, Calgary overtook Winnipeg, and Vancouver had passed Regina.[53] These changes were no doubt partly the result of wartime migrations to manufacturing centres and partly the consequence of a decline in the immigrant population due to death and, to a lesser extent, remigration to Hungary.[54]

The only 1951 census figure that reflects on the rate of integration of the whole Hungarian-Canadian group is the official number of residents in the country with Hungarian as their mother tongue. This is given as 42,402, down from 46,287 ten years earlier. The decline, despite the influx of post-war arrivals, probably stems from the fact that many of the old, Magyar-speaking Hungarian Canadians had died since 1941, and few of their Canadian-born children were native speakers of Magyar. By subtracting the number of immigrant Hungarians from that of Magyar-speaking Canadians, we can also get an idea of the size of the second- and third-generation Hungarian-Canadian population still retaining the language of their forefathers. For the whole of Canada their number is 14,504. The provincial breakdowns are led by Saskatchewan (5,668), Ontario (5,154), and Alberta (1,795).[55] Once again, the figures for Saskatchewan are of interest as they indicate the remarkable persistence of Hungarian culture among the province's Hungarian-Canadian population. In 1951 there were more Canadian-born Magyar-speaking people there than there were Hungarian immigrants. Elsewhere immigrants outnumbered Canadian-born Hungarian Canadians who still considered Magyar to be their native language by at least two to one.[56]

Achievements in Literature and the Arts

Neither Kósa's study nor the census statistics say anything about the "old" Hungarian-Canadian society's accomplishments in the realm of arts and letters. Moreover, no scholarly study has ever been published on this subject. Yet, from the meagre information available, one can safely conclude that the Hungarian-Canadian effort in these fields was considerable.

Poetry has always been close to the hearts of Hungarians, and Hungarian Canadians were no exception in this regard. They had often expressed their hopes or had drowned their sorrows and homesickness in verse. In 1940 Ruzsa listed nearly twenty Hungarian-Canadian poets and poetesses in his book, and gave samples from the poetry of several of them.[57] Watson Kirkconnell had translated a few of these poets, including Gyula Izsák, Sarolta Petényi, and Rózsa Kovács.[58]

In prose writing, the Hungarian-Canadian record in the decades under discussion here is poorer. No novelist of note had emerged, partly because of the problem of publishing books for Hungarian-Canadian audiences. In the realm of scholarly and historical writing, Czakó had produced a number of short studies in English, while Sántha published a few historical works. A more ambitious but less methodical chronicler of the "old" Hungarian-Canadian experience was Ruzsa.[59]

The old Hungarian-Canadian stock's record in the fields of visual arts and music is much more impressive. It is not possible to discuss even briefly all of those who had helped to make it so. It must suffice to give only a few examples. The foremost of these was the late Nicholas Hornyánszky, an internationally known etcher, painter, and educator, especially famous for his printmaking and for his role in the founding and expanding of the Society of Canadian Painter-Etchers and Engravers. As professor at the Ontario College of Art in Toronto, Hornyánszky had an important impact on a younger generation of Canadian painters.[60] Among musicians, Géza de Kresz should be mentioned. His first Canadian achievement was the founding, in 1929, of the Hart House String Quartet. Kresz went back to Hungary in 1936 but returned to Canada soon after the war. Subsequently he taught at the Royal Conservatory of Music in Toronto. Kresz's most important contribution was in the realm of educating Canadian musicians, particularly violinists.[61]

Neither Hornyánszky, nor Kresz, nor most of the other talented and successful Hungarian artists or musicians belonged to the same class of people that made up much of the old Hungarian-Canadian society. Yet, they were proud of their nation and did not deny their Hungarian background. Both Kresz and Hornyánszky, but especially the latter, participated in Hungarian-Canadian organizational life. Both as public figures and as successful individuals they played the role of cultural ambassadors of their ethnic group to the mainstream of Canadian life. In doing so they and others like them helped to prepare for a greater degree of acceptance of Hungarians in Canadian society. Nevertheless, the most important of such "image makers" for the Hungarian group had been a Canadian, Watson Kirkconnell, the noted scholar, poet, and educator who had done a great deal to popularize Hungarian literature, especially poetry, in Canada.[62]

While a handful of Hungarian-Canadian artists and musicians were improving their ethnic group's image through virtuoso achievement, the masses of Hungarian Canadians were slowly earning a good reputation through hard work, frugal life, and devotion to their families, and by being law-abiding citizens.[63] In doing so, they were helping to create conditions in which the next waves of Hungarian immigrants could attain social and economic positions undreamed of during the first half of the twentieth century. In a sense, then, the immigrants of the interwar period were pioneers who prepared the ground for a better future.

NOTES

1. Eisner Papers, Frank Hoffmann to Eisner, 15 April 1943; *The United Church of Canada Year Book, 1940*, p. 138.

2. *KMU*, 11 July 1941. On the 26th of June an air-raid was carried out against northeastern Hungary by a few aircraft whose identity was not positively established. At the time, the incident was blamed on Russia, and Hungary entered the war on Germany's side. After the war many historians argued that the raid had been the work of Nazi provocateurs anxious to involve Hungary in the war. There is no substantial evidence to support their claim. See N.F. Dreisziger, "New Twist to an Old Riddle: The Bombing of Kassa (Kosice), June 26, 1941," *Journal of Modern History*, 44, 2 (June, 1972), pp. 232-42; Dreisziger, "Contradictory Evidence Concerning Hungary's Declaration of War on the USSR in June 1941," *Canadian Slavonic Papers*, 29, 4 (December, 1977), pp. 481-8.

3. Eisner Papers, Dr. Eugene Molnár to Eisner, 30 September 1942.

4. PAC, Report on Reorganization of Nationalities Branch, undated Department of National War Services memorandum, RG 26, vol. 13. After the outbreak of the war in 1939 many English Canadians called for the closing of the entire ethnic press. That this did not happen was probably partly the work of Watson Kirkconnell, a self-appointed spokesman for new Canadians, who emphasized in his numerous publications that the vast majority of immigrant ethnics were loyal to Canada. See Watson Kirkconnell, *Canada, Europe and Hitler* (Toronto, 1939); Kirkconnell, *A Slice of Canada: Memoirs* (Toronto, 1967), Chapters 20, 24. Also, N.F. Dreisziger, "Watson Kirkconnell: Transla-

tor of Hungarian Poetry and Friend of Hungarian-Canadians,"
Canadian-American Review of Hungarian Studies, IV, 2 (Fall, 1977),
pp. 134ff.

5. One organization that aimed to achieve this purpose was the Council of
Friendship, which became active in many central Canadian centres by
the end of the 1930's. The Council's chief supporter was Mrs. Percival
Foster of Toronto. Two of her dedicated Hungarian helpers were
Ferenc Kovács of Hamilton and Nicholas Hornyánszky of Toronto. See
Gibbon, *Canadian Mosaic*, p. 360; and Ruzsa, *A Kanadai Magyarság*,
pp. 214, 381.

6. PAC, Report on Reorganization. The purpose of the CCCC was defined
in November, 1943, as follows: "to create among Canadians of French
and British origin a better understanding of Canadians of recent European origin and to foster among the latter a wider knowledge and appreciation of the best traditions of Canadian Life." (*Ibid.*, p. 4.) See also
an undated, anonymous government memorandum entitled Advisory
Committee on Co-operation in Canadian Citizenship, file on Interde-
partmental Committees, PAC, RG 35, 7, vol. 26.

7. Mihály Fehér, "Adatok a Montreáli Magyar Egyházak és Egyesületek
Nagybizottsága müködéséhez" [Data to the Activities of the Grand
Committee of Hungarian Churches and Associations of Montreal], ms,
undated, put at my disposal through the kindness of Dr. M. Mattya-
sovszky-Zsolnay. Also, Eisner Papers, Eisner to Gusztáv Nemes, 11
June 1942.

8. Eisner Papers, Eisner to Nemes, 11 June 1942; PAC, RG 26, vol. 6, file
24-H-3, Hornyánszky to Tracy Phillips, 27 July 1942; Eisner Papers,
Eisner to Eugene Molnár, 13 August 1942; Tracy Phillips to the President of Sun Life Insurance Co., 29 August 1942, PAC, Department of
Immigration and Citizenship Records, RG 26, vol. 5, file 34-E-2, vol. 1.

9. Eisner to V.J. Kaye, 18 September 1942, PAC, RG 26, vol. 5, file 34-E-2
vol. 1; and Eisner to Phillips, 22 September 1942, *ibid.*

10. Eisner Papers, Eisner to Sántha, 27 October 1942. In Calgary, the
CCCC's efforts were spurred by the local Hungarian Calvinist minister.

11. Eisner Papers, Eisner's correspondence with István Fajcz, Albert
Mezei, and Emeric Duha, November-December, 1942. Eisner's papers
reveal that at least a couple of educated Hungarians did live in Sudbury
in 1942. Why they were not known to other Hungarians there is not explained.

12. *Ibid.*, Eisner's correspondence with Duha, November-December, 1942;
Fehér, "Adatok."

13. Béla Eisner, "Report of my Good-Will Visit to the Communities of
Hungarian Origin in Certain Industrial Areas of the Province of Ontario and Districts of the Prairie Provinces," ms (Montreal: Cultural
Council of Canadians of Hungarian Origin backed by the Committee
on Co-operation in Canadian Citizenship, 1942), pp. 18-24. In northern

Ontario's mining communities Eisner found the working conditions poorer and morale weaker.

14. Hamilton, Niagara Falls, Sudbury, Timmins, and Welland. (*Ibid.*, pp. 10-17). Niagara Falls topped the list with an 80 per cent estimate. In two Ontario communities, Port Colborne and Welland, Eisner found small groups of people (estimated to be 5 per cent and 3 per cent respectively) who belonged to the "extreme right."

15. *Ibid.*, pp. 42ff.

16. *Ibid.*, pp. 45-67. Eisner proposed a comprehensive assault on this problem. He called for a program of educating native Canadians through publicizing the aims of the CCCC. He felt that local committees, made up of leaders of ethnic organizations, should monitor cases of discrimination and report them to the government. Since the basis for discrimination was often the immigrant's lack of knowledge of English, Eisner called for free language training for all newcomers to Canada. Eisner's other recommendations included the curtailment of the immigration of single men, government encouragement of, and even some limited financial support for, ethnic umbrella organizations and the ethnic media. Eisner also wanted to see some measures taken to reduce the scarcity of religious leaders.

For a briefer version of Eisner's findings and recommendations, see his manuscript "Toward a United Canada: Some Problems of the Hungarian-Born Canadians," 17 October 1944, in Eisner Papers. For a few comments on wartime conditions among Hungarians in the Toronto area, see the documents attached to N. Hornyánszky's letter to Tracey Phillips, 16 May 1942, PAC, RG 26, vol. 6.

17. Hungarian-Canadian farmers on the Prairies, while working just as hard and contributing just as much to the Canadian economy, were generally too short of cash to help the war effort with their savings. Eisner, "Toward a United Canada," pp. 8, 11.

18. "Names of Hungarian-born Canadians of Regina, Saskatchewan, Serving in his Majesty's Armed Forces," Eisner Papers. The Reverend Hoffmann reported from Saskatoon that fifty young men had joined the forces from the congregations he was serving. *United Church of Canada Year Book, 1942,* p. 148.

19. Statistical tables provided on non-English or French-speaking enlistments in the Canadian Forces. PAC, RG 26, vol. 13. The provincial breakdowns were as follows: Ontario, 421; Saskatchewan, 361; Alberta, 131; Manitoba, 63; Quebec, 58; British Columbia, 37.

20. Hornyánszky writing in *KMU*, 13 July 1943. Also, Phillips to Hornyánszky, 23 August 1943, PAC, RG 26, vol. 6, file 34-H-3.

21. *KMU*, 18 and 25 December 1945. The Hungarian House was to stay away from politics.

22. *KMU*, 10 October 1944.

23. The four churches participating were Roman Catholic, Reformed, Bap-

tist, and United. The organizations involved were the Toronto Hungarian House, the Toronto branch of the Brantford Sick-Benefit Federation, the Toronto Hungarian Democratic Association, and the local chapter of the Kossuth Sick-Benefit Federation. In addition, agents of four newspapers (*Canadian Hungarian News, American Hungarian People's Voice, American Liberty,* and *Canadian Hungarian Worker*) were also present. *KMU,* 27 April 1945.

24. *KMU,* 18 May 1945.

25. The government's views were expressed to Gusztáv Nemes of the *News* by an official of the Department of War Services. *KMU,* 4 May 1945.

26. *Ibid.,* 20 July, 17 and 31 August 1945.

27. *Ibid.,* 2 April, 17 and 24 May 1946.

28. *Ibid.,* 21 June 1946.

29. *Ibid.,* 8 November 1946, 25 April 1947.

30. "Mi az igazság az 'egység' körül" [What is the truth about "unity"], letter by B. Török, *KMU,* 3 February 1948. Török accused the "minority elements" (i.e., the left) in the UCHRC of using the organization for their own propaganda purposes. Also, *KMU,* 24 February 1948.

31. *KMU,* 18 March and 4 April 1948. The *News'* editors denied the charges.

32. *Ibid.,* 4 April 1947; interview with Steinmetz. A court case against the Hungarian House by a group of concerned Hungarians was dismissed on grounds that the house's constitution did not prevent its executive from appropriating part of the collected funds for its own purposes. (*KMU,* 13 February 1948.)

33. *50 Years: St. Elizabeth of Hungary Church* (Toronto, [1978]), pp. 13, 22; interviews with Sister Mary and Sister Columba.

34. Interview with Sister Mary; *973-1973: 1,000 Years of Hungarian Christianity* (Toronto, 1973), p. [24].

35. Fehér, "Adatok," pp. 69-78; *KMU,* 4 May 1943. Among the other Protestant congregations, the largest seems to have been Hamilton's Reformed Church. In 1944 it had a total membership of 495 and a yearly income of about $4,000. Toronto's Reformed congregation had 194 active members (1943). Each congregation had Sunday school and several social and cultural clubs affiliated with it. A new Reformed congregation in southern Ontario was founded in 1948 in Delhi. (*KMU,* 16 February and 2 March 1943, 25 February 1944, and 23 March 1948. Also, Borsay, "Origins of the Tobacco District Hungarian Presbyterian Church," p. 1.

36. *United Church of Canada Year Book, 1941,* p. 144; *United Church of Canada Year Book, 1946,* p. 149.

37. Archives of the United Church of Canada (AUCC), Report of the Commission on City Missions and Non-Anglo-Saxon Work, 4 February 1944, Board of Home Missions, United Church of Canada, vol. 16. Also, *ibid.,* Memorandum on Non-Anglo-Saxon Work and City Institutions, 3 February 1944.

38. For a brief outline of the history of several Hungarian-Canadian Roman Catholic congregations in Ontario, see *973-1973: 1,000 Years of Hungarian Christianity*, pp. 20-8.

39. Károly Steinmetz writing in *KMU*, 4 September 1942; Tamás, *Magyar iskolák Kanadában*, pp. 18, 24ff. The picture is not entirely negative. It seems that in growing Hungarian-Canadian centres flourishing schools existed alongside some of the stronger religious associations, such as the Roman Catholic parishes and largest Calvinist congregations of Montreal, Toronto, and Hamilton. (Interviews with Sister Mary and Sister Columba.) The school maintained by Fehér's congregation continued to offer classes three times a week. (Fehér, *Montreáli*, p. 77.) In the West, the school at Stockholm continued to function. (Sántha, *Three Generations*, p. 85.)

40. Eisner Report, pp. 43ff. AUCC, Commission on City Missions, 4 February 1944.

41. Kósa, "Hungarian Immigrants," pp. 361, 364.

42. Kósa, *Land of Choice*, pp. 6ff.

43. *Ibid.*, Chapter 2.

44. *Ibid.*, Chapter 3. Kósa observed considerable "conspicuous consumption" among the Hungarian-Canadian rich.

45. *Ibid.*, pp. 36-9.

46. *Ibid.*, pp. 45ff. The people who succeeded in overcoming these odds and found a suitable Hungarian wife did so often with the help of their sib relations.

47. *Ibid.*, pp. 53-7.

48. *Ibid.*, pp. 57-60.

49. *Ibid.*, pp. 67ff.

50. *Ibid.*, pp. 69-74.

51. *Ibid.*, pp. 80-95.

52. *Census of Canada*, 1951, II, Table 60.

53. *Ibid.*

54. After 1945 numerous left-wing Hungarians returned to their native land expecting post-war Hungary to offer better social and political treatment to her lower classes. Durovec, "Harmincöt" (see Chapter Five, note 62).

55. Calculations based on figures in *Census of Canada*, 1951, I, Table 54; II, Table 60.

56. Other census statistics cannot be broken down to members of the old Hungarian stock, or for the second- and third-generation groups. In fact, they are available only for the whole Hungarian-speaking population of Canada. But it may be of interest that in this category men still comprised 56 per cent of the total (*ibid.*, I, Table 53), and that 54 per cent of the whole group lived in towns and cities (*ibid.*, Table 55). In Ontario, the home of most Hungarian Canadians, the percentage of urban residents was 68.4, while in Saskatchewan, it was still only about 17 per cent (*ibid.*).

57. Ruzsa, *A Kanadai Magyarság*, pp. 403-29.

58. Watson Kirkconnell, "A Canadian Meets the Magyars," *The Canadian-American Review of Hungarian Studies*, 1, 1 (Spring, 1974), p. 10.

59. *Ibid*. Also, Ruzsa, p. 400. Sántha's and Ruzsa's works are mentioned in the Appendix: A Note on Sources.

60. Paul Kellner, "Hungarian Participation in Canadian Culture," ms (Ottawa, 1965), pp. 44ff. Copies of this manuscript are in the National Library and the Library of the Department of the Secretary of State, both in Ottawa. A Hungarian-Canadian sculptor of note was Béla Zoltványi, whose works adorn many churches in Quebec and elsewhere. Joseph Hilpert was a noted portrait painter in Toronto. (Ruzsa, pp. 388, 391.)

61. Undated, anonymous manuscript on Kresz, Box 30a, *CHN* Records. Ruzsa, pp. 388ff. Kellner, "Hungarian Participation," pp. 43ff. Other noted musicians were Pál Márky, pianist; Ervin Haris, János Rimanóczy, and Ibolyka Gyárfás, violinists; and Lajos Balogh, organist. (Ruzsa, pp. 388ff.)

62. See Dreisziger, "Watson Kirkconnell: Translator of Hungarian Poetry," pp. 117-43.

63. The data derived from the 1941 census speak to the low criminality of the Hungarian-Canadian population. According to this census, the group's rate of admission to penitentiaries per 100,000 population was 13. The national rate was 18, with rates for the individual ethnic groups ranging from 5 to 107. Hurd, *Racial Origins* (1941), Table 77, p. 151.

SEVEN

Toward a Golden Age: The 1950's

N.F. Dreisziger

THE ÉMIGRÉS

Unbeknown to its members, during the late 1940's Hungarian-Canadian society stood on the threshold of a new age. The epoch, commencing with the coming of the first wave of post-war immigrants during 1949-51, was characterized foremost by a substantial increase in the Hungarian-Canadian community's size. Along with this growth came further urbanization and even greater concentration of the group in industrial Ontario. Hungarian-Canadian society became much more diversified socially and culturally. In its organizational life, two old trends continued: a high degree of atomization and extreme politicization. But what characterized this new era above all was frenzied activity, great achievements, and even greater expectations.

The Post-war Immigration
In the five years after the end of World War II, 430,000 immigrants came to Canada from war-torn Europe. Most of these early arrivals came from Britain. The influx of Central and East European "displaced persons" did not get under way until after gradual changes were made in Canadian admission policies during 1947. The new regulations made the entry of certain classes of Hungarian refugees possible.[1]

Detailed statistics exist on this post-war movement of Hungarians to Canada. During 1946-48 only a few came; presumably they were sponsored people joining relatives in Canada. During the 1948-49 fiscal year the movement gathered some momentum with almost 1,400 Hungarians entering the country. The following year nearly 1,600 came, and in 1950-51 some 2,000 arrived. The influx reached its peak in the 1951-52 fiscal year when 4,500 Hungarians entered Canada.[2]

Statistics also reveal the composition of this migration. In the 1950-51 fiscal year, for example, about 57 per cent of the total arrivals were males over eighteen, 30 per cent were adult females, the rest were children. As far as occupational divisions were concerned, many of the arrivals, some 36 per cent of them, were officially classified as belonging to the "farming class," 21 per cent were "unskilled and semi-skilled," 15 per cent belonged to the "skilled class," and the rest to various classifications including "female domestic servants."[3] Evidently these figures don't do justice to the number of middle- and upper-class Hungarians who came to Canada in this period. The fact is that many educated people denied their schooling in order to improve their chances of admittance as farm workers or ordinary labourers.

The destination of slightly more than half of the 1950-51 Hungarian arrivals was Ontario. Nearly a third of them were bound for Quebec, about 9 per cent for Alberta, and the rest mainly for the other western provinces.[4] Where the new arrivals had really ended up is indicated by the 1951 census. Of the 5,500 Magyar-speaking immigrants who came to Canada between 1946 and June of 1951, 62 per cent resided in Ontario, 17 per cent in Quebec, and close to 9 per cent in Alberta. The remaining 12 per cent were divided among British Columbia, Manitoba, Saskatchewan, and the Maritimes.[5] Clearly, Ontario was the most favoured destination of the newcomers; Quebec was a distant second. At the same time, the Prairie Provinces had lost their attractiveness, and the Maritimes remained a *terra incognita* to the vast majority of Hungarians. As far as cities were concerned, by far the most desirable seems to have been Toronto. Nearly 1,100 of the new arrivals were found living there in 1951. Montreal was second with about 800, and Hamilton third with 250. Elsewhere in the country, only Winnipeg attracted more than two hundred of the "new stock" of Hungarian immigrants.[6]

Upon arrival, the post-war immigrants were usually housed in temporary quarters in one of Canada's metropolitan centres. They were let go on their own as soon as jobs became available for them. In some cases the placement of newcomers was slow, and it was not until the summer of 1952 that jobs were found for most of them. Contact between the "old" and "new" Hungarians usually happened first during the latter's stay in temporary residences, as the leaders and rank-and-file of the "old" organizations sought to aid their newly arrived countrymen. In Montreal, for example, the Hungarian United Church started English classes for the newcomers, and the Grand Committee of Hungarian Churches and Associations helped them to get clothing, furniture, apartments, and jobs.[7] These initial contacts seem to have been pleasant enough; only later did class and cultural differences cause problems between the new and the old stock. As has been mentioned, a substantial portion of the new wave of immigrants was made up of upper- and upper-middle-class people whose beliefs, traditions, and mannerisms differed greatly from those of working people. Fate had turned the tables on many one-time residents of Hungary who found themselves in Canada in the early 1950's: the former poor who had left the country were now "Canadians" with good incomes and a fair amount of wealth, while the former rich were now dispossessed newcomers. Furthermore, the latest arrivals often had to depend on their "social inferiors" for advice and help and had to accept menial jobs, which many of the old-timers could scorn by then. The situation tended to breed mutual spite and resentment, and often was not conducive to a healthy community life.[8]

Émigré Organizations: The International Scene

The new immigrants' most noticeable impact on Hungarian-Canadian society came in the realm of organizational life. The explanation lies partly in Hungarian traditions, and partly in political circumstances. While Hungary's lower classes rarely maintained political organizations, the middle and upper classes had traditionally been highly organized. It was not different with the bulk of the new immigration. Furthermore, many of the newcomers considered their departure from Hungary as a temporary exile, which was to be used for preparations for a collective return to the mother country as soon as the opportunity presented itself. Consequently, the new immigration placed greater stress on political organization than did any previous wave of Hungarian immigrants to Canada.

A portion of the post-1945 Hungarian emigration was organized internationally. Its chief organs closely resembled the political spectrum of interwar and wartime Hungary. At the apex stood the Hungarian National Council, "a quasi government-in-exile" with headquarters in New York.[9] Its executive committee was made up of the post-war Hungarian emigration's most illustrious politicians, publicists, and diplomats. Another influential association was the League of Hungarian Veterans (Magyar Harcosok Bajtársi Közössége or MHBK), whose membership included about one hundred former general staff officers and several thousand former members and officers of the Royal Hungarian Army. Two left-of-centre international organizations of Hungarians in exile were the Hungarian Peasant Federation and the Hungarian Social Democrats. The official political arm of the Hungarian Catholics in emigration was the Hungarian Christian Popular Movement. Other émigré leagues or associations were the Hungarian Liberation Movement, the Hungarian Council for United Europe, the Central European Christian Democratic Union, the Association of Hungarian Federalists, Actio Catholica, the Association of Free Hungarian Journalists, the Union of Hungarian (Parliamentary) Deputies, the Hungarian Boy Scout Association, the remains of two socialist and one extreme nationalist parties or factions, a couple of monarchist groups, and three national student organizations. In addition to these organs of émigrés from Hungary, Hungarians from the successor states formed "committees" of their own, working toward the liberation of Upper Hungary, Transylvania, Sub-Carpathia, and southern Hungary.

These organizations operated in most countries that admitted post-war immigrants and had their headquarters in such European and North American centres as Munich, Paris, London, Rome, New York, and Cleveland. All of them were emphatically anti-Communist and refused to admit leftist radicals. Most of them also excluded former Nazi collaborators, "at least *pro forma*." Other common characteristics of these organizations were, as an American secret service report put it in 1951, an "intense political activity not devoid of intrigue, rather limited financial resources, and a desire to obtain the official or semi-official support of the Western powers. . . ." One manifestation of this intense activity was the explosive growth of the Hungarian émigré press after the war. In 1951 American intelligence men knew about more than forty recently established émigré newspapers or periodicals.[10]

The Old Organizations in Transition

The impact of this extremely politicized emigration began to be felt in Hungarian-Canadian organizational life soon after the arrival of the first displaced persons. Contrary to what might be expected, not all aspects of this impact were disruptive. The war and post-war era had driven from Hungary a diverse group of people, some of whom were able to make a valuable contribution to an ethnic community such as the Hungarian-Canadian. Foremost among these were priests and ministers who left Hungary in the wake of the war. Their arrival in Canada contributed to the growth most Hungarian-Canadian churches experienced during the 1950's.[11]

The coming of qualified religious leaders, along with a large number of newcomers anxious for pastoral care in their own language, all in a period of rising incomes for the old Hungarian-Canadian stock, combined to produce progress and prosperity in the Hungarian ethnic group's churches and in church-affiliated affairs. The prosperity manifested itself, above all, in the establishment of new parishes and congregations and in the opening of new houses of worship. The former phenomenon seems to have been most prominent in the tobacco district of Ontario, where between 1948 and 1952 at least three Hungarian ethnic parishes were organized. The opening of church buildings, on the other hand, took place right across Canada. Between 1949 and 1955 Roman Catholic churches were built or purchased in Hamilton, Winnipeg, Courtland (Ontario), and Stockholm; Protestant churches were opened in Calgary, Delhi, Toronto, and Montreal.[12] Not to be outdone, Ontario's small Hungarian Greek Catholic community managed to acquire two church buildings of its own, one in Hamilton and the other in Courtland.[13]

The old Hungarian-Canadian lay institutions, often expanded by new membership and leaders, also continued to function and even to flourish through these years. Some of them did not attract many new members, even where these would have been readily available. The associations of the old left, still numerous and active, were unlikely candidates for gaining the loyalty of men and women who had fled the advance of the Russian armies or who had left Hungary later because of their conflicts with the Communists.[14] But other organizations also suffered from a lack of interest on the part of the newcomers. In an age of widely available insurance coverage, ethnic sick-benefit societies seem to have found it increasingly difficult to compete for wider support.[15] The days of self-help organizations were certainly not over, as the waning role of sick-benefit organizations appears to have been balanced by the increased popularity of credit unions. One of the first of these seems to have been the Hungarian Credit and Savings Union of Vancouver, which began its activities in 1951 with only a handful of members. Less than a decade later it was to have 280 shareholders and a capital fund of $80,000. The Union's main aim was to protect Hungarians from the evils of loan-sharking.[16]

The various "Hungarian house" associations also continued their activities during the period under discussion. One of the most active of these seems to have been Toronto's. By the early fifties it was a provincially incorporated institution with an annually elected executive. A 1954 report defined the house's aims as being the improvement of Hungarian Canadians' material and social circumstances, the cultivation and preservation of Hungarian culture, the sponsoring of cultural, social, and sports events, the passing on of the Hungarian heritage to the second generation, the dispensing of advice to members, the maintenance of a job placement service, the combatting of the problems associated with aging, misfortune, and relocation, and the protection of the immigrant's human rights. The house also claimed to act as a link between its members and Canadian society and the Canadian government.[17] It was an ambitious program whose realization was evidently beyond the human and material resources of a single ethnic organization. In fact, except for an active social and sport life, the Toronto Hungarian House made little impact on the life of the Hungarian-Canadian community at large.[18]

More effective than any of the Hungarian house clubs were the umbrella organizations that came into being in Montreal and Winnipeg during the war. Of the two, Montreal's probably was the more influential. It continued to have about a half dozen institutional members that acted in unison on important issues. In their social and cultural life, however, the various member associations were independent, and some of them, especially the Hungarian Social Club, were very active.[19]

New Organizations

While the old immigrants' churches, self-help associations, Hungarian houses, and grand committees continued to function during the 1950's, the striking feature of the emerging new Hungarian-Canadian society was the birth of a host of new organizations, created almost invariably by the new arrivals. Many of these were the more or less official branches of the post-war emigration's international organs. A case in point is the

Hungarian Canadian Scout movement, which began its vigorous life during the early fifties. The stress placed upon this movement by the new immigrants stemmed mainly from the fact that the scouts, much cherished by the pre-1945 Hungarian society, were suppressed in post-war Hungary. The effective organizational work needed to keep the movement alive and functioning in Canada was assured with the arrival, during the early 1950's, of several former Hungarian scoutmasters and organizers.[20] Like the Hungarian Scout movement, the Hungarian war veterans and Hungarian gendarmerie veterans also established what might be called "Canadian branches." Similarly, at least one of the movements for the liberation of occupied Hungarian territories had an organization in Canada.[21]

While some of these organizations proved ephemeral and others had very little impact on the Hungarian-Canadian scene, a handful became stable and viable institutions which, in time, became cornerstones of the new Hungarian-Canadian society's social and cultural life. Perhaps the best example of these new organizations was the Helicon Society of Toronto, whose principal goal has been defined as the development of "cultured Hungarian life in Canada," to use the words of one of its founders. The society aimed also to cultivate and preserve the "thousand-year-old Hungarian traditions, mentality and national ideology." To accomplish these goals, it embarked on a vigorous program of lectures, panel discussions, concerts, and art exhibits. The Helicon Society began collecting books for a library and, as finances permitted, assisted in the publication of the works of Hungarian-Canadian authors.[22]

A couple of years after the establishment of the Helicon, there emerged another organization of new arrivals in Toronto, the Rákoczi Association. While the leadership of the two organizations overlapped, the Rákoczi Association was more exclusive – it was formally the organization of veterans of the Royal Hungarian Army. The only other substantial difference from the Helicon was the fact the younger association did not seek a large membership and preferred to stay in the background. Nevertheless, it wielded some influence through the cultivation of the friendship of young, rising politicians involved in municipal or provincial affairs.[23] Still another organization brought about mainly through the efforts of former officers of the Hungarian Army was the Széchenyi Society of Calgary. Unlike the two Toronto organizations, this society carried out its work throughout much of Canada; it later became primarily a fund-raising institution dedicated to the support and promotion of Hungarian studies.[24]

A Nation-wide Federation

The beginning of the 1950's witnessed a new attempt at establishing an umbrella organization for Canada's Hungarian churches and associations. This attempt was more successful than previous ones, as it resulted in the present-day Hungarian Canadian Federation (HCF). The federation was not the creature of the new immigration, although several new arrivals were actively involved in its establishment. It should be pointed out, as well, that the new nation-wide organization came about without the support of a large and in the past very influential part of the Hungarian-Canadian political spectrum – the left. Nevertheless, fortuitous circumstances, foremost among them the Cold War, enabled the federation to gain recognition as the chief umbrella organization of the Hungarian ethnic group.

The new HCF's origins go back to the time of the national relief movement's demise. As may be recalled, the movement had split during the winter of 1947-48. Subsequently, the conservatives brought about the Council of Hungarian Churches and Clubs for Suffering Hungarians. This council did not save the relief movement, but it served as a concrete precedent for an umbrella organization which had forgone the participation of the left.[25]

The need for an organization that could claim to speak on behalf of the Hungarian-Canadian community remained. This fact was bluntly brought to the attention of a few of the group's leaders in the summer of 1951, when a small Hungarian-Canadian delegation representing a number of central Canadian organizations appeared before Prime Minister Louis St. Laurent to bring to his government's attention the reign of political terror being unleashed on Hungary by her new Stalinist regime. St. Laurent received the delegation with sympathy, but he suggested that such representations might better be made through a nation-wide organization that could speak on behalf of all Hungarian Canadians.[26]

St. Laurent's advice seems to have been the catalyst that prompted the Hungarian-Canadian community to decisive action. Through the collaboration of Montreal's Grand Committee and a few organizations in Toronto, a provisional national federation was set up under the name Canadian Hungarian National Federation (CHNF). The CHNF's interim executive then issued an invitation to the leaders of Hungarian organizations to come to a founding convention.[27] The convention, held on December 15, 1951, in the basement of Toronto's Hungarian Catholic church, contrasted sharply with the pomp and elegance of the convention that established the first Hungarian-Canadian federation in Winnipeg twenty-four years earlier. But the humble surroundings probably had a sobering effect on those present, and the results were salutary. The meeting adopted the HCF's by-laws and elected a regular executive. Two vital issues, the problem of relations between the old and the new arrivals and the question of revenues, seem to have been well-handled. Room was made for new immigrants in the HCF's top organs, but the predominance of the old stock was not jeopardized. As far as finances were concerned, the founders of the federation decided not to collect membership dues from individual Hungarian Canadians. Instead, they imposed a modest levy on member organizations calculated on the basis of size.[28]

The new HCF's progress during the first six months of its existence was impressive. By May, 1952, twenty-five churches and close to forty clubs had joined it. They represented about 13,700 Hungarian Canadians, mainly heads of families.[29] Evidently, many clubs had remained outside, and some that had joined at first changed their stand later. At another time and under different circumstances the absence of the left from the federation's ranks would have been a disadvantage. In the political climate of the early 1950's, it was probably an asset. Owing to the Cold War, Hungarian-Canadian society's top organization and the Canadian government were close on the political spectrum, and the HCF's credentials as the ethnic group's official voice were not likely to be questioned. Moreover, the new federation, unlike its most prominent predecessor, the Canadian Hungarian Federation of 1928-31, had a solid demographic footing in central Canada, which by 1951 was the geographic centre of the new Hungarian-Canadian community. And, unlike the earlier federation, the new HCF was cautious about finances. It collected a very small levy, a few cents per member from each organization, and tried to live within its modest means. Consequently, the financial fiascos of the first Hungarian-Canadian federation were not repeated.[30] Without an adequate income, however, there was little for the new federation to do except to send the occasional petition to the federal government. Only in 1956 did an event occur that allowed the HCF to enter the limelight of ethnic politics. But before 1956 is discussed, it is necessary to look at still another facet of Hungarian-Canadian organized life in the early 1950's, the ethnic media.

The Press in Transition

It may be recalled that on the eve of the new era three periodicals made up the Hungarian-Canadian community's press: the *Canadian Hungarian News*, the *Canadian Hungarian Worker*, and the *Tárogató*. These were the remnants of the plethora of publications launched during the interwar years, particularly in the late 1920's. In 1951 the *Tárogató* also ceased publication, leaving the *News* and the *Worker* as the old Hungarian stock's only press organs. Although facing the prospect of a diminishing readership, these newspapers were to continue publishing for many more years. In time they were joined by a new crop of serials, started and maintained partly by the new immigrants. Between 1949 and 1955 two religious and more than a half dozen secular periodicals were launched. Of the latter only two could be said to have attained prominence and longevity, the small but persevering *Sporthiradó* (Sport News) and *Kanadai Magyarság* (Canadian Hungarians), which became one of the large-circulation weeklies of the 1960's and 1970's. The two religious periodicals, *Új Élet* (New Life) and *Csendes Percek* (literally: Quiet Minutes), also survived. The former was a Reformed publication, the latter was sponsored by the United Church.[31] For some time, the Roman Catholic paper *Szív* (Heart) was also published in Canada.

In addition to the press, Hungarian-Canadian society's larger centres were increasingly served by weekly radio broadcasts lasting usually for half an hour. During the period under discussion such programs seem to have existed for some time at least in Brantford, Calgary, Hamilton, Montreal, and Toronto, and in Tillsonburg, in the tobacco district.[32]

THE REFUGEES

The most important event in the history of Canada's Hungarian community was the Hungarian Revolution of 1956 and the coming of nearly 38,000 refugees to this country. One reason for the revolution's importance is the fact that it received a great deal of attention in Canada. For the first time, a Hungarian event was given extensive coverage in the country's media and became the subject of consideration in the highest councils of government. The explanation for the great impact of this event lies in the political climate of the Cold War, and, in part, in the media's and the public's thirst for news of the unexpected and heroic. The government's response to the Hungarian events of 1956 has been studied in depth, and it is now possible to explain Ottawa's unprecedented magnanimity in the question of the refugees.

Prime Minister St. Laurent's sympathies for the insurrectionists notwithstanding,[33] Canada could do nothing to help the people of Hungary in their struggle for independence. Western intervention in Hungary was regarded as inadvisable for fear of a global war; moreover, even effective diplomatic intervention proved impossible because, by early November, the Western alliance had become hopelessly split over the question of Anglo-French intervention in Egypt. Mainly because of the Suez crisis, the Soviets were allowed to deal with Hungary as they pleased. Not being able to attain their country's independence, many Hungarians felt compelled to achieve their own personal safety by fleeing to the West. So many of them sought refuge in neighbouring Austria that they overtaxed that small country's capacity to provide food and shelter. As the exodus of refugees continued through the fall, the nations of the West came under increasing pressure to admit some refugees for permanent settlement. The country that reacted most energetically to the plight of the refugees in Austria was Canada.[34]

The Canadian government's reaction to the Hungarian refugee problem has to be viewed in the context of Canada's economic and political situation in 1956. The mid-fifties were years of economic growth and high immigration, when admission of refugees could not be regarded as being out of step with economic realities and demographic policies. Moreover, Canada was facing an election year in 1957, which meant that both the government and the opposition parties were anxious to appease national opinion. Not knowing for sure what that opinion was on the refugee problem, at first the government proceeded cautiously. It placed Hungarian refugees in a preferred position with respect to processing for admission. As the weeks passed, it became obvious that this measure did not satisfy the Canadian public. The demand for a more vigorous policy mounted. Several Canadian churches, the opposition parties, and part of the press, including the influential Toronto *Globe and Mail*, called for decisive government action.[35] As a result, at the end of November the federal government announced its decision to proceed with a generous program of refugee admission. The new policy's main feature was free passage for all refugees who wished to settle in Canada and who met the government's admission standards.[36]

While the reactions of the Canadian public and government to the Hungarian events of the autumn of 1956 were being shaped, the Hungarian-Canadian community was experiencing one of the most memorable periods of its history. The revolution brought the group to a moment of heightened emotions and ethnic awareness. Hungarian Canadians reacted to the events in Hungary with vigour and concern everywhere, but probably nowhere so emotionally and energetically as in Toronto, the group's largest centre by 1956.[37]

Toronto's Hungarian Canadians greeted the first news of the events in Hungary with enthusiasm. All routine social and cultural activities were suspended and frenzied work was undertaken in hope of furthering the cause of the revolution. Much of the community's program was directed at focusing national and even international attention on the struggle in Hungary. For this purpose demonstrations were organized, handbills were printed and distributed, a delegation was sent to Ottawa, petitions and proclamations were sent to the United Nations General Assembly, and cables were dispatched to the foremost leaders of the Western world and non-aligned nations. Another aspect of Hungarian-Canadian activity concentrated on protesting Soviet intervention in Hungary. The protest rallies included a motorcade past the Russian embassy in Ottawa.[38]

But action was not confined to demonstrations, petitions, and representations. Steps were taken to collect blood to be sent to Hungary, and abortive preparations were made for the establishment of a volunteer unit to join the freedom fighters in Budapest. Both the call for blood donors and the appeal for volunteers were met by enthusiastic response; but of course neither could influence the outcome of events in Hungary. The former was a generous act with no strategic significance, the latter was a quixotic scheme typical of those emotion-filled days. Naturally, the massive intervention of Soviet troops in Hungary early in November dashed all hopes of effective aid to the freedom fighters.

The Fund-raising Effort

The revolution's collapse brought a change in Hungarian-Canadian activities. The efforts to help Hungary were gradually transformed into drives to help the revolution's refugees. The 1956 relief movement had its origins during the days when the revolution stood triumphant. It seems to have all started with a general appeal to help Hungary. In response to this appeal, and before the start of any fund-raising effort, donations started to pour into the various centres of Hungarian activity. Later, a formal fund-raising drive was launched. In this, Hungarian Canadians and Canadians of all backgrounds collaborated, more than in any of the earlier schemes.[39]

The occasion called for a major fund-raising effort, a truly national campaign. Hungarian Canadians lacked the experience and the institutional structure needed for the purpose. They were also unco-ordinated: in addition to the main fund-raising drive, virtually every church and club had a relief campaign of one sort or another of its own. The organizers were deluged with inquiries, requests, and offers of help and advice from scores of ethnic and civic associations and hundreds of excited individuals, and this did not make matters any easier. But the biggest problem was the lack of clear division between fund-raising and other pro-Hungarian activities. The result was confusion.[40]

After a while the main fund-raising drive, initiated by the HCF, became affiliated with the Canadian Red Cross. Although this organization acted, first and foremost, as a trustee for the funds collected, its workers helped to campaign for money and its officials tried hard to reduce the confusion. Through Red Cross efforts the campaign was reorganized and its aims were redefined. All activities not related to fund-raising were diverted to other Hungarian or Canadian welfare or other organizations. Channels of communications were defined, and experienced Canadian welfare organizations were brought in to handle specific aspects of the campaign. The leadership was also reorganized. Hungarians were replaced by prominent Canadians, many of them women, who in turn could call upon influential Canadian individuals or institutions to help. In the end, close to $900,000 was collected. The campaign's success was not so much the result of work by the fund-raisers as a result of the emotions stirred by the revolution and the plight of the refugees.[41]

The Coming of the Refugees

The mass movement of Hungarian refugees to Canada began after the announcement by the Canadian government, at the end of November, of its generous admission program. To facilitate the movement, Ottawa streamlined existing immigration regulations, arranged for the temporary housing in Britain, France, and the Netherlands of 10,000 refugees wishing to come to Canada, and made arrangements for the transportation of these and thousands of others across the Atlantic. During the first months of 1957, a special "Air Bridge to Canada" or ABC scheme had been initiated by Ottawa to bring regular immigrants to Canada. Over 200 chartered flights brought nearly 17,600 immigrants. The majority were British citizens wishing to settle in Canada, but there were a great many Hungarians among them as well. Two weekly flights from Vienna brought Hungarian refugees only, as did several ships chartered specially for this purpose. The number of refugees resettled in Canada steadily grew. By the end of 1956, 4,167 had reached this country. This figure had more than doubled by the end of January, 1957. And by the end of 1957, over 36,700 refugees had come. Their number grew only very slowly thereafter. The cost to the Canadian taxpayer was in excess of $14 million.[42]

Bringing the refugees to Canada was only the first step in the process of their resettlement. The second step, their initial integration into Canadian life, was a more difficult undertaking. It was accomplished through the joint efforts of Canadian government and welfare agencies on the one hand and the Hungarian-Canadian community on the other. The contribution of each was indispensable to the success of the program.

Among the governments, the federal administration in Ottawa played the most important role. It provided the overall leadership as well as much of the money needed. As Ottawa had no jurisdiction in many aspects of resettlement, it encouraged and financially assisted the various provinces in the task of meeting the needs of the newcomers. For example, the federal government and Ontario worked out a scheme to share the initial cost of housing, clothing, and caring for the health of all refugees who came to Ontario. To implement the arrangement, Queen's Park established reception centres, or lodges, which accommodated refugees until they could obtain jobs and make alternate arrangements for housing. Similar reception centres were established elsewhere in the country, with the largest being in Montreal, Winnipeg, and Abbotsford, British Columbia.[43]

A less visible yet equally important role in the reception of the refugees was played by Hungarian-Canadian society's organizations and members. While the various levels of government concentrated on the administrative and financial aspects of refugee reception, the ethnic community took care of the human aspect. Much of this task was accomplished in an informal and spontaneous manner, as most Hungarian Canadians welcomed the refugees with a mixture of curiosity, awe, and affection. In the process of satisfying their own curiosity and paying their respect to the newcomers, Hungarian Canadians established relationships with the refugees which, for the initial period at least, greatly facilitated the latter's integration into Canadian society.

When the influx of refugees started, Hungarian-Canadian society once again swung into action with zeal similar to that which had been attained during the first days of the revolution. Welcoming committees were established, reception centres were set up, car-pools were organized to transport people from airports; food, clothing, and temporary shelter were provided to those newcomers who were not lodged in a government hostel. The refugees were helped in the purchase of furniture and in the finding of apartments and jobs. Many Hungarian Canadians took newcomers into their homes and treated them as guests until they could find alternate accommodation for themselves. Many of the people treated in this manner were relations or friends of the hosts, but often complete

206

strangers received the same magnanimous treatment.[44] It has been suggested that the refugees were received as if they had all been kinsfolk joining their Canadian relatives.[45]

Much of the work of helping the refugees was done by the Hungarian-Canadian churches. Their buildings became used as reception centres, meeting halls, placement offices, language training centres, or simply as drop-in centres for homesick newcomers. The work was done by untiring priests, ministers, sisters, and volunteer workers. In Toronto, the St. Elizabeth of Hungary church and hall was a beehive of activity for months, but the other churches were also very active catering to the needs of their followers. In any case, religious differences did not seem to have mattered much, as the newcomers tended to turn to wherever they received the most sympathy as well as friendly and effective help. It should be added that the churches' work did not end when the new arrivals found jobs and exchanged their temporary quarters for apartments of their own. Counselling, language training, and other welfare work continued, as did public relations with Canadian authorities conducted on behalf of those newcomers who, often in ignorance of Canadian customs and laws, got into trouble with the police.[46]

It is difficult to assess the value of this type of help extended to the new arrivals by the ethnic community. It was Hungarian Canadians who made the Canadian welcome to the refugees meaningful. The fact that the bewildered newcomers were greeted by friendly and helpful co-nationals must have had a reassuring effect on them, as did the fact that they could receive consolation and encouragement in a familiar atmosphere and in their own language. In many ways, then, the participation of the Hungarian-Canadian community in the resettlement of the refugees cushioned the shock that awaits a newcomer in the receiving country. It was a service that Canadian governments and welfare agencies by themselves could not have performed with similar facility.[47]

The Hungarian refugees who came to Canada were mostly young people. Nearly half of them were under the age of twenty-nine. Only about 30 per cent of them were over forty-five years of age. There was an imbalance in their sex distribution as well: men outnumbered women almost three to two.[48] About two-thirds of the refugees were Roman Catholics. The remainder was made up of members of various Protestant denominations and Jews.[49]

From the Canadian point of view, age, sex, and religious affiliation mattered less than the newcomers' occupational affiliation. In this regard many segments of Canadian society had certain expectations. Some of Canada's industrial and transportation companies hoped that the refugees would meet their needs for unskilled labourers. Other Canadians expected the newcomers to increase the supply of domestic servants. Those who cherished these hopes were disappointed, as the mass of refugees was made up mainly of semi-skilled and skilled workers, professional people, and a large number of students.[50] Indeed, so many

Hungarian students came to Canada in the wake of 1956 that they were regarded as a special class of refugees, and one group of them received very special treatment.

The Sopron Foresters

The number of Hungarian university students who arrived in Canada by the opening of the academic year in 1957 has been estimated at close to 1,000.[51] A part of this student population dispersed to various parts of the country either to continue their studies or to obtain employment. Over 100 engineering students enrolled at the University of Toronto. Smaller groups entered other universities. Most of them did so with government assistance, but on the same academic terms as Canadian students. The exception to this rule was a group of 200 students of the Sopron School of Forestry. This group, along with twenty-nine of their professors, had come to Canada together and were incorporated into the University of British Columbia as a special division of the UBC Forestry Faculty.[52] Canada suddenly acquired a Hungarian institution of higher learning. It was a unique experiment in the annals of Canadian immigration history.

After their flight from Hungary, the Sopron students and faculty made an attempt to reconvene and re-establish their institution under Austrian auspices. Although government officials in Vienna were sympathetic to the plan, they did not sanction it for fear of Soviet retaliation for what might be construed as a violation of Austrian neutrality. Accordingly, the possibility of relocating in another country was explored. After negotiations with the Minister of Immigration, the Hon. John W. Pickersgill, and other Canadian representatives, a decision was reached to move the school to British Columbia. Soon, most of the school's students, accompanied by many of their professors and their dependents, embarked on a voyage to Canada. After arrival, they travelled in a special train from Saint John to Abbotsford, stopping for enthusiastic receptions on the way in every large city. The group spent the rest of the academic year in Powell River, B.C., learning English and familiarizing themselves with Canadian forestry practices.[53] In September, 1957, the Sopron School resumed its functioning at the University of British Columbia. It retained a great deal of autonomy, including the use of Hungarian as the language of instruction. The school's senior class graduated in the spring of 1958, and the UBC Sopron School of Forestry closed its gates in 1961 when the last of its students received their diplomas. In the words of Dr. N.A.M. MacKenzie, then president of the University of British Columbia, the experiment "was successful beyond the expectations or imagination of any of us."[54]

Problems in Adjustment

Starting a new life in Canada was not easy for the majority of Hungarian refugees. Innumerable problems were encountered by them. Some of these were the same as those faced by every Hungarian immigrant to Canada: the difficulties of learning a new language and adjusting to a different social, cultural, and economic environment. Other problems were peculiar to the refugees. The 56-ers had become accustomed to a social system very different from Canada's. Communist Hungary was a welfare state in which the individual's dependence on the state was deliberately fostered, and certain elements of society, such as working-class youths and college students, were purposely pampered. Hungarian students, for example, were not expected to work during the summers, let alone perform menial tasks unrelated to their fields of study. When financial circumstances forced them to do so in Canada, they were annoyed.[55]

True, no Hungarian newcomers to Canada had ever received such a warm welcome and so much government assistance as had the 56-ers. It might be said that, compared to the previous waves of immigrants, they had it easy. But their quick admission and friendly reception probably caused some problems. The pre-1945 immigrants presumably had a chance to agonize over their decision to leave Hungary before their departure. The post-war arrivals had chafed for years in refugee camps and had had a chance to work out the psychological trauma of emigration before coming to Canada. For many of them, immigration must have been a relief from the miserable life in camps. The 56-ers, in contrast, came before they could recover from the shock caused by the dramatic events that had changed their lives. In addition, the type of reception extended to them upon arrival in Canada probably aroused undue expectation in them with regard to their future prospects. For the refugees, the trauma that accompanies leaving one's native land and the frustrations caused by the difficulties of integration tended to come not during and immediately after arrival, but months or even years later.[56]

Intellectuals, professional men, and students faced difficulties in addition to those caused by a sudden, unplanned transfer to a new cultural environment and a different social system. They had problems stemming from the host country's differing professional standards and practices. The case of the Soproners amply illustrates this point. Forestry practices in Hungary and Canada greatly differed. Hungarian silviculture was very intensive – it emphasized forest preservation and reforestation. In Canada, extensive forestry was practised. Logging was highly mechanized, while reforestation technology was primitive. In Hungary logging operations were very limited and modern logging machinery was virtually non-existent. There were differences in the training of foresters as well. On Canada's West Coast, a forest engineer was essentially a civil engineer working in the forest. His Hungarian counterpart was a "kind of industrial engineer taking care of . . . engineering problems inherent in (the) development of forests."[57] These differences hindered the professional acclimatization of Hungarian foresters and also led to crises regarding their accreditation.[58] With the passage of time these problems were overcome, and most members of the Sopron group successfully integrated into both their profession and Canadian society.[59]

Impact on Hungarian-Canadian Society

The most obvious impact that the influx of refugees had on Hungarian-Canadian society was demographic. Never before did so many Hungarians come to Canada in such a short time. The result was a substantial growth in most Hungarian-Canadian centres, as well as the establishment of a few new Hungarian-Canadian communities. Where the refugees dispersed is revealed by the 1961 census. It recorded 34,396 Magyar-speaking individuals who had come to Canada between 1956 and 1961. The vast majority of these, slightly more than 90 per cent, had settled in Canada's urban centres.[60] As far as provincial distribution was concerned, Ontario led the way. It had received nearly half (47 per cent) of the newcomers. Quebec followed with nearly 23 per cent, British Columbia with 12, and Alberta with about 9 per cent. Manitoba received only about 2,000 of the refugees, while Saskatchewan got less than half that number. Once again, all but a few of the newcomers avoided the Maritimes.[61]

As might be suspected, the metropolitan area that experienced the largest influx of refugees was Toronto. Nearly 8,700 of them had settled in that city by 1961. A close second was Montreal with slightly more than 7,100. Vancouver came third with about 2,200 and Winnipeg fourth with 1,740. These were followed by Calgary (1,436), Hamilton (1,346), Edmonton (942), and Ottawa (706).[62] For most of these cities' Hungarian-Canadian communities, the increase meant the doubling, tripling, or even quadrupling of the local immigrant Hungarian population.[63] The influx had also led to the birth of Hungarian communities in cities where virtually none had existed before. The best example is Ottawa, but there are a few others as well.[64]

A less tangible and much less documentable impact that the refugees had on Hungarian-Canadian society was the socio-political one. The influx of refugees began affecting Hungarian-Canadian society's social development and politics already during the winter of 1956-57. No studies have been published on this process, as indeed it might be too early to examine it from a historical point of view. The most obvious manifestations of the refugees' impact were the new Hungarian-Canadian institutions which sprang up in the wake of the events of 1956.

The influx of both the post-World War I and World War II immigrants had resulted in the establishment of many new organizations. It was not very different with the 1956 refugees. Like their 1945 predecessors, the 56-ers were internationally organized; but they had fewer organizations. Only one major refugee political organization has survived to this day in Canada: the Freedom Fighters Federation of Canada, a member of the World Federation of Freedom Fighters.[65] Various student organizations had functioned for many years both within and out-

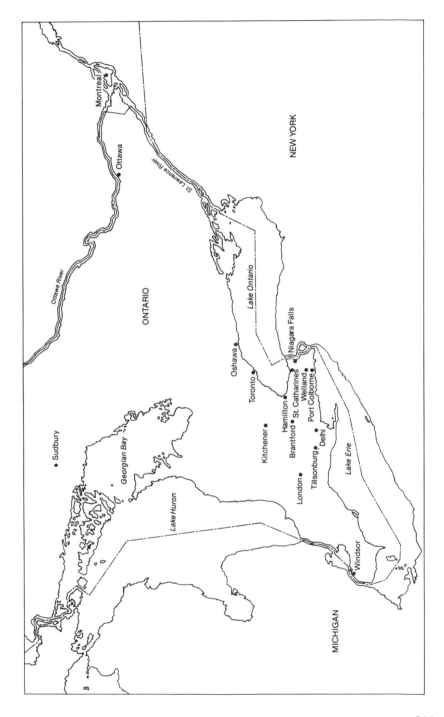

side of the Federation of Hungarian University and College Students, which became an exile organization after 1956. But as refugee students graduated, these organizations gradually became mere social clubs or disappeared altogether.[66]

Despite their roots in a political uprising and struggle, the refugees contributed relatively little to that proliferation of Hungarian-Canadian political organizations that had started around 1950. Perhaps by 1956 there was only very limited need for new political associations, as there were a great number and variety of them in existence. There was a need for additional cultural and professional groupings, and it was precisely this need that the refugees helped to fill.

The years after 1956 saw the establishment of cultural groups such as choirs, dance ensembles, and theatre groups. This development was not new in Hungarian-Canadian history, but the standards achieved constituted a new departure. While there may not have been much difference in the dedication with which many Hungarian Canadians participated in these undertakings before and after 1956, the expertise of the directors, choir masters, conductors, and choreographers elevated the new groups' standards to a semi- or even professional level.[67] In smaller centres, where specialization was not warranted by numbers, Hungarian cultural associations took on a more general form and embarked on more variegated types of activities.[68]

Another type of post-1956 Hungarian-Canadian organization was the association of various groups of Hungarian professional men and women. Writers, teachers, engineers, foresters, and agronomists established their societies with differing success and longevity. The most active of these seem to be the Hungarian Canadian Engineers' Association and the Hungarian Canadian Authors' Association. Both have members in many Canadian cities.[69]

The coming of the refugees also had a substantial effect on Hungarian-Canadian society's press. Like the arrival of the immigrants of the late 1920's, and those of the post-World War II era, the influx of the 56-ers sparked a rapid expansion of publishing activities. The growth took on many different forms. *Canadian Hungarians*, for example, switched from weekly to semi-weekly frequency. Another newspaper, *Magyar Élet* (Hungarian Life), transferred its operations from Buenos Aires to Toronto. The competition became even keener when still other papers appeared on the market. Some, like *Egységes Magyarság* (United Hungarians), tried to serve a particular region, in this case southern Ontario's Niagara Peninsula. Others appealed to a certain sub-group within Hungarian-Canadian society. The bi-weekly *Menorah*, for example, was started to serve Canada's greatly increased Hungarian Jewish community. Still other serials attempted to capitalize on the interest in social events, literature, and the arts. In Ontario alone, at least six Hungarian serial publications saw the light of day between 1957 and 1961. Only a few of them proved viable undertakings.[70]

Part of the reason for this sudden flowering of Hungarian-Canadian society's press was the dedication and determination of a handful of newcomers who wanted to make their voices heard among Hungarians in Canada and elsewhere. But the more important reason was the sheer growth in the Hungarian-Canadian community's size. The same growth that resulted in the launching of highly specialized undertakings in cultural life also created a larger market for the printed word. This kind of effect was evident in many walks of Hungarian-Canadian life. The influx of thousands of newcomers into the group's larger centres created conditions in which not only the ethnic organizations and press could prosper, but churches could fill their pews and schools increase their enrolments. With the coming of two large waves of Hungarian immigrants within a single decade, with the arrival among Hungarian Canadians of persons with rich and diverse educational and professional backgrounds, the group's prospects for the future looked better than ever before. At the end of the 1950's it seemed that Hungarian-Canadian society was on the threshold of a golden age.

NOTES

1. The provisions of the government's policy of admitting displaced persons in certain occupational categories are outlined in the *Report of the Department of Labour for the Fiscal Year Ending March 31, 1948* (Ottawa, 1949), pp. 59-61. For a general treatment of Ottawa's attitudes to the immigration of post-war refugees, see Dirks, *Canada's Refugee Policy*, Chapter 7.

2. *Report of the Department of Citizenship and Immigration for the Fiscal Year Ended March 31, 1951* (Ottawa, 1951), Table 7, pp. 36ff. *Report of the Department of Citizenship and Immigration for the Fiscal Year Ended March 31, 1953* (Ottawa, 1953), Table 2, p. 27.

3. *Report of the Department of Citizenship and Immigration* (1951), Table 10, pp. 42ff.

   In connection with the composition of this immigration of Hungarian-born persons it should be mentioned that the group was ethnically not homogeneous. Only about 71 per cent of the arrivals were Magyars; the rest are classified in the statistics as "Hebrew," "German," and a sprinkling of Czechs, Poles, and Yugoslavs. (*Ibid.*, Table 8, pp. 38ff.)

4. *Ibid.*, Table 10, pp. 42ff.

5. *Census of Canada*, 1951, II, Table 60.

6. *Ibid.*, Table 61.

7. Fehér, "Adatok," p. 86. For a report on the help extended to newcomers in other centres, such as Calgary and Winnipeg, see *KMU*, 5 October 1948.

8. *Ibid.* Also, interview with Sister Mary. Even the differing habits of the

two groups caused some friction. One Hungarian-Canadian minister has related to the author that to the old-time members of his congregation he had always been the "Reverend" and "Sir," even after years of close co-operation. To the newly arrived Hungarians, however, he soon became "Charlie." The implied intimacy was greatly resented by the old-timers. (Steinmetz interview.)

9. Confidential Research and Analysis Report on Emigré Hungarian Organizations and Leaders, 22 May 1951, Records of the U.S. Department of State, National Archives of the United States, Washington, D.C. The following is based on this report and on information provided to me by Miklós Korponay and Tivadar Borsi, both of Toronto.

10. *Ibid.*

11. Among the priests and ministers who came to Canada during the late 1940's and early 1950's were several Jesuit fathers who later played important roles in the life of Hungarian-Canadian parishes in Ontario and elsewhere. The Greek Catholic community, most of the time without a single priest before 1948, received three refugee priests between 1949 and 1953. A handful of newly arrived intellectuals, following in the tradition of Hoffmann and Czakó, became ministers of the United Church of Canada after their arrival. For further details, see *50 Years: St. Elizabeth of Hungary Church,* p. 13; Beskyd, *In the Vineyard of Christ: Yearbook of the Eparchy of Toronto,* pp. 502-4, 507-9; *The United Church of Canada Year Book, 1952,* p. 145; and Borsay, "Origins of the Tobacco District Hungarian Presbyterian Church," p. 1.

12. *KMU,* 22 April 1949; *Kanadai Magyarság (KM),* 5 July 1952, 19 September 1953, 7 May 1955, 14 July 1956. Elsewhere, church buildings were remodelled or additions were built. Naturally, in some of the old centres of Hungarian-Canadian life, the progress in organized religious life had little or nothing to do with the arrival of newcomers. The early 1950's also saw a resurgence of Hungarian Jewish religious life in Canada. Its focal point seems to have been Toronto, where a congregation of Jewish immigrants was established. Nevertheless, the great expansion in Hungarian Jewish religious activity came after the arrival of the 1956 refugees and the establishment of still other congregations for Hungarian-speaking members of Canada's Jewish community. (Information from Mr. George Egri.)

13. Beskyd, *In the Vineyard of Christ,* pp. 504ff.

14. The Independent Mutual Benefit Federation continued to increase its membership throughout the 1950's, but it seems that some of its expanding branches were non-Hungarian and that many of its Hungarian chapters were recruiting non-Hungarians to expand their membership. (*Az Uttörö,* 26 June 1958.)

15. Interview with Kertész and Jakus.

16. *KMU,* 8 May 1951 and 2 January 1959.

17. *KMU*, 27 February 1954.
18. In 1949 the Hungarian House launched the Toronto Hungarian Sport Club and sponsored its activities for a year, after which the club became independent. The house also gave help to newcomers and had a fund for its own members to help them with funeral expenses in case of death. (*KMU*, 24 September and 1 October 1955.) For some information on the activities of other, similar associations, see *KM*, 25 December 1954. At least two Hungarian communities, those in Welland and Delhi, had "houses" larger than Toronto's.
19. In 1954 the Hungarian Social Club purchased a farm on the St. Lawrence River and used it as a resort. The following year about 2,000 Hungarians visited the ground, according to figures provided by the club. *KM*, 29 October 1955, 11 August 1956; also Fehér, *Montreáli,* p. 68.
20. Kellner, "Hungarian Participation in Canadian Culture," pp. 57ff. Private information from Dr. Miklós Mattyasovszky Zsolnay of Montreal.
21. *1,000 Years of Hungarian Christianity,* p. [33]. *KM*, 14 February 1953.
22. Gyula Torzsay-Bíber, "Magyar Helikon Társaság huszonhárom évének története" [Twenty-three Years' History of the Hungarian Helicon Society], draft of an essay kindly put at my disposal by Dr. Torzsay-Bíber. For another view of the Helicon's early work see Kellner, "Hungarian Participation," pp. 54ff. Originally, the Helicon was to be a part of the emigration's network of international organizations. It was to be the "cultural front" for the supporters of the exiled Hungarian politician Tibor Eckhardt. But of the several Helicon societies established in North America, only Toronto's proved viable. In time, it became independent of all international emigré organizations. (Information from Messrs. Borsi and Korponay.)
23. Interview with Korponay.
24. *1,000 Years,* p. 30; Kellner, "Hungarian Participation," pp. 59ff.
25. *KMU*, 24 February 1948.
26. Fehér, "Adatok," p. 4.
27. *Ibid.* Cf. draft of the notice of the convention, *CHN* Records, Box 30a. The notice was signed by six prominent persons: two Catholic priests, two Protestant ministers, and two members of the intelligentsia (Pál Sántha, István Békesi, Jenö Ruzsa, Kálmán Tóth, Béla Böszörményi Nagy, and Tivadar Borsi). Böszörményi Nagy, who became the HCF's regular president, soon left Canada to take up an academic post in the U.S. Borsi became the HCF's general secretary, adding that post to a similar one he held in the Helicon Society. (Private information from Borsi and Korponay.)
28. In the newly elected HCF, executive members of the "old stock" outnumbered newcomers four to three. In the federation's supreme organ, the Presidential Council, the ratio was almost three to one. Further-

215

more, 90 per cent of the organizations that had joined the HCF by May, 1952, were those of the old immigrants. (Memoranda, dated 13 and 15 May 1952, *CHN* Records, Box 30a.)

29. A more precise breakdown of the HCF's member organizations in 1952 is as follows: Catholic parishes, sixteen; Protestant congregations, nine; clubs, thirty-six; institutions, three. The Catholic parishes accounted for most members, nearly 8,000 people. (Undated memorandum, *CHN* Records, Box 30a.)

30. Like its 1928 predecessor, the HCF lacked a press organ of its own. But it had the support of the Winnipeg-based *News*, which made the establishment of a new newspaper unnecessary and, indeed, not advisable. (Memorandum, 13 May 1952, *CHN* Records, Box 30a.)

31. Gusztáv Nemes, "Kanadai Magyar Újság" [Canadian Hungarian News], ms, kindly put at my disposal by Mr. Nemes. The two religious journals and one of the lay periodicals were printed by Mr. Nemes's printing office. *Magyar Élet* [Hungarian Life], one of the bulkiest weeklies in recent years, was also started in the period under discussion here, but did not move to Canada until later.

32. *KMU*, 16 September 1948 and 14 December 1954; *KM*, 2 February 1952, 4 April and 2 May 1953, 26 March and 9 July 1955.

33. Dale C. Thomson, *Louis St. Laurent: Canadian* (Toronto, 1967), p. 482.

34. Dirks, *Canada's Refugee Policy,* pp. 191ff.

35. *Ibid.,* pp. 194-6. It is interesting that the Ontario government was ready to act – to charter ships and aircraft to bring over Hungarian refugees – when criticism of the scheme in rural Ontario and positive action on the matter in Ottawa made involvement by Ontario unwise and unnecessary. (*Ibid.,* pp. 198ff.)

36. *Ibid.,* pp. 198ff.

37. Fortunately, there is a fairly detailed account of events in this city during the fall and early winter of 1956. See Audrey Wipper, "A Study of the Reactions of Hungarian Canadians to the Hungarian Crisis with Special Emphasis on Activities in the Toronto Region," a Defence Research Board study prepared for the Department of Citizenship and Immigration, ms (1958). Wipper first was a volunteer worker for the Hungarian relief drive and later worked at a refugee reception centre.

38. *Ibid.,* pp. 13-15 and Chapters 3-6.

39. While on the whole sympathetic to the plight and cause of the freedom fighters, most Canadians were reluctant to see their country involved in a quarrel or war with the Soviet Union over Hungary. But when it came to helping refugees, Canadians were ready to collaborate with all factions of Hungarian-Canadian society. (*Ibid.,* pp. 17ff.)

40. *Ibid.,* pp. 67-82.

41. *Ibid.,* pp. 83-94. Information from Dr. György Nagy. According to Dr. Nagy, most of the donations came during the first few weeks of the fund-raising drive.

42. Dirks, *Canada's Refugee Policy,* pp. 199-202. In March, 1960, the official government tally of Hungarian refugee arrivals stood at 37,727. (Memorandum, 9 March 1960, PAC, Devlin Papers, Canadian National Railway Records, vol. 5723.) For statistics on Hungarian arrivals between 1956 and 1959, see the *Report of the Department of Citizenship and Immigration, 1959-60,* pp. 30ff.

43. Dirks, *Canada's Refugee Policy,* pp. 204-8. Dirks concentrates on the reception of the refugees in Ontario. Details regarding their reception in Manitoba are given in a memorandum by A.M. Larson, 30 May 1957, PAC, Devlin Papers, CNR Records, vol. 5687. For some information on the situation in Quebec, see Fehér, *Montreáli,* pp. 152ff. On British Columbia, see Norris, *Strangers Entertained: A History of the Ethnic Groups of British Columbia,* p. 169.

44. Wipper, "Reactions of Hungarian Canadians," pp. 95-100. *KM* periodic report on the efforts to help the refugees, November and December 1956. The author and his family were the first refugees to arrive in Welland, Ontario, and were accorded a truly generous welcome by the local Hungarian-Canadian community.

45. Wipper, "Reactions of Hungarian Canadians," p. 99.

46. Interviews with Sister Mary and with the late László Kálmán; Fehér, *Montreáli,* p. 102. Wipper, "Reactions of Hungarian Canadians," pp. 95-8. Hungarian refugees travelling on railways are known to have pulled the emergency brakes in washrooms, mistaking them for handles of water tanks which, in Hungarian residential water closets, are located near the ceiling. CNR officials found it necessary to affix the sign *"vészfék"* on emergency brakes in toilets. (PAC, Devlin Papers, CNR Records, Vol. 5687.) This was just one example of Hungarians committing unlawful acts in complete ignorance of Canadian practices.

47. One exception seems to have been the International Institute in Toronto, which provided effective help to a great many refugees. Information from Dr. György Nagy.

48. Dirks, *Canada's Refugee Policy,* p. 203; *Census of Canada,* 1961, I, Part 3, Table 125.

49. Dirks, *Canada's Refugee Policy,* p. 203. According to Dirks' source, one-fifth of the refugees were Jewish, which, if correct, would make them the second largest religious group among the refugees. Indeed, census statistics indicate a tenfold growth in the Hungarian-Canadian Jewish community between 1951 and 1961. (*Census of Canada,* 1951, II, Table 34; *Census of Canada,* 1961, I, Part 3, Table 110.)

50. Dirks, *Canada's Refugee Policy,* pp. 203ff.

51. Carlos E. Kruytbosch, "Flight and Resettlement of the Sopron Forestry Faculty: A study in group integration and disintegration" (M.A. thesis, University of British Columbia, 1958), p. 194, n. 10.

52. Laszlo Adamovich and Oszkar Sziklai, *Foresters in Exile: The Sopron Forestry School in Canada* (Vancouver, 1970), p. 21. For a briefer English language account, see Kalman J. Roller, "Accomplishments of

217

Sopron Foresters After Ten Years in Canada," *The Forestry Chronicle*, 45, 1 (February, 1969), pp. 1-4. Professor Roller has also written a much more detailed history of the Sopron story in Hungarian, which is printed in the Soproners' journal: *Kapocs* (Link), II, 2 (August, 1966).

53.   Adamovich and Sziklai, *Foresters in Exile*, pp. 13-18. Dirks, *Canada's Refugee Policy*, pp. 204ff. At about the same time seventy-two students of the Sopron School of Mining and Engineering arrived in Toronto in hope of gaining collective admission to the University of Toronto. Many of them were admitted for the following academic year, as individuals and not as a group. (*KM*, 3 January 1957; Dirks, *Canada's Refugee Policy*, pp. 205ff.)

54.   N.A.M. MacKenzie, in his foreword to Adamovich and Sziklai, *Foresters in Exile*, p. IX.

55.   Adamovich and Sziklai, *Foresters in Exile*, p. 19.

56.   Two published studies deal with the integration of Hungarian refugees in Canada: E.K. Koranyi, A. Kerenyi, and G.J. Sarwer-Foner, "On Adaptive Difficulties of Some Hungarian Immigrants: A Socio-psychiatric Study," *Medical Services Journal*, XIV, 6 (June, 1958), pp. 383-405; and T. Cnossen, "Integration of Refugees: Some Observations on the Hungarian in Canada," Research Group for European Migration Problems *Bulletin*, Supplement 7 (June, 1964), pp. 3-23. Both studies stress that many of the refugees had assumed that "they had come to a rich and wealthy country which would take care of them, give them a job, tell them what to do, house them, feed them and make all decisions for them." (Koranyi *et al.*, p. 392; also quoted in Cnossen, p. 13.) The first study listed offers much useful data on the refugees' psychic and psychiatric problems. Most of these seem to have occurred in patients who had gone through particularly traumatic experiences (imprisonment, torture, the execution of loved ones, etc.), or who had a record of psychiatric disorders. The trauma of shock and psychiatric problems often resurfaced because of the "stress that immigration presented" and "adaptive problems." The adaptive problems of the Soproners are discussed in Kruytbosch, "Flight and Resettlement," and in Larry A. Rotenberg, "The Sopron Experiment: A Study of the Psychiatric Aspects of Migration" (University of British Columbia Doctor of Medicine thesis, 1962).

57.   Adamovich and Sziklai, *Foresters in Exile*, pp. 23-5; cf. Roller in *Kapocs*.

58.   The Soproners were not granted the equivalent of a UBC engineering degree but only a B.Sc. in Forestry, a degree they considered inferior to the Sopron forestry degree. They also had trouble gaining accreditation from the B.C. Professional Forest Engineers' Association. It is interesting to note that since the early 1960's, North American forestry practices have become more intensive, and that a number of new forestry schools have developed curricula similar to that of the Sopron School. (Adamovich and Sziklai, *Foresters in Exile*, p. 25.)

59. The Sopron group's achievements are evaluated and outlined in the works of Roller and Adamovich and Sziklai.

60. *Census of Canada*, 1961, I, Part 3, Table 125. The discrepancy between this and the official Department of Immigration and Citizenship figures can be explained by a combination of factors: some refugees, especially those who had left without their families, had returned to Hungary; some may have died since 1956; a few may have left Canada for destinations other than Hungary; and there may be errors in the official statistics.

61. *Ibid.,* Table 126.

62. *Ibid.,* Table 127.

63. The following are percentage increases in the immigrant Hungarian population of the largest Hungarian-Canadian centres between 1956 and 1961:

Toronto	167%
Montreal	120%
Hamilton	57%
Vancouver	237%
Calgary	135%
Winnipeg	330%

(Calculations based on figures provided in *ibid.*)

64. Such as Victoria, B.C., and Kingston, Ontario. The census also recorded the appearance for the first time of several scores of Hungarians in such places as Halifax, Quebec City, and the Yukon Territory.

65. *1,000 Years of Hungarian Christianity*, p. 26.

66. During the mid-1960's the author was an active member of the University of Toronto's Hungarian Students' Association. By 1966 this club was the only Canadian organization of its kind to maintain links with the federation of (exile) Hungarian students. The Toronto group ceased functioning a few years later. A few very active Hungarian youth clubs continue functioning in Canada, but they are quite unlike the clubs that had been sustained by the original 56-ers.

67. Two outstanding examples seem to be the Kodály Choir and the Hungarian Theatre, both of Toronto. The former developed into a large ensemble with choir, orchestra, and dance group, while the latter has delighted Hungarian audiences with Hungarian plays and operettas for many years.

68. The organization that comes to mind is the Hungarian Literary Society of Winnipeg, which led a very active social and cultural life through the 1960's and 1970's. (Information from Mr. E. Haraszty and Dr. Kristof, both former members of the society's executive.)

69. *KM*, 23 April and 9 July 1958. Private information from John Miska and Gyula Bethlendy, officers of the authors' and engineers' associations respectively.

70. McLaren, *Ontario Ethno-Cultural Newspapers,* pp. 81-9. *KM*, 22 December 1956, 26 March 1958, 31 January 1959.

EIGHT

A Century of Evolution: Conclusions

N. F. Dreisziger

In 1960 Hungarian settlement in Canada was seventy-five years old. Since the arrival of the first Hungarian immigrants on the Prairies, Canada had grown from a young, sparsely populated country into a populous and prosperous nation. During the same time, Hungary had undergone several major political and social transformations that markedly affected the lifestyles and attitudes of the successive waves of Magyar emigrants. During this three-quarters of a century the Hungarian-Canadian ethnic group had grown from small rural settlements to a sizable minority whose members could be found in all walks of life in many parts of Canada.

Internal Migrations and Demographic Changes

The three main themes of the Hungarian-Canadian group's demographic evolution have been growth, dispersal, and increasing urbanization. Growth came mainly as a result of immigration, and it took place in great spurts. The vast majority of Hungarian immigrants to Canada still living today arrived during either the 1920's or the 1950's. Natural population growth also took place at an uneven pace. It accelerated when the members of a particular immigrant stream reached the child-rearing age. The movement from the countryside to the cities was also rather erratic. Its rate was influenced by economic conditions in Canada and the degree of propensity among newcomers to prefer life in the cities. The urbanization of Hungarian Canadians took place mainly in the 1920's and 1950's, periods of economic expansion in Canada and of high immigration from Hungary.

The processes of growth and settlement in urban areas took place simultaneously with a steady dispersal of Hungarians throughout much of Canada. Each of Canada's decennial censuses has noted the appearance of Hungarians in more and more census districts; and each wave of Hungarian immigrants resulted in the emergence of clusters of Magyar residents in cities or regions hitherto avoided by them. The residential dispersal of Hungarian Canadians was actually a process of regrouping – concentrations of Hungarians dwindled in some parts of the country and new concentrations emerged in others. The most dramatic example of such residential transformation has been the shifting positions of Saskatchewan and Ontario as places of Hungarian concentration in Canada. In 1921 the former province was the home of two-thirds of all Hungarian Canadians, while the latter had only 11 per cent of them. Forty years later, Saskatchewan's Hungarian-Canadian population made up only 13 per cent of the Canadian total, while Ontario's had grown to 47 per cent.[1]

Demographic Trends since 1960

The 1950's witnessed some of the most striking changes in the Hungarian group's demographic development. Between the censuses of 1951 and 1961, Canada's Hungarian population increased by 65,760 souls, representing a 109 per cent growth. Never before had the group increased so much in the course of a single decade. Slightly more than a third of the increase was due to natural population growth. The fact was that the Hungarian group had experienced another "baby boom" during this eventful decade, as the children of the interwar immigrants entered the child-bearing age and recent arrivals established families.[2]

The growth experienced in the 1950's did not continue much beyond 1961. From that year to the next census in 1971, the Hungarian group increased by only 5,670 people, representing a mere 4.5 per cent growth rate.[3] A drastic decline in immigration and fertility and, presumably, an increased death rate combined to slow down the group's numerical growth appreciably. It is unlikely that the 1981 census results will reveal a changed situation. As immigration from Hungary continues to be confined to a trickle, and as more and more of the immigrants of the 1920's die and those of the 1950's reach old age, growth in the Hungarian population will be minimal. But the 1980's may witness another "baby boom" when the children born in the 1950's will be establishing families.

Regarding the geographic distribution of Hungarian Canadians, the post-1960 decades have seen the continuation of earlier trends. One of these is increasing concentration in central Canada. In 1951 53 per cent of Hungarian Canadians already lived in Ontario and Quebec. By 1961 this figure had increased to almost 60 per cent. Particularly impressive were the gains made by Ontario. By the time of the 1971 census, that province was the home of 49.8 per cent of Hungarian Canadians.[4] A corollary to the growing population shift to central Canada is the decline of the Prairie Provinces' combined Hungarian population. In 1951 Manitoba, Saskatchewan, and Alberta served as the home to 37.4 per cent of Hungarian Canadians. By 1961 this figure had declined to 29.2 per cent, and by 1971, to 26.9 per cent. Of the three Prairie Provinces, only Alberta experienced a growth in Hungarian population in recent decades. Further west, British Columbia attracted more and more

221

Magyars, while in the East, Quebec's Hungarian population declined quite sharply during the 1960's. As a result, Quebec slid from being the province with the third largest Hungarian population to fifth position.[5]

As far as urbanization is concerned, the post-1960 period has brought no departure from the patterns established very early in the Hungarian-Canadian group's history. The general trend toward city life was no doubt greatly accentuated by the influx in the 1950's of semi-skilled and skilled workers, professionals, and intellectuals, who were essentially city dwellers. As a result, the Hungarian-Canadian urbanization ratio leaped from 55 per cent in 1951 to nearly 75 per cent ten years later. By 1971, this figure had climbed to 80.8 per cent.[6] Barring cataclysmic changes in the economic or social development of Canada, the trend among Hungarian Canadians toward increased urbanization can be expected to continue in the decades ahead.

Socio-cultural Change

Vast changes have taken place in Hungarian-Canadian social and cultural characteristics in the nearly one hundred years since the establishment of the first Hungarian colonies. To a large extent, these changes were the consequences of the radical social and political transformations that occurred in Hungary. It is no great exaggeration to say that with every wave of immigrants a very different type of Hungarian came to Canada. The settlers of the pre-1914 era were predominantly simple peasants. The post-World War I immigrants, while officially "agriculturalists," were in fact a group with much more diverse social, political, and even cultural backgrounds. The displaced persons of the Cold War era contained an unusually large contingent of middle- and even upper-class people, while the 1956 refugees consisted of the various elements in Hungary's newly forged socialist society. Each of these immigrant streams brought with it different value systems, attitudes, and ideologies.

Naturally, the host country's changing environment also had an important impact on Hungarian-Canadian society. The diversification of Canada's economy, the growth of her manufacturing and service industries, the improvement of transportation and communications, the rise in living standards, the advent of the welfare state, the expansion of the public education system, the increased influence of the media, especially radio and television: all have had far-reaching effects on the lifestyles, culture, and community life of Hungarian Canadians. The transformation of Canada's economy facilitated the dispersal of Hungarians, and in many cases made it necessary. As farming became more and more mechanized, many Hungarians were forced to leave the Prairies for other parts of the country. At the same time, new arrivals from Hungary could not settle in or near existing Hungarian colonies but had to take up residence in distant parts of the country. Successive crises of the economy forced many Hungarian Canadians to take up roots repeatedly and try their luck in other parts of the country. This process inevitably led to the weakening of kinship ties, the severance of friendships, and the loss of connection with ethnic institutions. Under such conditions the maintenance of ethnic values and traditions became difficult, and their transmittance to the next generation next to impossible. The coming of an era of greater economic prosperity during and after the Second World War also posed threats to the maintenance of ethnic traditions. The consequent social stratification among immigrants tended to disrupt the cohesion of their groupings and organizations. It even helped the disintegration of their residential concentrations: more successful families left the ghettos and settled in more affluent neighbourhoods.

Technological change also had far-reaching effects and facilitated the dispersal of Hungarian Canadians. Particularly important seems to have been the advent of the automobile. Before its widespread availability, Hungarian immigrants to Canada's cities tended to settle near their ethnic church and shopping district. Their new mobility enabled them to select their places of residence on the basis of other considerations. Not surprisingly, many significant residential concentrations of Hungarians disappeared in the course of the last four decades. Another technological achievement of our age, television, has probably had an equally damaging effect on Hungarian ethnic life. Being the medium which, together with the radio, takes the culture of the North American host society into the home, it has the potential of destroying the last sanctuary of ethnic culture.

The assimilative impact of a non-Hungarian neighbourhood and the audio-visual media is further enhanced by the public school system. School not only separates children from their parents, kinfolk, and other co-ethnics, but also inculcates in them values and traditions often different from those cherished at home. Growing up among children of other cultures, attending school from five years of age to early adulthood, and being exposed to outside culture even in the family livingroom, the enculturation of second-generation Hungarians into the ethnic subculture has become virtually impossible. Sunday school taught in the Magyar language, occasional attendance at ethnic functions, and a stint in the Hungarian scout (summer) camp can only make a slight and superficial contribution to the cultural upbringing of second- and third-generation Hungarian Canadians.

While the general differences in the culture, political outlook, and social composition of the main Hungarian immigrant streams were to a large extent determined by changing conditions in Hungary, the transformation of individual Hungarian Canadians' customs, mannerisms, and values was effected by the process of acculturation. No individual went untouched by it, as each newcomer sooner or later, in one way or another, had to adjust, at least to some extent, to his new socio-economic environment. The degree of adjustment required for successful functioning in the new homeland varied greatly according to time and circumstance. Homesteading in pre-1914 Canada usually required a lesser degree of cultural adjustment than functioning as a white-collar or even a blue-collar worker in one of Canada's bustling cities. Social change before 1914 was slower than it is in the age of the motor car and television: but it is also true that the old-timers were less equipped to handle rapid adjustment than, for example, the refugees, many of whom had lived through more than one radical transformation of their political and social world even before coming to Canada.

Adjustment manifested itself in many ways, including the acquisition of language skills, Canadian work habits, citizenship status, and an increasingly effective functioning outside the cultural boundaries of the Hungarian-Canadian community. With adjustment started the complex process of assimilation. Beginning with the shedding of the garments brought from the old country, and often ending with the loss of the immigrant's original value system and language skills, this process has affected all Hungarian Canadians in different ways and to a varying extent. Particularly far-reaching were its effects on second-generation people.[7]

Each of the Hungarian immigrant streams to Canada underwent, to some degree at least, the processes of adjustment and assimilation. Evidence of the effect is revealed by census data: figures regarding knowledge of English, language retention statistics, etc. These indicate – and this information is corroborated by other sources – that assimilation took place more slowly among the early immigrant groups. Nevertheless, even the pioneer communities succumbed to it in time. It is obvious that Hungarian ethnic life could not have flourished in Canada for nearly a hundred years had the pre-1914 settlers not been reinforced by the inter-war arrivals who in turn were replenished by the post-1945 refugees.

The replenishment of an already established Hungarian-Canadian sub-culture by new arrivals had led, both in the 1920's and in the 1950's, to a kind of cultural revival – a great flourishing of social and institutional life, as well as some stress and disharmony in community affairs. The "revival" of the late 1920's was cruelly stifled by the Depression, but the one that began around 1950 resulted in what will probably be known as the "golden age" of Hungarian-Canadian history. If past experience is any indication of the future, it seems evident that this new age will end one day, and the continued existence of the Hungarian-Canadian sub-culture will depend on the arrival of still another wave of Hungarian immigrants. Without such reinforcement, there might not be another resurgence, or effective culture maintenance. Within the foreseeable future Hungarian-Canadian society might have to face the prospect of extinction as a culturally distinct ethnic community.[8]

Institutions and Politics

From the early days of Hungarian settlements on the Canadian Prairies to the present, Hungarian Canadians have maintained a great variety of institutions. The most important of these have been the churches, which have rendered invaluable spiritual and practical services to their congregations and, through them, to the country as a whole. Hungarian-Canadian history has many heroes, and most of them are unrecognized. They include the men and women who worked tirelessly to serve their churches and their people. They have given hope to the disappointed, eased the pain of the homesick and the lonely, and encouraged many to persevere in the struggle for a new existence. Although the Hungarian-Canadian churches can be faulted for fostering ethnic disunity, there can be little doubt that without them Hungarian community life would have been poorer and the loneliness of the individual Hungarian immigrant more painful.

Important functions have been performed through the ages by Hungarian-Canadian lay organizations. Many of the old-timers' institutions had existed partly or mainly for the purpose of protecting immigrants from the hardships of economic insecurity. With the coming of greater prosperity and state-sponsored welfare, the need for mutual insurance and other self-help organizations declined. Nevertheless, the number of Hungarian-Canadian associations continued to grow as later arrivals, rather than joining the old-timers' institutions, often established new ones. This growth was especially pronounced during the Cold War era, when a highly politicized emigration caused the proliferation of political organizations.

Both the religious and the lay institutions, as well as the Hungarian-Canadian press, had important and varying roles to play in the processes of integration and acculturation. They facilitated the newcomer's initial adjustment to Canadian conditions. By providing advice and information to him in his native language, they had made his lot easier; by the same token, however, they substantially reduced the immigrant's need for a good knowledge of English. In a sense, then, these institutions probably hindered or delayed many a Hungarian immigrant's ultimate adjustment. They could often seem to have reduced the pace of acculturation through reinforcing the newcomer's (and his children's) ethnic heritage, and indirectly, through enabling most Hungarian Canadians to function, part of the time at least, within a familiar Hungarian social and cultural environment. But the most important overall achievement of Hungarian-Canadian institutions has been the cushioning of the shocks involved in the processes of adjustment and acculturation.

Most Hungarian-Canadian institutions have been plagued by myriad problems. One of their basic difficulties is inherent in all voluntary organizations: there is nothing to prevent their members from dissolving them after a while, or leaving them and setting up rival organizations. Another basic difficulty lies probably in the Hungarian national traits of excessive individualism and pride, which make co-operation within institutions difficult. Consequently, Hungarian-Canadian organized life from the earliest days to the present has been characterized by atomization.

Geography, residential instability, religious divisions, social differences, and political rivalries also caused problems. Throughout most of their history, Hungarian Canadians have lived widely scattered in this big country. Many of them have had to relocate repeatedly in search of economic opportunities. Furthermore, Hungarian Canadians have been divided along religious lines and, especially since the 1920's, social differences have been increasingly evident among them. Ideological rifts have also plagued Hungarian-Canadian society throughout the better part of its long existence. Still another though less obvious problem has been the question of leadership. Although leaders were usually appreciated, the rise of any individual Hungarian Canadian head-and-shoulders above his fellows was resented and even prevented by one means or another.[9] Before the Second World War only a few educated Hungarians could immigrate to Canada, and as a result Hungarian-Canadian organizations had an inadequate reserve of potential leaders, especially the type who could act as spokesmen for their people in the society at large. After the Second World War the situation became the reverse. By the 1950's potential leaders abounded to such an extent that existing organizations could hardly accommodate them.

These difficulties enfeebled many Hungarian-Canadian associations and resulted in their instability. But the greatest problem seems to have been the continuity from one generation to the next and from one immigration stream to the other. The situation in this respect is not entirely negative, as there are numerous organizations, founded by the interwar or even pre-1914 arrivals, which have been taken over in recent decades by the immigrants of the 1950's. Nevertheless, the danger exists that with the passing away of the great number of Hungarians who came during the 1949-59 period there might be too few Hungarian Canadians willing and able to continue the organizational work of their predecessors. Should this happen, decades of dedicated work will be undone, many Hungarian-Canadian churches, halls, schools, and libraries will vanish, and a valuable subculture will begin to disappear from the country.

In many respects, the Hungarian-Canadian community has never had so much going for it as it has in the past few decades. Most of its members seem to have a reasonable standard of living. There is an abundance of well-educated, highly trained persons among them.[10] They enjoy more respect in Canada than the Hungarian immigrants of the interwar and pre-1914 periods. Hungarian-Canadian society, moreover, is no longer split by a struggle between radicals and conservatives. The leftists of the 1930's and 1940's have been greatly weakened by desertions, internal wrangles, deaths, and, above all, by the passing of the social and economic conditions which had existed during the Depression and the war years. Yet, all is not well within the Hungarian ethnic group. The spectre of assimilation looms large on the horizon. Despite the decline of the "old left," ideological unity has eluded most Hungarian-Canadian centres, as political differences continue to exist even among those who fled Hungary after the imposition of a Stalinist dictatorship. Moreover, the Hungarian-Canadian community is presently threatened by potential political dissension over the issue of relations with the government of Hungary.

Relations with Hungary

In the past, Hungary's governments rarely concerned themselves with Hungarian-Canadian affairs. Before 1918 the handling of Hungary's external affairs was done by the Austro-Hungarian imperial authorities in Vienna. Since 1918 Hungary has been plagued by frequent social and political upheavals, which have prevented her leaders from paying much attention to the affairs of Hungarian immigrants abroad. Nevertheless, during two distinct periods the Budapest authorities systematically sought contacts with Hungarian Canadians and many of their organizations: the interwar years and, more recently, the 1970's.

After the First World War Hungary's conservative regimes embarked on a policy of cultivating links with the right-of-centre political groupings of Hungarian emigrants in the West. Their policy manifested itself in such measures as support for the conservative Hungarian immigrant press, advice to immigrants and immigrant organizations, tours by Hungarian dignitaries, and the encouragement of visits by Hungarian immigrants to their native land. These measures were generally welcomed by Hungarian Canadians, except for leftist radicals who resented the aid Budapest rendered to their political rivals. In a sense, then, the interwar Hungarian government's interest in Hungarian-Canadian affairs reinforced the ideological rift that existed in Hungarian-Canadian society during this period.

With the coming of the Second World War, contacts between Hungary's authorities and Hungarian-Canadian organizations virtually ended and were not resumed in the immediate post-war era. With the establishment of a Stalinist regime in Hungary, the atmosphere improved for official contacts between Budapest and certain elements of the Hungarian-Canadian left; but relations between Hungary's new masters and the majority of Hungarian Canadians reached a low point. Hungary's Communists regarded the post-1945 Hungarian emigrants as "renegades" or "war criminals," and showed no interest in having contacts with them or any of their organizations. This attitude seemed to suit a large segment of Hungarian-Canadian society, whose members viewed their country's Stalinist regime with hostility.

In the 1960's, however, Hungary's political leaders adopted a more conciliatory attitude toward Hungarians abroad. Visits by Hungarian immigrants to Hungary were encouraged. Even most post-1945 and 1956 refugees were welcome to spend their vacations (and dollars) in Hungary.

Moreover, the Hungarian government in recent years has sought to open a dialogue with the vast majority of Hungarian Canadians and their organizations. The chief instrument of this so-called "bridge building" is Hungary's bustling tourist industry, but official and unofficial visits by people from Hungary, the distribution of free literature, cultural exchanges, and so on are also becoming more prevalent. Under ordinary circumstances, closer ties between a Canadian ethnic group and the native country's authorities could prove mutually beneficial, but given the ideological rift separating the bulk of Hungarian-Canadian society and Hungary's rulers, such ties may create difficulties. The fact seems to be that some Hungarian Canadians welcome Budapest's initiatives. They are apparently willing to let bygones to be bygones and are anxious to enlist the aid of a potentially powerful agency in the struggle to preserve and enhance Hungarian culture in Canada. Others resent the Hungarian government's efforts. They see such efforts as part of a Communist cultural offensive, designed above all to serve a cause which is alien to Hungarian Canadians and, as a matter of fact, to all loyal Canadian citizens. Given these circumstances, it is not surprising that the scope and nature of relations with Hungary's officialdom have already been the subject of much controversy among Hungarian Canadians in recent years. They are likely to be the source of even more dissension in the foreseeable future.

Contributions to Canada

Immigration is a process of give and take. When one country accepts as immigrants the nationals of another, usually benefits accrue to both the host nation and the people being admitted. There can be little doubt, in the case of Canada's Hungarian immigrants, that this indeed has been the case. What Canada gave to her Hungarian newcomers depended on a host of complex and varying circumstances. In the early years, particularly before 1914, Canada provided its Magyar immigrants with homesteads, jobs, and opportunities to earn a better living than was possible for a poor peasant in East Central Europe. But pre-1914 Canada and, for a long time, the whole of the Canadian frontier offered very little in the way of cultural and social amenities. As one Hungarian old-timer from the Prairies put it: Canada gave many material benefits but very few spiritual blessings.[11]

To the post-1945 refugees, Canada offered more: political freedom, a greater variety of economic opportunities, and a certain measure of social and cultural fulfilment within the already flourishing Hungarian-Canadian subculture. Of course, not all of the later arrivals' expectations were satisfied. Much like the old-timers, many of the new immigrants remained strangers within Canadian society, as they could rarely achieve close social ties with native-born Canadians. Consequently, the attainment of social acceptance often remained an aspiration for second-generation Hungarian Canadians. But those immigrants, usually the young, who were capable of more complete adjustment to the new environment could aspire to the same material, social, and cultural advancement as the average native-born Canadian. The road to this stage of affairs was a bumpy one: in the pre-World War II era the privilege of being treated as full-fledged Canadians had often been beyond the reach even of second-generation Hungarian Canadians.[12]

It should be noted that, besides offering her Hungarian immigrants freedom, economic opportunities, and eventually the prospect of social equality, at least indirectly Canada has benefited Hungarians everywhere. Through her Hungarian residents, she has been a source of aid and comfort to many Magyars in East Central Europe. In days when the free flow of information from the West was barred by authoritarian governments, many a Hungarian's only link with the Western democratic world had been his or her Hungarian-Canadian friends or relatives. Thousands of Hungarian Canadians have also helped their needy relations in the old country with money and relief parcels. Hundreds of Hungarian Canadians, moreover, help to maintain international organizations of Hungarian immigrants, thereby reinforcing Hungarian ethnic life in countries of the New World and Western Europe.

In return for the benefits Canada bestowed on Hungarians, they have given this country first and foremost that which they brought with them from their homeland: skills, talents, knowledge, sometimes even a little wealth, but more often than not nothing more than a strong back and two willing hands. The members of the first immigration stream were short on urban refinements but made up for this with their willingness and capacity to do backbreaking labour and a determination to succeed even under the most trying conditions. Later arrivals were often in possession of specialized skills currently in demand in Canada. Over the nearly hundred years of their history, Hungarian Canadians supplied Canada with the type of manpower most needed. In the age of frontier development, farmers, miners, and navvies came; in the industrial age, skilled workers and professional people were numerous among Hungarian immigrants.

Whether on the farmstead, in the mines, in logging camps, on construction sites, in factories, or in offices and laboratories, Hungarian Canadians struggled hard to fulfil their expectations of a better life for themselves and their children. Many of them have become successful. Some have distinguished themselves in the arts, the professions, business, or sports. In doing so, they have advanced Canada's economic and cultural development. In the realm of collective achievements, the Hungarian-Canadian record is not easily visible or measurable. There certainly are not many remarkable physical or cultural landmarks in Canada that can be readily attributed to the collective efforts of Hungarian- Canadians.[13] In this respect, Hungarians are no different from other Canadian ethnic groups of comparable size. Few if any of these groups have had extensive influence on a significant aspect of Canadian life, but the members of each contribute to the development of this country through their individual efforts.

In reality, however, the contributions of Hungarian Canadians to Canada's advancement make up more than the sum total of their personal achievements. Through their hard work and perseverance, Hungarian Canadians have gained respect not only for themselves but also for other minorities. By doing so they have no doubt reinforced many Canadians' belief in cultural pluralism or multiculturalism and in ethnocultural tolerance. Moreover, by cherishing their old customs and traditions and by sharing these with Canadians at large, Hungarian Canadians have helped to diversify Canada's cultural, religious, and social life. It is not an exaggeration to say that their main impact has probably been the enrichment of the quality of Canadian existence. Through their own struggle for human fulfilment, then, Hungarian Canadians have helped to make Canada a country in which the immigrant's hope – indeed, everyone's hope – for a better future has a greater chance of attainment.

NOTES

1. See *Census of Canada*, 1961, Bulletin 1.2-5, Table 35-1.
2. The number of Canadian-born Hungarians had expanded from 29,300 in 1951 to over 53,000 in 1961. In the same period the number of immigrant Hungarians had increased from about 31,000 to nearly 73,000. (*Census of Canada*, 1951, II, Table 37; and *Census of Canada*, 1961, I, Part 2, Table 49.
3. *1971 Census of Canada, Profile Studies, Ethnic Origins of Canadians* (Ottawa, 1977), Table 1.
4. Data based on statistics provided in *Census of Canada*, 1951, I, Table 32; *Census of Canada*, 1961, *Population*, I, Part 1, Table 35; *Census of Canada*, 1971, *Population, Ethnic Groups* (Ottawa, 1973), Table 2.
5. Data based on statistics provided in *ibid*. The 1971 provincial breakdowns are as follows: Ontario, 65,695; Alberta, 16,245; British Columbia, 16,000; Saskatchewan, 13,830; Quebec, 12,570; Manitoba, 5,405.
6. Data based on statistics provided in *Census of Canada*, 1951, I, Table 33; *Census of Canada*, 1961, *Population*, I, Part 2, Table 36; and *Census of Canada*, 1971, *Population, Ethnic Groups*, Table 3. In 1971 Canada's total population was 76 per cent urbanized. It is interesting that the process of urbanization among Hungarians took place most rapidly in Saskatchewan, where the Hungarian group's urbanization ratio had grown from 18 per cent in 1951 to 49 per cent twenty years later.
7. Adjustment does not necessarily result in assimilation or any of its advanced stages, but often adjustment can facilitate the process of assimilation. Marriage to a member of the host society, for example, implies a certain degree of social adjustment, but can be contracted by an individ-

ual who had not forsaken the essence of his immigrant heritage. Such a marriage, however, usually hinders the transmittance of the immigrant ethnoculture to the children, and hence becomes a cause of their assimilation.

8. Because of the lack of adequate research on ethnic groups in Canada, it is not possible to estimate the relative rate of assimilation of Hungarian Canadians and other immigrant groups. There is some evidence, however, which would support the hypothesis that Hungarians are losing their ethnic identity faster than several other groups. A recent comprehensive study of ten different ethnic communities in five large Canadian cities revealed, for example, that among Greeks, Italians, Chinese, and Ukrainians the retention of the ancestral language is considered more important than among Hungarians. Similarly, on the question of the need for ethnic children to receive instruction in their native language, Hungarians responded less enthusiastically than all the other groups surveyed. For further discussion of these subjects, see K.G. O'Bryan *et al., Non-Official Languages: A Study in Canadian Multiculturalism* (Ottawa, 1975), especially pp. 215-84, 296-306, 383-402.

9. Steinmetz interview.

10. In 1965 Kellner observed that in five selected occupational categories (artists, physicians and dentists, professional engineers, scientists, management personnel) Hungarians ranked second among seven selected ethnic groups (including the Dutch, German, Jewish, and Polish). Kellner, "Hungarian Participation in Canadian Culture," pp. 35ff. For further statistics on Hungarian physicians and dentists, see *ibid.*, p. 40.

11. Interview with Sister Mary.

12. For a fictionalized treatment of the subject, see John Marlyn, *Under the Ribs of Death* (Toronto, 1957).

13. Early examples of such physical landmarks are the massive churches erected by the peasant pioneers. Some of the Hungarian houses or cultural centres would be illustrations of the collective achievements of later immigrants. A recent example of what might be called a "cultural landmark" is the program in Hungarian studies at the University of Toronto, established as a result of the efforts of the Széchenyi Society of Calgary. The program, consisting of courses in Hungarian language and literature, is financed from the proceeds of an endowment grant; it is the first of its kind at a North American university.

Appendix:

A Note on Sources

N. F. Dreisziger and M. L. Kovacs

Research materials relating to ethnic history are diverse and numerous. They can be divided into two basic categories: those emanating from within the ethnic community and those which derive from outside of it. Examples of the first type are records created by ethnic institutions, correspondence accumulated by community leaders, and the reminiscences of ordinary immigrants. In the second category belong a wide variety of sources ranging from records of private agencies which had dealings with immigrants to police files, court records, and census statistics.

While the variety of the first of these types of sources is great, their quality, completeness, and usefulness often leave much to be desired. Unlike famous statesmen and diplomats, ordinary immigrants rarely accumulate personal records, and their notes and other writings hardly ever survive very long. Unfortunately, the same is true of their organizations. As a rule, these are the products of one particular wave of immigrants, and they often vanish without a trace when their founders pass away. Even if they leave some of their records behind, these can offer only an incomplete picture of the organization's experience. As a result, historians have to rely mainly on sources produced about the ethnic group by outside institutions and non-group members. Often these sources, also, are incomplete and scattered and require careful evaluation.

Sources of information on Hungarian-Canadian history appear to be particularly scarce and not easily accessible. Owing to a variety of circumstances, comparatively few Hungarian-Canadian organizations seem to have kept and preserved records properly reflective of their activities. And even fewer of their records have reached archival repositories. When this study was undertaken, for example, not a single substantial collection of Hungarian-Canadian institutional documents could be found in any of Canada's numerous archives. At the present there is one such collection, the papers of the *Canadian Hungarian News* of Winnipeg, which are now deposited in the Public Archives of Canada (PAC). This collection contains some of the records of the first truly nation-wide federation of Hungarian Canadians. Other smaller or less significant collections of Hungarian-Canadian institutional or private papers are only now finding their way into archives such as the PAC's Ethnic Archives section and the recently established archives of the Multicultural History Society of Ontario.

Fortunately, we have been able to carry out research in privately held papers put at our disposal by individuals concerned about the completeness of our study. These are mentioned in footnotes. Another type of source material, recorded interviews, was used for most parts of this book. Occasionally, information was obtained in a more or less informal manner. Owing to limitations of space, our informants are not always identified. Much information was derived from the Hungarian-Canadian press.

In the category of primary sources created by non-Hungarian Canadian agencies or individuals, the most important are those originating from the Canadian federal government. Many of these have been published, others are available only in manuscript form. Still others, such as census returns, most RCMP files, and Department of Justice records, remain closed to researchers. Among the manuscript sources which are open, the most useful information can be gleaned from the records of the following departments and agencies: the Departments of the Interior and of Agriculture (for the pre-1914 period), the Department of Immigration and Colonization and the Canadian National Railways Company (for the interwar period), the Department of National War Services and the Department of Citizenship and Immigration (for the World War II and subsequent eras). Some of these sources have been published in such government publications as the annual *Sessional Papers* of Parliament, *Departmental Reports*, and other similar collections of official documents. An extremely useful printed source of information is the census results published by Statistics Canada, formerly the Dominion Bureau of Statistics. To a lesser extent, and less often, provincial records are also useful. One example is the records of the Saskatchewan Royal Commission on Immigration and Settlement. Among other Canadian institutional records, those kept in church archives are useful.

Other records relevant to Hungarian-Canadian history derive from Hungarian authorities concerned with emigration from Hungary or with Hungarians settled abroad. Practically all Hungarian county archives contain documentary material useful for the study of early Hungarian-Canadian settlements. The most important government records are found in the Hungarian National Archives in Budapest. The archives of the Archdioceses of Kalocsa and Esztergom and those of the Reformed Church of Hungary in Debrecen also yielded some valuable information. Unfortunately, access to post-1918 government records is restricted in Hungary and it is only by good fortune that copies of a few documents pertaining to the interwar era were obtained. Among these were some reports of the Royal Hungarian Consulate in Winnipeg on the situation of Magyar immigrants in western Canada on the eve of and during the first years of the Great Depression.

Secondary literature on Hungarian-Canadian history seems to be even more limited than primary source material. The first monographic study of this subject by a professional scholar appeared only in 1957, some seventy years after the start of Hungarian immigration to the country. It was John Kósa's *Land of Choice: Hungarians in Canada* (Toronto: University of Toronto Press, 1957), a sociological study based on interviews with 112 randomly selected Hungarian Canadians in southern Ontario. The next monograph appeared seventeen years later from the pen of one of the present authors: Martin Louis Kovacs, *Esterhazy and Early Hungarian Immigration to Canada* (Regina: Canadian Plains Studies, 1974). Still another monograph by Professor Kovacs on the Bekevar-Kipling settlement, *Peace and Strife: Some Facets of the History of an Early Prairie Community* (Kipling, Saskatchewan: Kipling District Historical Society, 1980), was published while this study was being prepared. In addition to these books, there is a volume of life histories, told in the words of the informants, compiled by Professor Linda Dégh: *People in the Tobacco Belt: Four Lives* (Ottawa: National Museum of Man, 1975). As far as periodical literature on Hungarian Canadians is concerned, the situation is no better. There are a few articles, authored mainly by Kósa or Kovacs. The most substantial of these is the latter's "The Hungarian School Question," in Kovacs (ed.), *Ethnic Canadians* (Regina: Canadian Plains Studies, 1978), which treats some aspects of Hungarian-Canadian socio-cultural life on the Prairies in the 1908-1914 period.

Although some information can be obtained from the great many books and articles written by Canadian scholars on immigrants and their offspring in Canada and by Hungarian writers about Hungarians abroad, it is safe to say that the extent of scholarly publishing on our subject is very limited. Nevertheless, the work done and research material accumulated so far has been sufficient for the purposes of an overview. Perhaps it is not too much to hope that the present effort also represents a step toward the achievement of a synthesis on Hungarian-Canadian history.

The fact that the existing scholarly literature is supplemented by the work of non-professional Hungarian-Canadian researchers and writers seems to indicate broad popular interest in the group's history. Among those who distinguished themselves are three clergymen. The late Monsignor Paul Sántha, who held a Ph.D. degree in church history, published a concise but well-researched history of his parish, as well as several articles relating mainly to Hungarian settlements in Saskatchewan. The Reverend Mihály Fehér wrote a detailed history of his Montreal Reformed congregation, while the late Reverend Jenő Ruzsa published a general history. Although Ruzsa's work, *A Kanadai Magyarság Története* (The History of Canada's Magyars) (Toronto: by the author,

1940), reflects its author's lack of adequate time, funds, and training for historical research, it is an indispensable source of information especially for the interwar era. In addition to the writings of these and a few other Hungarian Canadians, several books by Hungarian visitors to Canada contain relevant information. Although these works are almost invariably journalistic and often unreliable in their statements of fact, they can be useful to the cautious historian. Still another type of source material is constituted by the reminiscences of Hungarian immigrants to Canada. Since many of these were published in Hungary by persons who had been unsuccessful in Canada, these works tend only to illustrate their authors' largely but not completely untypical reactions to the immigrant experience in this country.

Two other, often very useful types of secondary sources for historians dealing with a large subject such as ours are government-commissioned "background studies" and theses prepared by graduate students. As far as Hungarian-Canadian history is concerned, two works must be mentioned in the first of these categories. One is Kósa's bulky manuscript, "Immigration and Adjustment of Hungarians in Canada" (ca. 1955); the other is Paul Kellner's "Hungarian Participation in Canadian Culture" (Ottawa, 1965). Both are useful surveys but suffer from the fact that they were researched in haste and lacked adequate budgets. Kósa's manuscript formed the backbone of his book mentioned above. In the second category, that of graduate theses, no work really stands out in usefulness. We are not aware of any Ph.D. theses completed on Hungarian-Canadian subjects in the social sciences or the humanities. At least two have been undertaken recently, indicating a growing interest in the field by graduate students.

Bibliography

Adamovich, Laszlo, and Oszkar Sziklai. *Foresters in Exile: The Sopron Forestry School in Canada.* Vancouver: University of British Columbia, 1970.

Avery, Donald. *'Dangerous Foreigners': European Immigrant Workers and Labour Radicalism in Canada, 1896-1932.* Toronto: McClelland and Stewart, 1979.

Berry, John W., Rudolf Kalin, and Donald M. Taylor. *Multiculturalism and Ethnic Attitudes in Canada.* Ottawa: Minister of State for Multiculturalism, 1976.

Blumstock, Robert, ed. *Bekevar: Working Papers on a Canadian Prairie Community.* Ottawa: National Museum of Man, 1979.

Bŏdy, Paul. "Travel Reports on Hungarian Settlements in Canada 1905-1928," *The Canadian-American Review of Hungarian Studies,* II, 1 (Spring, 1975), pp. 21-32.

Bölöni Farkas, Alexander. *Journey in North America.* Translated and edited by Theodore and Helen Benedek Schoenman. Philadelphia: American Philosophical Society, 1977.

Bradwin, Edmond. *The Bunkhouse Man,* with an introduction by Jean Burnet. Toronto: University of Toronto Press, 1972.

Canada. Department of the Secretary of State. Multiculturalism Directorate. *The Canadian Family*

---

* Limitations of space and the availability of up-to-date bibliographies have prompted us not to include a comprehensive list of secondary works in this study. Those wishing to examine the complete literature on our subject might start with I.L. Halasz de Beky's *The Hungarians in Canada: A Bibliography* (Toronto: published by the author, 1977); Joseph Szeplaki's *Hungarians in the United States and Canada: A Bibliography* (Minneapolis: Immigration History Research Center, University of Minnesota, 1977); and John Miska's very recent *Ethnic and Native Canadian Literature, 1850-1979: A Bibliography of Primary and Secondary Materials* (Lethbridge, Alberta: Microform Biblios, 1979).

Tree: Canada's Peoples. Don Mills, Ontario: Corpus Information Services in co-operation with the Multiculturalism Directorate and the Canadian Government Publishing Centre, 1979.

Cnossen, T. "Integration of Refugees: Some Observations on the Hungarians in Canada." Research Group for European Migration Problems. *Bulletin*, Supplement no. 7 (June, 1964). pp. 3-23.

Dégh, Linda. *People in the Tobacco Belt: Four Lives.* Ottawa: National Museum of Man, 1975.

Dirks, Gerald E. *Canada's Refugee Policy: Indifference or Opportunism?* Montreal: McGill-Queen's University Press, 1977.

Dojcsak, G.V. "The Mysterious Count Esterhazy," *Saskatchewan History*, XXVI, 2 (Spring, 1973), pp. 63-72.

Dreisziger, N.F. "Watson Kirkconnell: Translator of Hungarian Poetry and Friend of Hungarian Canadians," in N.F. Dreisziger (ed.), *Hungarian Poetry and the English-Speaking World: A Tribute to Watson Kirkconnell* (Ottawa: Hungarian Readers' Service, 1977), pp. 117-144.

England, Robert. *The Central European Immigrant in Canada.* Toronto: Macmillan, 1929.

____. *The Colonization of Western Canada. A Study of Contemporary Land Settlement (1896-1934).* London: P.S. King and Son, 1936.

Esterhazy, P.O. *The Hungarian Colony of Esterhaz, Assiniboia, North-West Territories, Canada.* Ottawa, 1902.

Gibbon, John Murray. *Canadian Mosaic: The Making of a Northern Nation.* Toronto: McClelland and Stewart, [1938].

Hedges, James B. *Building the Canadian West: The Land and Colonization Policies of the Canadian Pacific Railway.* New York: Macmillan, 1939.

Hurd, W. Burton. *Origin, Birthplace, Nativity and Language of the Canadian People.* Ottawa: King's Printer, 1929.

____. *Racial Origins and Nativity of the Canadian People.* Ottawa: King's Printer, 1937.

____. *Racial Origins and Nativity of the Canadian People.* Ottawa: King's Printer, 1947.

Kirkconnell, Watson. "A Canadian Meets the Magyars," *The Canadian-American Review of Hungarian Studies,* 1, 1 (Spring, 1974), pp. 1-11.

____. *A Slice of Canada: Memoirs.* Toronto: University of Toronto Press, 1967.

Kósa, John. "A Century of Hungarian Emigration, 1850-1950," *American Slavic and East European Review,* XVI, 4 (December, 1957), pp. 501-14.

____. "Hungarian Immigrants in North America: Their Residential Mobility and Ecology," *Canadian Journal of Economics and Political Science,* XXII, 3 (August, 1956), pp. 358-70.

____. *Land of Choice: Hungarians in Canada.* Toronto: University of Toronto Press, 1957.

____. "The Knowledge of English among Hungarian Immigrants in

Canada," in Imre Bernolak *et al., Immigrants in Canada* (Montreal, 1955), pp. 23-9.

Koranyi, E.K., A. Kerenyi, and G.J. Sarwer-Foner. "On Adaptive Difficulties of Some Hungarian Immigrants: A Sociopsychiatric Study," *Medical Services Journal,* XIV, 6 (June, 1958), pp. 383-405.

Kovacs, M.L., and A.J. Cropley. *Immigrants and Society: Alienation and Assimilation.* Sydney, Australia: Macmillan, 1975.

Kovacs, Martin Louis. *Esterhazy and Early Hungarian Immigration to Canada.* Canadian Plains Studies No. 2. Regina: Canadian Plains Research Center, 1974.

————, ed. *Ethnic Canadians: Culture and Education.* Regina: Canadian Plains Research Center, 1978.

————. "From Peasant Village to the Canadian Prairies," *Proceedings of the First Banff Conference on Central and East European Studies,* Thomas M.S. Priestly, editor (Edmonton, 1977), pp. 364-72.

————, ed. *Hungarian-Canadian Perspectives: Selected Papers.* Ottawa: Hungarian Readers' Service, 1980. Special issue of *The Canadian-American Review of Hungarian Studies,* VII, 1 (Spring, 1980).

————. "The Hungarian School Question," in Kovacs (ed.), *Ethnic Canadians,* pp. 333-58.

————. *Peace and Strife: Some Facets of the History of an Early Prairie Community.* Kipling, Saskatchewan: Kipling District Historical Society, 1980.

Macdonald, Norman. *Canada: Immigration and Colonization: 1841-1903.* Toronto: Macmillan, 1966.

Marchbin, Andrew A. "Early Emigration from Hungary to Canada," *Slavonic and East European Review,* XIII (July, 1934), pp. 127-38.

Martin, Chester. *"Dominion Lands" Policy.* Toronto: McClelland and Stewart, 1973.

Norris, John. *Strangers Entertained: A History of the Ethnic Groups of British Columbia.* Vancouver: British Columbia Centennial Committee, 1971.

O'Bryan, K.G., J.G. Reitz, and O. Kuplowska. *Non-Official Languages. A Study in Multiculturalism.* Ottawa: Minister Responsible for Multiculturalism, 1975.

Palmer, Howard. *Land of the Second Choice: A History of Ethnic Groups in Southern Alberta.* Lethbridge, Alberta: The Lethbridge Herald, 1972.

Papp, Susan M., ed. *Hungarians in Ontario.* Toronto: Multicultural History Society of Ontario, 1979-80. Special issue of *Polyphony, the Bulletin of the Multicultural History Society of Ontario,* 2, 2-3 (1979-80).

Patrias, Carmela. *The* Kanadai Magyar Ujsag *and the Politics of the Hungarian Canadian Elite.* Toronto: Multicultural History Society of Ontario, 1978.

Pirot, Jules. *One Year's Fight for the True Faith in Saskatchewan: Or the Hungarian Question in Canada in 1910.* Toronto, 1911.

Pivanyi, E. *Hungarian-American Historical Connections from Pre-Columbian Times to the End of the American Civil War.* Budapest, 1927.

Quinn, David B., and Neil M. Chesire. *The New Found Land of Stephen Parmenius: The Life and Writings of a Hungarian Poet, Drowned on a Voyage from Newfoundland 1583.* Toronto: University of Toronto Press, 1972.

Sántha, Paul. *Three Generations, 1901-1957: The Hungarian Colony at Stockholm, Saskatchewan.* Stockholm: published by the author, [1959].

Index

Abbotsford: 143, 150, 206
Acculturation: 68
Adjustment: 66-68, 186-187, 208-210, 218 (n. 56)
Ady, Endre: 15, 24
Air Bridge to Canada: 205
Aldina: 116
Anda, Géza: 25
Apponyi, Count Albert: 160
Árpád dynasty: 7-8
Assimilation: 83, 186-187, 223-224, 231 (n. 8)
Austin, Leo J.: 180
Austria: 17, 28, 37, 203
Az Otthon (see Press): 121, 127

Bácskai-Peyerle, Béla: 126, 159
Bakfark, Bálint: 25
Bakonyi, E.L.: 77
Balassa, Bálint: 24
Balogh, Lajos: 194 (n. 61)
Bartók, Béla: 25
Békesi, István: 215 (n. 27)
Bekevar: 64, 70, 73-79 passim, 86 (n. 30), 151
Belgians: 144
Benchonzie: 72, 79
Bender: 76
Borsi, Tivadar: 215 (n. 27)
Böszörményi Nagy, Béla: 215 (n. 27)
Brantford: 95, 96, 124, 158, 203
Britain: 18
Budapest: 15, 16, 19, 39, 99, 128, 161, 204, 227-228

Buffalo: 128
Bukovina: 66, 106

Calgary: 107, 121, 146, 150, 172, 187, 198, 203, 210
Camps for the unemployed: 142
Canadai Magyar Farmer (see Press): 80-81, 125
Canadai Magyar Néplap (see Press): 125
Canadian Hungarian Association (1908): 79
Canadian Hungarian Cultural Club: 106
Canadian Hungarian Democratic Federation: 167 (n. 62), 177
Canadian Hungarian Federation: 129-130, 160, 161
Canadian Hungarian Fraternal Association (1910-1916): 79-81
Canadian Hungarian Immigrant Protection Bureau: 99-100
Canadian Hungarian National Federation (1936): 160
Canadian Hungarian National Federation (1951): 201
Canadian Hungarian Sick-Benefit Federation: 124
Canadian National Railways: 128
Canadian North-West Land Company: 63
Canadian Pacific Railway: 62, 63, 128
Canadian Red Cross: 178, 205

Cars (See Motorcar)
Catholic Funeral Society of Regina: 106
Church Union: 120
Churches (see Religious life)
Cleveland: 127
Cold War: 202, 203, 225
Committee on Co-operation in Canadian Citizenship: 171-173
Communists: 16-17, 19-24, 41, 46-47, 48, 49, 124, 151, 154-155, 158, 162, 170, 171, 172, 174, 178, 199, 226, 228
Community life: 73-75, 116-117, 182-183
Contributions to Canada: 228-230
Council of Hungarian Churches and Clubs for Suffering Hungarians: 201
Courtland: 198
Croats: 29-32
Crowsnest Pass: 95
Csávossy, József: 129
Csendes, Imre: 181
Csendes Percek (see Press): 202
Csutoros, István: 129
Cupar: 79
Czakó, Ambró: 121, 170, 177-178, 182, 188
Czechoslovakia: 17, 20, 41, 46, 100
Cziffra, György: 25

de Dóry, Géza: 63
de Kresz, Géza: 188
Deák, Ferenc: 13-14
Delhi: 144, 183, 198
Demographic characteristics: 110-112, 144-149, 187-188, 210, 221-222
Department of Immigration and Colonization: 100
Department of National Defence: 142
Department of National War Services: 171, 173
Deportations: 141-142
Discrimination: 175, 191 (n. 16)
Dóry (see de Dóry)
Dózsa, György: 9

Eastern Canadian Hungarian Sick-Benefit Association: 124
Eckhardt, Tibor: 215 (n. 22)

Edmonton: 107, 146, 158, 210
Education: 70-71, 78, 80-81, 91 (n. 81), 122, 181, 193 (n. 39), 223
Egységes Magyarság (see Press): 211
Eisner, Béla: 172-175
Enculturation: 68
Endrész, György: 161
Érdujhelyi, Menyhért: 80
Erkel, Ferenc: 25
Esterhaz: 64, 66, 69
Esterhazy: 64, 77, 79
Esterhazy, Paul Oscar: 61, 63, 64, 67
Evangélikus Élet (see Press): 126
Evangélikus Otthon (see Press): 126

Family: 70-71, 114, 185
Federation of Hungarian University and College Students: 211
Fehér, Mihály: 126, 172
Figyelő (see Press): 126
First Hungarian Sick-Benefit Society of Lethbridge: 94, 95, 123
First Hungarian Sick-Benefit Society of Winnipeg: 95, 106, 123
First Hungarian Workers' Sick-Benefit Association of Hamilton: 124
First World War (see World War I)
France: 18
Freedom Fighters Federation of Canada: 210

Galt: 95
Galt, Sir Alexander T.: 94
German-Hungarian Club: 104
Germans: 28, 29-32, 37, 95, 145
Gönzy, Sr., Lajos: 77
Grand Committee of Hungarian Churches and Associations of Montreal: 172-173, 176, 196
Great Depression: 130, 139-162 passim, 174
Gyárfás, Ibolyka: 194 (n. 61)
Gyertyafény (see Press): 126

Habsburgs: 10-15, 28
Hamilton: 95, 96, 102-103, 120, 122, 124, 127, 151-152, 153, 154, 158, 177, 178, 180, 196, 198, 203, 210
Haris, Ervin: 194 (n. 61)
Hédly, Jeromos: 126

Hilpert, Joseph: 194 (n. 60)
Hiradó (see Press): 159
Hoffmann, Frank (Ferenc or Francis): 42, 121, 126, 151, 181
Hordossy, Iván: 99, 125
Hornyanszky, Nicholas (Miklós): 172, 176, 188
Horthy, Miklós: 16-19, 41
Horváth, Miklós: 172
Howell: 70, 71, 79
Hugessen, Senator A.K.: 178
Hungarian Canadian Authors' Association: 211
Hungarian Canadian Engineers' Association: 211
Hungarian Canadian Federation: 200-202
Hungarian Canadian Scout movement: 200
Hungarian consulates in Canada: 102-103, 106, 116, 123, 127, 154
Hungarian Credit and Savings Union of Vancouver: 199
Hungarian culture: 24-25
Hungarian Helicon Society: 200, 215 (n. 22)
Hungarian houses: 124-125, 157; in Toronto: 176, 179, 199
Hungarian Literary Society of Winnipeg: 219 (n. 68)
Hungarian National Council: 197
Hungarian Relief of West-Canada: 129
Hungarian school question (1910-11): 80-82
Hungarian Sick-Benefit Association of Brantford: 124
Hungarian Theatre: 219 (n. 67)
Hungary: 27-51, 30, 33, 99, 100-101, 127-128, 145, 160, 162, 169, 170, 178, 181, 201, 203, 227; attitude to emigration: 37; Compromise of 1867: 14; contemporary politics: 21-24; emigration: 27-51; immigration from: 61-63, 98-99, 195-196, 205-206; minorities: 14-15, 29-32; Revolution of 1848-49: 13-14, 28, 33; Revolution of 1956: 21, 48-49, 57 (n. 65), 203-204; Soviet occupation: 19-20, 169; World War I: 44-45; World War II: 16, 18-19, 46, 169-171, 177, 178-179
Hunsvalley: 63
Huntington: 143
Hunyadi, János: 9

Illyés, Gyula: 25
Immigrant Protection Bureau: 99
Immigrant Protection Bureau of Winnipeg: 125
Immigration regulations: 98-99, 205
Independent Sick-Benefit Federation: 158
Institutions (see Organizations)
Istvánffy, Miklós: 129
Izsák, Gyula: 188

Jancsó, Miklós: 25
Jászi, Oszkár: 15
Jews: 18, 19, 29-32, 47, 103, 104, 207, 211, 214 (n. 12), 217 (n. 49)
Jókai, Mór: 24
József, Attila: 25
"Justice for Hungary" flight: 161-162, 167 (n. 71)

Kádár, János: 21-24
Kálmán, Imre: 25
Kanadai Magyar Hirlap (see Press): 126
Kanadai Magyar Munkás (see Press): 126, 182, 202
Kanadai Magyar Népszava (see Press): 126
Kanadai Magyar Újság (see Press): 99-100, 125-127, 159, 170, 176, 182, 202, 232
Kanadai Magyarság (see Press): pre-World War I: 125; post-World War II: 202, 211
Kaposvar: 64, 69, 74, 77, 79, 80, 151
Karman, Todor: 25
Károlyi, Count Mihály: 15-17, 41, 121, 182
Kelowna: 143
King St. Stephen Roman Catholic Sick-Benefit Association: 123
Kipling: 63, 76, 77, 126
Kirkconnell, Watson: 24, 188, 189, 189 (n. 4)
Kis Újság (see Press): 126-127, 159
Kitchener: 122, 152
Kodály, Zoltán: 25

Kodály Ensemble: 219 (n. 67)
Körösi-Csoma, Sándor: 26
Kósa, John: 183
Kossuth, Lajos: 12-15
Kossuth Sick-Benefit Association:
    158, 177, 178
Kovács, Ferenc: 126, 128
Kovács, János: 64, 128-129
Kovács, Rózsa: 188
Kovácsi, Kálmán: 75, 79-81, 90
    (n. 61)
Kovácsi, Lajos: 79-81
Koynok, Kálmán: 159
Kresz (see de Kresz)
Krúdy, Gyula: 24
Kun, Béla: 16-17, 19, 41

Land distribution: 75
Langevin, Archbishop Adelard: 80-81
Langruth: 154
Language skills: 67-68, 78, 83, 149
Leadership: 118, 154, 226
League of Hungarian Veterans: 197
Leask: 116
Léhar, Ferenc: 25
Lethbridge: 94-96, 107, 123, 124
Liberal Party of Canada: 79-81, 92
    (n. 86), 157
Liszt, Ferenc: 25
Literature: 90 (n. 61)
Living conditions and lifestyles:
    95-96, 112-118, 139-141, 152,
    184-186
Logging camps: 112
Louis the Great of Hungary: 9
Lukácsffy, Kristóf: 76-77

MacKenzie, N.A.M.: 208
Magyar, Sándor: 160
Magyar Élet (see Press): 211
Magyarság (see Press): 159
Márky, Pál: 194 (n. 61)
Marriage: 185-186
Martin, Paul: 178
Matthias Corvinus: 9
Mátyásföld: 66
McGuigan, Archbishop James C.:
    180
Mécs, László: 24
Menorah (see Press): 211
Michel: 95
Migration chain: 37-38

Migrations: 142, 220-221
Mikszáth, Kálmán: 24
Mindszenty, Cardinal: 20, 23
Minnedosa: 63
Misatim: 154
Modernization (see Technological
    change)
Moholy-Nagy, László: 25
Molnár, Ferenc: 24
Montreal: 102, 103-104, 116, 121-123,
    127, 145, 153, 157, 172, 180,
    187, 196, 198-199, 203, 206,
    210
Moricz, Zsigmond: 24
Motorcar, impact of: 76-77, 223
Munkácsy, Mihály: 25

Nagy, Imre: 20-22
National Federation of American
    Hungarians: 128
Nazi sympathizers: 171, 198
Nemes, Gusztáv: 182
Németh, László: 25
New Hungary: 63
New York: 127
Niagara Falls: 95
Norbury: 116
Norfolk County (Ontario): 144
North Sydney: 95

Okanagan Valley: 143
Oliver: 143
Organizations: 73, 78-81, 103-104,
    116-117, 119-130, 150-161
    passim, 171-173, 176-179,
    197-202 passim, 210-213, 224-227
    (see also Religious life, Press)
Ormandy, Eugene: 25
Örszem (see Press): 126
Oshawa: 102
Osoyoos: 143
Ottawa: 171, 210
Otthon: 64, 71, 74, 75, 77, 121, 151
Ottoman Turks: 9-11, 14, 27

Paizs, Ödön: 102
Papp, János: 121
Parmenius, Stephen: 26
Pennsylvania: 62, 63
Perényi, Zsigmond: 126
Petényi, Sarolta: 188
Petőfi, Sándor: 24

Picnics: 73
Pinke, Imre: 64
Pinkefalva: 66
Pirot, Jules: 80-81
Plunkett: 70, 77, 79
Poetry: 90 (n. 61), 188
Port Colbourne: 96, 102, 154, 159
Powell River: 208
Press: 71, 79-81, 125, 154, 158-159, 182, 202, 211, 225; religious periodicals: 121, 126-127, 202; leftist press: 126, 182, 202
Prud'homme: 66, 77

Rabbit Lake: 116
Radio broadcasting: 159, 203
Railways, impact of: 76
Railways Agreement (1926): 98
Rajcs, Zoltán: 66
Rákóczi Association: 200
Rákóczi, Ferenc: 11
Rákosi, Mátyás: 19-21
Református Hiradó (see Press): 126
Refugees (1956): 203-204, 205-213
Regina: 106, 121, 128, 145, 151, 157, 158, 174, 175, 187
Relations with Hungary: 127-128, 227-228
Religious life: 69-70, 80-81, 103-104, 119-122, 150-154, 179-181, 198, 207, 214 (n. 11, 12), 225
Rimanóczy, János: 194 (n. 61)
Rites of passage: 71-72
Riverton: 154
Romania: 17, 23, 28, 39, 41, 44-46, 100, 106, 145
Romanians: 29-32
Rózsa, Miklós: 25
Rothmere: 116, 181
Russia (see Soviet Union)
Ruthenians: 29-32 (see also Ukrainians)
Ruzsa, Jenő: 122, 126, 151-152, 178, 188, 215 (n. 27)

St. Catharines: 102
St. László: 66, 77
St. Laurent, Louis: 201, 203
St. Luke: 64
St. Stephen, King of Hungary: 8
St. Thomas: 102

Sántha, Paul: 152-153, 178, 188, 215 (n. 27)
Saskatoon: 107, 121, 129, 151, 158
Saxon-Hill: 71
Schaffer, L.J.: 81
Schefbeck, István: 139
Schools (see Education)
Second Vienna Award (August, 1940): 18, 145
Self-Improvement Society of Welland: 96, 124
Semmelweiss, Ignác: 25
Serbs: 29-32
Sib system: 183-184
Sick-Benefit Federations: 124, 158-159
Sisters of Social Service: 122-123, 151, 180
Slovaks: 29-32, 63, 94
Smallholder Party: 20
Solti, Sir George: 25
Sopron School of Forestry: 208-210
South America: 32
Soviet Union: 20, 21, 22, 49, 158, 170-171
Spanish Civil War: 162, 168 (n. 73)
Spiritwood: 116
Sporthiradó (see Press): 202
Stalin, Joseph: 19-21
Steinmetz, Károly (Charles): 126, 152-153, 178
Stephens, Sir George: 63
Stockholm: 66, 69, 79, 107, 123, 151, 198
Sudbury: 173
Summerland: 143
Swedes: 66
Sydney: 95
Szabó, György: 128-129
Szabó, János: 64
Szalatnay, Márk: 95
Szalay, Emil: 161
Széchenyi, Count István: 12, 13, 15
Széchenyi Society: 200, 231 (n. 13)
Székelyföld: 66, 70
Székelys: 10, 66, 103-104
Széll, George: 25
Szent-Györgyi, Albert: 25
Szigeti, Joseph: 25
Szilárd, Leo: 25

Sziv (see Press): 202
Szőke, István: 178
Tárogató (see Press): 121, 170, 182, 202
Technological change: 75-77, 81, 223
Teleki, Pál: 18
Teller, Edward: 25
Thorold: 102
Tillsonburg: 203
Tonelli, Sándor: 35, 36
Török, Bertalan: 177
Toronto: 96, 103-104, 117, 121, 122, 127, 145-146, 151-152, 153, 157, 159, 160, 172, 176, 177, 180, 183, 187, 196, 198-199, 200, 201, 203, 204, 207, 210
Tóth, Kálmán: 215 (n. 27)
Trade unions: 174
Transylvania: 10, 23, 25
Trianon, Treaty of: 16, 41, 160
Turks (see Ottoman Turks)

Új Élet (see Press): 202
Újváry, János: 129
Ukrainians: 80, 154
United Canadian Hungarian Relief Committee: 177-179
United Church of Canada: 154, 180-181
United States: 28, 29, 32, 34-40, 43, 45, 49, 50, 61, 62, 64, 81, 83, 95, 96, 100, 115, 128, 153
University of British Columbia: 208
University of Toronto: 208
Urbanization: 77-78, 101-102, 108-109, 146, 210, 222

Vancouver: 143, 146, 187, 210

Vasarely, Victor: 25
Vay, Peter A.: 94-95
Vienna: 205
Világosság (see Press): 126
Visual arts: 188
von Neumann, John: 25
Vörösmarty, Mihály: 24

Wakaw: 63, 66, 73, 74, 79
Welland: 95, 96, 121, 122, 128, 145-146, 151, 153, 154
Welland Canal: 102
Whitewood: 63
Windsor: 95, 96, 121, 122, 145-146, 153, 160
Winnipeg: 78, 79, 95-96, 99, 102, 105, 115, 120, 121, 124, 126, 128-129, 140, 145, 151, 158, 160, 173, 174, 181, 187, 196, 198-199, 206, 210
Women: 67, 115-116, 148-149
Woodcutter, Francis: 66
World Federation of Overseas Hungarians: 160
World War I: 15, 81-83, 92 (n. 95), 93 (n. 96), 96-97
World War II: 18-19, 169-178; treatment of Hungarians: 82; relief effort: 176-179

Yorkton: 77, 151, 181
Young Magyar American (see Press): 159
Yugoslavia: 17, 41, 46, 100

Zathureczky, Ede: 25
Zoltványi, Béla: 194 (n. 60)
Zrínyi, Miklós: 24

BENNETT KOVRIG is Professor of Political Science and Chairman of the Department of Political Economy at the University of Toronto. He is the author of *The Hungarian People's Republic* (Baltimore: The Johns Hopkins Press, 1970), *The Myth of Liberation: East-Central Europe in U.S. Diplomacy and Politics since 1941* (Baltimore: The Johns Hopkins Press, 1973), and *Communism in Hungary from Kun to Kádár* (Stanford: Hoover Institution Press, 1979), as well as of articles in *Survey, Yearbook of International Communist Affairs, The Historical Journal, International Journal,* and so on.

PAUL BÖDY holds the position of Comprehensive Economic Development Planner, Department of City Development, City of Pittsburgh. He holds a Ph.D. in History from the University of Notre Dame and a Master of City and Regional Planning from Ohio State University. He is the author of *Joseph Eötvös and the Modernization of Hungary, 1840-1879* (Philadelphia: American Philosophical Society, 1972) and several articles on modern Hungarian intellectual and social history. He conducted studies and research for this book in Hungary with the assistance of a post-doctoral fellowship of the International Research and Exchanges Board in 1973-74.

M.L. KOVACS is Professor of History at the University of Regina. His major publications include *Esterhazy and Early Immigration to Canada* (Regina: Canadian Plains Studies, 1974), *Immigrants and Society* (Sydney, Australia: McGraw Hill, 1975; co-authored with A.J. Cropley), *Ethnic Canadians: Culture and Education* (Regina: Canadian Plains Studies, 1978), and *Peace and Strife: Some Facets of the History of an Early Prairie Community* (Kipling, Saskatchewan: Kipling District Historical Society, 1980). He is one of the founders of the Central and East European Studies Association of Canada and is the author of numerous articles and papers.

N.F. DREISZIGER is Associate Professor of History at the Royal Military College of Canada. His publications include *Hungary's Way to World War II* (Toronto: Helicon Society, 1968), *The Hungarian Revolution Twenty Years After* (Ottawa: Hungarian Readers' Service, 1976), and *Mobilization for Total War* (Waterloo, Ontario: Wilfrid Laurier University Press, 1981). He is the co-founder of the *Hungarian Studies Review* and the author of articles in such periodicals as the *Journal of Modern History, Canadian Historical Papers, The Historical Journal,* and *Canadian Ethnic Studies.*